Other Books and Series by Jeff Bowen

Applications for Enrollment of Chickasaw Newborn Act of 1905
Volumes I thru VII

Cherokee Intermarried White 1906 Volume I thru X

Applications for Enrollment of Creek Newborn Act of 1905
Volumes I thru XIV

Applications for Enrollment of Choctaw Newborn Act of 1905
Volume I, II, III, IV, V, VI, VII, VIII, IX, X & XI

Visit our website at **www.nativestudy.com** to learn more about these and other books and series by Jeff Bowen

APPLICATIONS FOR ENROLLMENT OF CHOCTAW NEWBORN ACT OF 1905

VOLUME XII

TRANSCRIBED BY
JEFF BOWEN

NATIVE STUDY
Gallipolis, Ohio
USA

Other Books and Series by Jeff Bowen

1901-1907 Native American Census Seneca, Eastern Shawnee, Miami, Modoc, Ottawa, Peoria, Quapaw, and Wyandotte Indians (Under Seneca School, Indian Territory)

1932 Census of The Standing Rock Sioux Reservation with Births And Deaths 1924-1932

Census of The Blackfeet, Montana, 1897- 1901 Expanded Edition

Eastern Cherokee by Blood, 1906-1910, Volumes I thru XIII

Choctaw of Mississippi Indian Census 1929-1932 with Births and Deaths 1924-1931   Volume I
Choctaw of Mississippi Indian Census 1933, 1934 & 1937, Supplemental Rolls to 1934 & 1935 with Births and Deaths 1932-1938, and Marriages 1936-1938 Volume II

Eastern Cherokee Census Cherokee, North Carolina 1930-1939 Census 1930-1931 with Births And Deaths 1924-1931 Taken By Agent L. W. Page Volume I
Eastern Cherokee Census Cherokee, North Carolina 1930-1939 Census 1932-1933 with Births And Deaths 1930-1932 Taken By Agent R. L. Spalsbury   Volume II
Eastern Cherokee Census Cherokee, North Carolina 1930-1939 Census 1934-1937 with Births and Deaths 1925-1938 and Marriages 1936 & 1938 Taken by Agents R. L. Spalsbury And Harold W. Foght Volume III

Seminole of Florida Indian Census, 1930-1940 with Birth and Death Records, 1930-1938

Texas Cherokees 1820-1839 A Document For Litigation 1921

Choctaw By Blood Enrollment Cards 1898-1914 Volumes I thru XVII

Starr Roll 1894   (Cherokee Payment Rolls) Districts: Canadian, Cooweescoowee, and Delaware Volume One
Starr Roll 1894 (Cherokee Payment Rolls) Districts: Flint, Going Snake, and Illinois   Volume Two
Starr Roll 1894 (Cherokee Payment Rolls) Districts: Saline, Sequoyah, and Tahlequah; Including Orphan Roll Volume Three

Cherokee Intruder Cases Dockets of Hearings 1901-1909 Volumes I & II

Indian Wills, 1911-1921 Records of the Bureau of Indian Affairs Books One thru Seven;
 Native American Wills & Probate Records 1911-1921

Other Books and Series by Jeff Bowen

Turtle Mountain Reservation Chippewa Indians 1932 Census with Births & Deaths, 1924-1932

Chickasaw By Blood Enrollment Cards 1898-1914 Volume I thru V

Cherokee Descendants East An Index to the Guion Miller Applications Volume I
Cherokee Descendants West An Index to the Guion Miller Applications Volume II (A-M)
Cherokee Descendants West An Index to the Guion Miller Applications Volume III (N-Z)

Applications for Enrollment of Seminole Newborn Freedmen, Act of 1905

Eastern Cherokee Census, Cherokee, North Carolina, 1915-1922, Taken by Agent James E. Henderson Volume I (1915-1916)
Volume II (1917-1918)
Volume III (1919-1920)
Volume IV (1921-1922)

Complete Delaware Roll of 1898

Eastern Cherokee Census, Cherokee, North Carolina, 1923-1929, Taken by Agent James E. Henderson Volume I (1923-1924)
Volume II (1925-1926)
Volume III (1927-1929)

Applications for Enrollment of Seminole Newborn Act of 1905 Volumes I & II

North Carolina Eastern Cherokee Indian Census 1898-1899, 1904, 1906, 1909-1912, 1914 Revised and Expanded Edition

1932 Hopi and Navajo Native American Census with Birth & Death Rolls (1925-1931) Volume 1 - Hopi
1932 Hopi and Navajo Native American Census with Birth & Death Rolls (1930-1932) Volume 2 - Navajo

Western Navajo Reservation Navajo, Hopi and Paiute 1933 Census with Birth & Death Rolls 1925-1933

Cherokee Citizenship Commission Dockets 1880-1884 and 1887-1889 Volumes I thru V

Copyright © 2013
by Jeff Bowen

ALL RIGHTS RESERVED
No part of this publication may be reproduced
or used in any form or manner whatsoever
without previous written permission from the
copyright holder or publisher.

Originally published:
Baltimore, Maryland
2013

Reprinted by:

Native Study LLC
Gallipolis, OH
www.nativestudy.com
2020

Library of Congress Control Number: 2020918113

ISBN: 978-1-64968-105-8

Made in the United States of America.

This series is dedicated to the descendants of the Choctaw newborn listed in these applications.

This map of Indian Territory shows how large the Choctaw and Chickasaw Nations' land base was that contained huge deposits of asphalt and coal. Just the size and territory involved was flooded with the "Grafters".

DEPARTMENT OF THE INTERIOR.

Commissioner to the Five Civilized Tribes.

NOTICE.

Opening of Land Office at Wewoka,
IN THE SEMINOLE NATION, INDIAN TERRITORY.

Notice is hereby given that on Monday, September 4, 1905, the Commissioner to the Five Civilized Tribes will establish a land office at Wewoka, in the Seminole Nation, Indian Territory, for the purpose of allowing citizens and freedmen of the Seminole Nation to select allotments of land for their minor children enrolled under the Act of Congress approved March 3, 1905 (33 Stat. L 1060), and for the further purpose of allowing citizens and freedmen of the Seminole Nation, whose allotments are incomplete, to select additional land in order to bring the value of their allotments up to the standard of $309.09, as nearly as may be practicable.

Each child whose enrollment in accordance with the Act of March 3, 1905, has been duly approved by the Secretary of the Interior, is entitled to receive an allotment of forty acres without regard to the character or value of the land selected.

Selection of allotments for minor children must be made by their citizen or freedmen parents or by a duly appointed guardian, or curator, or by a duly appointed administrator.

TAMS BIXBY,
Commissioner.

Muskogee, Indian Territory,
July 29, 1905.

This particular notice for the Seminole and Creek Newborn makes mention of the Act of 1905. It is likely that a similar notice was posted in the Choctaw and Chickasaw Nations for the registration of newborn children.

DEPARTMENT OF THE INTERIOR,
Commission to the Five Civilized Tribes.

Rules and Regulations Governing the Selection of Allotments and the Designation of Homesteads in the Choctaw and Chickasaw Nations.

1. Selections of allotments and designations of homesteads for adult citizens and selections of allotments for adult freedmen must be made in person except as herein otherwise provided.

2. Applications to have land set apart and homesteads designated for duly identified Mississippi Choctaws must be made personally before the Commission to the Five Civilized Tribes. Fathers may apply for their minor children and if the father be dead the mother may apply. Husbands may apply for wives. Applications for orphans, insane persons and persons of unsound mind may be made by duly appointed guardian or curator, and for aged and infirm persons and prisoners by agents duly authorized thereunto by power of attorney, in the discretion of said Commission.

3. At the time of the selection of allotment each citizen and duly identified Mississippi Choctaw shall designate as a homestead out of said selection land equal in value to one hundred and sixty acres of the average allottable land of the Choctaw and Chickasaw Nations, as nearly as may be.

4. Each Choctaw and Chickasaw freedman, at the time of selection shall designate as his or her allotment of the lands of the Choctaw and Chickasaw Nations, land equal in value to forty acres of the average allottable land of the Choctaw and Chickasaw Nations.

5. Citizens, freedmen and identified Mississippi Choctaws who are married, whether they have attained their majority or not, will be regarded as of age for the purpose of making selections.

6. Selections may be made by citizen and freedman parents for unmarried male children under twenty-one years of age and for unmarried female children under eighteen years of age, and a male citizen or freedman may make selection for his wife, if she is entitled to make selection, unless she shall, at the time or previously thereto, protest in writing.

7. Where the father of an unmarried minor citizen, freedman or identified Mississippi Choctaw is a non-citizen, the citizen, freedman or identified Mississippi Choctaw mother of such children must make selection in person in behalf of said children.

8. Selections of allotments and designations of homesteads for minor citizens and selections of allotments for minor freedmen may be made by the citizen father or mother or freedman father or mother, as the case may be, or by a guardian, curator, or an administrator having charge of their estate, in the order named.

9. Selections of allotments and designations of homesteads for citizen, and selections of allotment for freedmen, prisoners, convicts, aged and infirm persons and soldiers and sailors of the United States on duty outside of Indian Territory, may be made by duly appointed agents under power of attorney, and for incompetents by guardians, curators, or other suitable person akin to them.

10. Selections may be made and homesteads designated by duly identified Mississippi Choctaws, who have, within one year after the date of their identification as such, made satisfactory proof of bona fide settlement within the Choctaw-Chickasaw country, at any time within six months after the date of their said identification.

11. Persons authorized to make selections by power of attorney, as provided in rules 2 and 9 hereof, must be the husband or wife, or a relative not further removed than a cousin of the first degree of the person for whom such selection is made.

12. It shall be the duty of the Commission to the Five Civilized Tribes to see that selections of allotments and designations of homesteads for the classes of persons mentioned in rules 2, 6, 7, 8 and 9 hereof, are made for the best interests of such persons.

13. Selections of allotments for citizens, freedmen and identified Mississippi Choctaws who have died subsequent to September 25, 1902, and before making a selection of allotment, shall be made by a duly appointed administrator or executor. If, however, such administrator or executor be not duly and expeditiously appointed, or fails to act promptly when appointed, or for any other cause such selections be not so made within a reasonable and practicable time, the Commission to the Five Civilized Tribes shall designate the lands thus to be allotted.

14. In determining the value of a selection the appraised value of the land selected shall be increased by the appraised value of such pine timber on such land as has heretofore been estimated by the Commission to the Five Civilized Tribes.

15. Selections of allotments may be made only by citizens and freedmen whose enrollment has been approved by the Secretary of the Interior, and by persons duly identified by the Commission to the Five Civilized Tribes as Mississippi Choctaws, and by none others.

16. When a selection of land has been made by a citizen, freedman or identified Mississippi Choctaw, and the land so selected is claimed by a person whose rights as a citizen or freedman have not been finally determined, contest for the land so selected may be instituted by the person claiming the land, formal application for the land being first made as is required by the Rules of Practice in Choctaw and Chickasaw allotment contest cases.

THE COMMISSION TO THE FIVE CIVILIZED TRIBES.
TAMS BIXBY, Chairman.

Muskogee, Indian Territory, March 24, 1903.

The above statement published prior to 1905, was established for what was supposed to be a set of guidelines when it came to allotments. But with supplemental agreements and Congressional legislation, time frames as well as rules and regulations often changed and were not the same for every tribe.

INTRODUCTION

The *Applications for Enrollment of Choctaw Newborn Act of 1905*, National Archive film M-1301, Rolls 50-57, are found under the heading of Applications for Enrollment of the Commission to the Five Civilized Tribes. For this series, I have transcribed the application forms filled out by individuals applying for enrollment in the Five Civilized Tribes under the Dawes Commission. These applications contain considerably more information than stated on the census cards found in series M-1186. M-1301 possesses its own numerical sequence, separate from M-1186. To find each party's roll number you would have to reference M-1186.

The Choctaw as well as the Chickasaw allotments were likely some of the most sought after properties in Indian Territory. There was supposed to be a 25-year restriction on the sale or lease of any Indian lands so as to insure that the owners wouldn't be swindled, but that isn't what happened. This fact is borne out in the Dawes Commission General Allotment Act, of February 8, 1887, Section 5, which "Provides that after an Indian person is allotted land, the United States will hold the land 'in trust [1] for the sole use and benefit of the Indian' (or his heirs if the Indian landowner dies) for a period of 25 years. (Land held in trust by the United States government cannot be sold or in anyway alienated by the Indian landowner, since the United States government considers the underlying ownership of the land held by itself and not the tribe. After the period of trust ends, the Indian landowner is free to sell the land and is free from any encumbrance from the United States.)"[1] Instead, Native Americans were exploited by the devious. The Choctaw and Chickasaw Districts both had huge asphalt and coal deposits, so there was pressure from outsiders to acquire them from the minute they were discovered. After repeated attacks throughout the years and many legislative changes, President "Roosevelt finally signed the Five Tribes Bill at noon on April 26, 1906, the forces seeking to end all restrictions were disappointed. Section 19 removed restrictions from the sale of all inherited land but directed that no full-bloods could sell their land for twenty-five years. The Act also prohibited leases for more than one year without the approval of the Secretary of the Interior."[2]

Angie Debo described the opportunists that wanted these Native American allotments as, "Grafters". The parents of the newborns enumerated within this series would no sooner receive the approval for their child's allotment than there would be someone there with cash in hand holding a new deed or lease for the parents to sign their child's birthright away. Angie Debo said it best, "As the business incapacity of the allottees became apparent, a horde of despoilers fastened themselves upon their property." According to Debo, "The term 'grafter' was applied as a matter of course to dealers in Indian land, and was frankly accepted by them. The speculative fever also affected Government employees so that it was almost impossible to prevent them from making personal investments."[3]

---

[1] General Allotment Act, Act of Feb. 8, 1887 (24 Stat. 388, ch. 119, 25 USCA 331)
[2] The Dawes Commission and the Allotment of the Five Civilized Tribes, 1893-1914 by Kent Carter, pg. 173
[3] And Still the Waters Run, Angie Debo, p. 92.

INTRODUCTION

According to the Department of Interior in 1905, "It is estimated that there will be added to the final rolls of the citizens and freedmen of the Choctaw and Chickasaw nations the names of 2,000 persons, including 1,500 new-born children to be enrolled under the provisions of the act of Congress approved March 3, 1905."[4]

The quote below explains, in detail, the requirements for qualifying as a newborn Choctaw, "By the act of Congress approved March 3, 1905 (H.R. 17474), entitled 'An act making appropriations for the current and contingent expenses of the Indian Department and for fulfilling treaty stipulations with various Indian tribes for the fiscal year ending June 30, 1906, and for other purposes,' it was provided as follows:

'That the Commission to the Five Civilized Tribes is hereby authorized for sixty days after the date of the approval of this act to receive and consider applications for enrollment of infant children born prior to September twenty-fifth, nineteen hundred and two, and who were living on said date, to citizens by blood of the Choctaw and Chickasaw tribes of Indians whose enrollment has been approved by the Secretary of the Interior prior to the date of the approval of this act; and to enroll and make allotments to such children.'

'That the Commission to the Five Civilized Tribes is authorized for sixty days after the date of the approval of this act to receive and consider applications for enrollment of children born subsequent to September twenty-fifth, nineteen hundred and two, and prior to March fourth, nineteen hundred and five, and who were living on said latter date, to citizens by blood of the Choctaw and Chickasaw tribes of Indians whose enrollment has been approved by the Secretary of the Interior prior to the date of the approval of this act; and to enroll and make allotments to such children.'

"Notice is hereby given that the Commission to the Five Civilized Tribes will, up to and inclusive of midnight, May 2, 1905, receive applications for the enrollment of infant children born prior to September 25, 1902, and who were living on said date, to citizens by blood of the Choctaw and Chickasaw tribes of Indians whose enrollment has been approved by the Secretary of the Interior prior to March 3, 1905."[5]

Following is the scope of these transcriptions: Besides the applications themselves, researchers will find the identities of other individuals within these applications -- doctors, lawyers, mid-wives, and other relatives -- that may help with you genealogical research.

Jeff Bowen
Gallipolis, Ohio
NativeStudy.com

---

[4] Annual Reports of the Department of the Interior For the Fiscal Year Ended June 30, 1905, p. 609.
[5] Annual Reports of the Department of the Interior For the Fiscal Year Ended June 30, 1905, p. 593.

Applications for Enrollment of Choctaw Newborn
Act of 1905   Volume XII

Choc New Born 787
    Alice Mitchell   b. 11-9-03

Choctaw 2006.

Muskogee, Indian Territory, April 12, 1905.

Luster Mitchell,
    Kiowa, Indian Territory.

Dear Sir:

Receipt is hereby acknowledged of the affidavits of Jane Mitchell and Alcy Rose to the birth of Alice Mitchell, daughter of Luster and Jane Mitchell, November 9th, 1903, and the same have been filed with our records as an application for the enrollment of said child.

Respectfully,

Commissioner in Charge.

NEW BORN AFFIDAVIT

No

CHOCTAW ENROLLING COMMISSION

IN THE MATTER OF THE APPLICATION FOR ENROLLMENT as a citizen of the Choctaw Nation, of   Alice Mitchell   born on the 9 day of   November   190 3

Name of father   Luster Mitchell   a citizen of   U S   Nation, final enrollment No...........................   now Mitchell

Name of mother   Jane Murphy   a citizen of   Choctaw   Nation, final enrollment No.   5735

Kiowa I.T.   Postoffice.

Applications for Enrollment of Choctaw Newborn
Act of 1905   Volume XII

AFFIDAVIT OF MOTHER

UNITED STATES OF AMERICA
   INDIAN TERRITORY
DISTRICT   Central

I   Jane Murphy now Mitchell   , on oath state that I am   20   years of age and a citizen by   Blood   of the   Choctaw   Nation, and as such have been placed upon the final roll of the   Choctaw   Nation, by the Honorable Secretary of the Interior my final enrollment number being   5735   ; that I am the lawful wife of   Luster Mitchell   , who is a citizen of the   US   Nation, and as such has been placed upon the final roll of said Nation by the Honorable Secretary of the Interior, his final enrollment number being — and that a   Female   child was born to me on the   9   day of November   190 3; that said child has been named   Alice Mitchell   , and is now living.

WITNESSETH: Jane Mitchell

  Must be two witnesses ⎰ John Philips
  who are citizens   ⎱ Sina Gus

Subscribed and sworn to before me this, the   28   day of   February   , 190 5

                                        HB Rowley
                                           Notary Public.

My Commission Expires:
Nov 22nd 1905

Affidavit of Attending Physician or Midwife

UNITED STATES OF AMERICA,
   INDIAN TERRITORY,
Centl   DISTRICT

I,   Alcy Rose   a   midwife on oath state that I attended on Mrs. Jane Murphy now Mitchell   wife of   Luster Mitchell   on the   9   day of   November , 190 3, that there was born to her on said date a   Female   child, that said child is now living, and is said to have been named   Alice Mitchell

                                       her
                                 Alcy x Rose   midwife   ~~M. D~~.
                                 mark

Subscribed and sworn to before me this the   28   day of   February   1905

                                    HB Rowley
                                      Notary Public.

WITNESSETH:
  Must be two witnesses ⎰ Tom Philip
  who are citizens and
  know the child.   ⎱ Sina Gus

Applications for Enrollment of Choctaw Newborn
Act of 1905 Volume XII

We hereby certify that we are well acquainted with Alcy Rose a mid wife and know her to be reputable and of good standing in the community.

Must be two citizen witnesses. { Tom Philip
Sina Gus

BIRTH AFFIDAVIT.

DEPARTMENT OF THE INTERIOR.
COMMISSION TO THE FIVE CIVILIZED TRIBES.

IN RE APPLICATION FOR ENROLLMENT, as a citizen of the Choctaw Nation, of Alice Mitchell , born on the 9th day of Nov , 1903

Name of Father: Luster Mitchell   a citizen of the United States ~~Nation~~.

nee Jane Murphy

Name of Mother: Jane Mitchell   a citizen of the Choctaw Nation.

Postoffice   Kiowa Ind. Ter.

AFFIDAVIT OF MOTHER.

UNITED STATES OF AMERICA, Indian Territory, }
Central   DISTRICT.

I, Mrs Jane Mitchell , on oath state that I am 21 years of age and a citizen by Blood , of the Choctaw Nation; that I am the lawful wife of Luster Mitchell , who is a citizen, ~~by~~ of the United States ~~Nation~~; that a Female child was born to me on 9th day of November , 1903; that said child has been named Alice Mitchell , and was living March 4, 1905.

Jane Mitchell

Witnesses To Mark:
{

Subscribed and sworn to before me this 8th day of April , 1905

C.E. Culbertson
Notary Public.

Applications for Enrollment of Choctaw Newborn
Act of 1905   Volume XII

AFFIDAVIT OF ATTENDING PHYSICIAN OR MID-WIFE.

UNITED STATES OF AMERICA, Indian Territory,
 Central   DISTRICT.

I,   Alcy Rose   , a   Midwife   , on oath state that I attended on Mrs.   Jane Mitchell   , wife of   Luster Mitchell   on the   9th   day of November, 1903; that there was born to her on said date a   Female   child; that said child was living March 4, 1905, and is said to have been named Alice Mitchell

                                                        her
Witnesses To Mark: Alcy x Rose
{ Dellie Mitchell   mark
{ M.A. Mitchell

Subscribed and sworn to before me this   8th   day of   April   , 1905

                            C.E. Culbertson
                            Notary Public.

Choc New Born 788
    Crawford Billy   b. 2-2-04

                                                                              Choctaw 2082.

                        Muskogee, Indian Territory, April 12, 1905.
Austin Billy,
    Talihina, Indian Territory.

    Receipt is hereby acknowledged of the affidavits of Susan Billy and Austin Billy to the birth of Crawford Billy, son of Austin and Susan Billy, February 2nd, 1904, and the same have been filed with our records as an application for the enrollment of said child.

                      Respectfully,

                                          Commissioner in Charge.

Applications for Enrollment of Choctaw Newborn
Act of 1905 Volume XII

7 NB 788

Muskogee, Indian Territory, June 16, 1905.

Austin Billy,
    Talihina, Indian Territory.

Dear Sir:

    Receipt is hereby acknowledged of the affidavits of Susan Billy and Phoeba Benton; also affidavits of Henry Johnson and George Milton to the birth of Crawford Billy, son of Austin and Susan Billy, February 2, 1904, and the same have been filed with our records in the matter of the enrollment of said child.

Respectfully,

Chairman.

7-NB-788.

Muskogee, Indian Territory, June 6, 1905.

Austin Billy,
    Talihina, Indian Territory.

Dear Sir:

    There is enclosed herewith for execution affidavit of the attending physician or midwife in the matter of the application for the enrollment of your infant child, Crawford Billy.

    It is noted from the application heretofore filed in this office that you attended upon your wife at the time of birth of the applicant. If there was a physician or midwife also in attendance you will please secure his or her affidavit, but if you were the only one in attendance it will be necessary for you to secure the affidavits of two persons, who are disinterested and not related to the applicant, who have actual knowledge of the facts that the child was born, the date of his birth; that he was living on March 4, 1905, and that Susan Billy is his mother.

    This matter should receive your immediate attention, as no further action can be taken until these affidavits are filed with the Commission.

Respectfully,

VR 6-2.   Commissioner in Charge.

Applications for Enrollment of Choctaw Newborn
Act of 1905   Volume XII

BIRTH AFFIDAVIT.

DEPARTMENT OF THE INTERIOR.
COMMISSION TO THE FIVE CIVILIZED TRIBES.

IN RE APPLICATION FOR ENROLLMENT, as a citizen of the Choctaw Nation, of Crawford Billy, born on the 2 day of February, 1904

Name of Father: Austin Billy   a citizen of the Choctaw Nation.
Name of Mother: Susan Billy   a citizen of the Choctaw Nation.

Postoffice   Talihina I.T.

AFFIDAVIT OF MOTHER.

UNITED STATES OF AMERICA, Indian Territory, }
    Central   DISTRICT.

I, Susan Billy, on oath state that I am 30 years of age and a citizen by Blood, of the Choctaw Nation; that I am the lawful wife of Austin Billy, who is a citizen, by Blood of the Choctaw Nation; that a male child was born to me on 2^d day of Feby, 1904, that said child has been named Crawford Billy, and is now living.

                          her
                Susan x Billy

Witnesses To Mark: mark
  { Austin W James
    D. Thomas

Subscribed and sworn to before me this 8 day of April, 1905.

                Sam T. Roberts Jr
                Notary Public.

AFFIDAVIT OF ATTENDING PHYSICIAN OR MID-WIFE.

UNITED STATES OF AMERICA, Indian Territory, }
    Central   DISTRICT.

I, Austin Billy, a ——————, on oath state that I attended on Mrs. Susan Billy, wife of my wife on the 2^d day of February, 1904; that there was born to her on said date a male child; that said child is now living and is said to have been named Crawford Billy

                Austin Billy

Witnesses To Mark:
  { D. Thomas

Applications for Enrollment of Choctaw Newborn
Act of 1905   Volume XII

Subscribed and sworn to before me this 8 day of   April   , 1905.

                                                     Sam T. Roberts Jr
                                                     Notary Public.

(The affidavit below typed as given.)

United States of America)
Central District, Ind Ter.) ss.

              Henry Johnson   Being duly sworn deposes and says .My name is Henry Johnson   , age   47   .My Post office is Talihina I T.I am a Choctaw Indian and a duly enrolled citizen.I know Austin Billy and his wife, Susan Billy.I know that they had a male child born to them on February 2nd 1904 and that said child bears the name of   Crawford Billy, and is alive at this date.I futher state that I am of no relation to either the Father or Mother and that I have no interest in the prosecution of this claim.

                                                   Henry Johnson

Subscribed and sworn to before me this sworn to before me this 13th day June 1905.

                                                   Jno J Thomas

My commission expires Mch 3oth 1909.

(The affidavit below typed as given.)

United States of America)
Central District, Ind Ter.) ss.

              George Milton   Being duly sworn deposes and says .My name is George Milton   , age   22   .My Post office is Talihina I T.I am a Choctaw Indian and a duly enrolled citizen.I know Austin Billy and his wife, Susan Billy.I know that they had a male child born to them on February 2nd 1904 and that said child bears the name of Crawford Billy, and is alive at this date.I futher state that I am of no relation to either the Father or Mother and that I have no interest in the prosecution of this claim.

                                                   George Milton

Subscribed and sworn to before me this sworn to before me this 13th day June 1905.

                                                   Jno J Thomas

My commission expires Mch 3oth 1909.

Applications for Enrollment of Choctaw Newborn
Act of 1905   Volume XII

BIRTH AFFIDAVIT.

DEPARTMENT OF THE INTERIOR.
COMMISSION TO THE FIVE CIVILIZED TRIBES.

IN RE APPLICATION FOR ENROLLMENT, as a citizen of the Choctaw Nation, of Crawford Billy, born on the 2nd day of Feb, 1904

Name of Father: Austin Billy   a citizen of the Choctaw Nation.
Name of Mother: Susan Billy   a citizen of the Choctaw Nation.

Postoffice   Talihina Ind. Ter.

AFFIDAVIT OF MOTHER.

UNITED STATES OF AMERICA, Indian Territory, }
Central   DISTRICT.

I, Susan Billy, on oath state that I am 30 years of age and a citizen by Blood, of the Choctaw Nation; that I am the lawful wife of Austin Billy, who is a citizen, by Blood of the Choctaw Nation; that a male child was born to me on 2nd day of Feby, 1904; that said child has been named Crawford Billy, and was living March 4, 1905.

                                her
                        Susan x Billy
Witnesses To Mark: mark
 { Alex McIntosh
 { Ben Willis

Subscribed and sworn to before me this 13th day of June, 1905

My commission expires March 30, 1909
Commission from U. S. Court - Antlers, I. T.   Jno J Thomas
MY OFFICE TALIHINA, I. T.   Notary Public.

AFFIDAVIT OF ATTENDING PHYSICIAN OR MID-WIFE.

UNITED STATES OF AMERICA, Indian Territory, }
Central   DISTRICT.

I, Phoeba Benton, a midwife, on oath state that I attended on Mrs. Susan Billy, wife of Austin Billy on the 2nd day of February, 1904; that there was born to her on said date a male child; that said child was living March 4, 1905, and is said to have been named Crawford Billy
                                her
                        Phoeba x Benton
                                mark

Applications for Enrollment of Choctaw Newborn
Act of 1905 Volume XII

Witnesses To Mark:
    { Dan Bryant
      Sam T Roberts Jr

    Subscribed and sworn to before me this 13th day of June , 1905

    My commission expires March 30, 1909   Jno J Thomas
    Commission from U. S. Court - Antlers, I. T.   Notary Public.
    MY OFFICE TALIHINA, I. T.

Choc New Born 789
    Mabel Dukes b. 9-15-03

                                Choctaw 2198.

                  Muskogee, Indian Territory, April 12, 1905.

Loren D. Dukes,
    Talihina, Indian Territory.

Dear Sir:

    Receipt is hereby acknowledged of the affidavits of Pallie Dukes and W. B. Miller to the birth of Mabel Dukes, daughter of Loren D. Dukes and Pallie Dukes, September 15, 1903, and the same have been filed with our records as an application for the enrollment of said child.

                  Respectfully,

                                    Commissioner in Charge.

BIRTH AFFIDAVIT.
DEPARTMENT OF THE INTERIOR.
COMMISSION TO THE FIVE CIVILIZED TRIBES.

    IN RE APPLICATION FOR ENROLLMENT, as a citizen of the   Choctaw   Nation, of Mabel Dukes , born on the 15 day of September , 1903

Name of Father: Loren Dukes   a citizen of the Choctaw Nation.
Name of Mother: Pallie Dukes   a citizen of the Choctaw Nation.

                      Postoffice   Talihina I.T.

Applications for Enrollment of Choctaw Newborn
Act of 1905   Volume XII

AFFIDAVIT OF MOTHER.

UNITED STATES OF AMERICA, Indian Territory, }
    Central   DISTRICT. }

    I, Pallie Dukes, on oath state that I am 23 years of age and a citizen by Intermarriage, of the Choctaw Nation; that I am the lawful wife of Loren D Dukes, who is a citizen, by Blood of the Choctaw Nation; that a female child was born to me on 15 day of September, 1903, that said child has been named Mabel Dukes, and is now living.

                                    Pallie Dukes

Witnesses To Mark:
  {

    Subscribed and sworn to before me this 8 day of April, 1905.

                                    Sam T Roberts Jr
                                          Notary Public.

AFFIDAVIT OF ATTENDING PHYSICIAN OR MID-WIFE.

UNITED STATES OF AMERICA, Indian Territory, }
    Central   DISTRICT. }

    I, W.B. Miller, a Physician, on oath state that I attended on Mrs. Pallie Dukes, wife of Loren Dukes on the 15 day of September, 1903; that there was born to her on said date a female child; that said child is now living and is said to have been named Mabel Dukes

                                    W.B. Miller M.D.

Witnesses To Mark:
  {

    Subscribed and sworn to before me this 8 day of April, 1905.

                                    Sam T Roberts Jr
                                          Notary Public.

Applications for Enrollment of Choctaw Newborn
Act of 1905   Volume XII

Choc New Born 790
    Clyde Sage   b. 11-25-04
    Claude Sage   b. 11-25-04
    Leroy Sage   b. 12-3-03

    No. 3   died prior to March 4, 1905

    No. 3   Hereon dismissed under order of the
           Comm to The FCT of July 18, 1905

    Notice of Decision forwarded applicant's
          father Aug 23, 1905

7-NB-790.

Muskogee, Indian Territory, May 31, 1905.

Sidney Sage,
    Talihina, Indian Territory.

Dear Sir:

    Referring to the applications for the enrollment of your infant children, Claud[sic] Sage and Clyde Sage, born November 25, 1904, it is noted that the same affidavits are filed in support of borth[sic] of these applications. Separate affidavits will be required in each case, which you will please supply, using the enclosed applications.

    In having these affidavits executed care should be exercised to see that all names are written in full, as they appear in the body of the affidavit, and in the event that either of the persons signing the affidavit are unable to write, signatures by mark must be attested by two witnesses. Each affidavit must be executed before a Notary Public and the notarial seal and signature of the officer must be attached to each separate affidavit.

                    Respectfully,

VR 31-8.   [sic]

Applications for Enrollment of Choctaw Newborn
Act of 1905   Volume XII

7-NB-790.

Muskogee, Indian Territory, June 10, 1905.

Sidney Sage,
    Talihina, Indian Territory.

Dear Sir:

    Receipt is hereby acknowledged of the affidavits of Carrie Sage and W. B. Miller to the birth of Clyde Sage and Claud Sage, children of Sidney and Carrie Sage, November 25, 1904, and the same have been filed with our records in the matter of the enrollment of said child.

Respectfully,

Chairman.

BIRTH AFFIDAVIT.

DEPARTMENT OF THE INTERIOR.
COMMISSION TO THE FIVE CIVILIZED TRIBES.

    IN RE APPLICATION FOR ENROLLMENT, as a citizen of the   Choctaw   Nation, of Clyde Sage   , born on the   25   day of   November   , 1904

Name of Father: Sidney Sage   a citizen of the   Choctaw   Nation.
Name of Mother: Carrie Sage   a citizen of the   Choctaw   Nation.

Postoffice   Talihina Ind. Ter.

AFFIDAVIT OF MOTHER.

UNITED STATES OF AMERICA, Indian Territory, }
    Central   **DISTRICT.** }

    I,   Carrie Sage   , on oath state that I am   38   years of age and a citizen by intermarriage   , of the   Choctaw   Nation; that I am the lawful wife of   Sidney Sage   , who is a citizen, by blood   of the   Choctaw   Nation; that a male   child was born to me on   25   day of   November   , 1904; that said child has been named   Clyde Sage   , and was living March 4, 1905.

Carrie Sage

Witnesses To Mark:
{

Applications for Enrollment of Choctaw Newborn
Act of 1905 Volume XII

Subscribed and sworn to before me this 6 day of June , 1905

Sam T. Roberts Jr
Notary Public.

AFFIDAVIT OF ATTENDING PHYSICIAN OR MID-WIFE.

UNITED STATES OF AMERICA, Indian Territory,
Central   DISTRICT.

I, WB Miller , a Physician , on oath state that I attended on Mrs. Carrie Sage , wife of Sidney Sage on the 25 day of November , 1904; that there was born to her on said date a male child; that said child was living March 4, 1905, and is said to have been named Clyde Sage

W.B. Miller M.D.

Witnesses To Mark:
{

Subscribed and sworn to before me this 6 day of June , 1905

Sam T. Roberts Jr
Notary Public.

BIRTH AFFIDAVIT.

DEPARTMENT OF THE INTERIOR,
COMMISSION TO THE FIVE CIVILIZED TRIBES.

IN RE Application for Enrollment, as a citizen of the Choctaw Nation, of Clyde and Claud Sage , born on the 25 day of November , 1904

Name of Father: Sidney Sage   a citizen of the Choctaw Nation.
Name of Mother: Carrie Sage   a citizen of the Choctaw Nation.

Post-Office: Talihina I.T.

Applications for Enrollment of Choctaw Newborn
Act of 1905   Volume XII

AFFIDAVIT OF MOTHER.

UNITED STATES OF AMERICA, }
    INDIAN TERRITORY.
  Central   District.

    I, Carrie Sage, on oath state that I am 38 years of age and a citizen by Intermarriage, of the Choctaw Nation; that I am the lawful wife of Sidney Sage, who is a citizen, by Blood of the Choctaw Nation; that a Twin Male child~~ren~~ ~~was~~ *were* born to me on 25 day of November, 1904, that said child~~ren~~ has been named Clyde Sage & Claud Sage, and is now living.

                              Carrie Sage

WITNESSES TO MARK:

    Subscribed and sworn to before me this 8 *day of* April, *1905*.

                              Sam T. Roberts Jr
                                NOTARY PUBLIC.

AFFIDAVIT OF ATTENDING PHYSICIAN OR MID-WIFE.

UNITED STATES OF AMERICA, }
    INDIAN TERRITORY.
  Central   District.

    I, W B Miller, a Physician, on oath state that I attended on Mrs. Carrie Sage, wife of Sidney Sage on the 25 day of November, 1904; that there was born to her on said date a Twin Male children ~~child~~; that said child is now living and is said to have been named Clyde Sage & Claude Sage

                              W. B. Miller M.D.

WITNESSES TO MARK:

    Subscribed and sworn to before me this 8 *day of* April, *1905*.

                              Sam T. Roberts Jr
                                NOTARY PUBLIC.

Applications for Enrollment of Choctaw Newborn
Act of 1905   Volume XII

BIRTH AFFIDAVIT.

DEPARTMENT OF THE INTERIOR,
COMMISSION TO THE FIVE CIVILIZED TRIBES.

IN RE Application for Enrollment, as a citizen of the   Choctaw   Nation, of   Leroy Sage , born on the   3   day of   December   , 1903

Name of Father: Sidney Sage   a citizen of the   Choctaw   Nation.
Name of Mother: Carrie Sage   a citizen of the approval pending Nation.

Post-Office: Talihina I.T.

AFFIDAVIT OF MOTHER.

UNITED STATES OF AMERICA, }
   INDIAN TERRITORY.
   Central   District.

I,   Carrie Sage   , on oath state that I am   37   years of age and a citizen by Intermarriage   Nation; that I am the lawful wife of   Sidney Sage   , who is a citizen, by Blood   of the Choctaw   Nation; that a   male   child was born to me on   3   day of December , 1903 , that said child has been named   Leroy Sage   , and is now living.

Carrie Sage

WITNESSES TO MARK:

Subscribed and sworn to before me this   8   day of October   , 1905.

Sam T Roberts Jr
NOTARY PUBLIC.

AFFIDAVIT OF ATTENDING PHYSICIAN OR MID-WIFE.

UNITED STATES OF AMERICA, }
   INDIAN TERRITORY.
   Central   District.

I,   C E Calhoun   , a   Physician   , on oath state that I attended on Mrs. Carrie Sage   , wife of Sidney Sage   on the 3^d day of   December , 1903; that there was born to her on said date a   male   child; that said child is now living and is said to have been named   Leroy Sage

C.E. Calhoun M.D.

Applications for Enrollment of Choctaw Newborn
Act of 1905   Volume XII

WITNESSES TO MARK:
{

Subscribed and sworn to before me this   8   day of   October   , 1905.

Sam T Roberts Jr
NOTARY PUBLIC.

7-NB-790

COPY

Muskogee, Indian Territory, August 23, 1905.

Sidney Sage,
    Talihina, Indian Territory.

Dear Sir:

You are hereby advised that it appearing from the records of this office, that your child, Leroy Sage died prior to March 4, 1905, the Commissioner to the Five Civilized Tribes on August 23, 1905, dismissed the application for the enrollment of said child as a citizen by blood of the Choctaw Nation.

Respectfully,
SIGNED
Tams Bixby
Commissioner.

7-NB-790

COPY

Muskogee, Indian Territory, August 23, 1905.

Mansfield, McMurray & Cornish,
    Attorneys for Choctaw and Chickasaw Nations,
        South McAlester, Indian Territory.

Gentlemen:

You are hereby advised that it appearing from the records of this office that Leroy Sage died prior to March 4, 1905, the Commissioner to the Five Civilized Tribes, on August 23, 1905, dismissed the application for the enrollment of said child, as a citizen by blood of the Choctaw Nation.

Respectfully,
SIGNED   *Tams Bixby*
Commissioner.

Applications for Enrollment of Choctaw Newborn
Act of 1905 Volume XII

It appearing from the within affidavits that Leroy Sage, born December 3, 1903, for whose enrollment as a citizen by blood of the Choctaw Nation, application was made under the Act of Congress approved March 3, 1905 (33 Stats., 1071), died March 12, 1904, it is hereby ordered that the application for the enrollment of said Leroy Sage as a citizen by blood of the Choctaw Nation be dismissed.

                                      Tams Bixby
                                      Commissioner.

Muskogee, Indian Territory,
    AUG 23 1905

Department of the Interior,
COMMISSION TO THE FIVE CIVILIZED TRIBES.

In the matter of the death of   Leroy Sage   a citizen of the   Choctaw Nation, who formerly resided at or near   Talihina   , Ind. Ter., and died on the   12   day of   March   , 1904

AFFIDAVIT OF RELATIVE.

UNITED STATES OF AMERICA,
   INDIAN TERRITORY,
   Central   District.

I,   Sidney Sage   , on oath state that I am   38   years of age and a citizen by Blood   , of the   Choctaw   Nation; that my postoffice address is   Talihina   , Ind. Ter.; that I am   Father   of   Leroy Sage   who was a citizen, by Blood   , of the Nation and that said   Leroy Sage   died on the   12   day of   March   , 1904

                                    Sidney Sage

Witnesses To Mark:
  {

Subscribed and sworn to before me this   8   day of   October   , 1904

                                    Sam T Roberts Jr
                                        Notary Public.

Applications for Enrollment of Choctaw Newborn
Act of 1905   Volume XII

AFFIDAVIT OF ACQUAINTANCE.

UNITED STATES OF AMERICA,
INDIAN TERRITORY,
Central District.

I, C.E. Calhoun, on oath state that I am 26 years of age, and a citizen by of the United States Nation; that my postoffice address is Talihina, Ind. Ter.; that I was personally acquainted with Leroy Sage infant who was a citizen, by Blood, of the Choctaw Nation; and that said Leroy Sage died on the 12 day of March, 1904

C.E. Calhoun M.D.

Witnesses To Mark:

Subscribed and sworn to before me this 8 day of October, 1904

Sam T Roberts Jr
Notary Public.

7-2298
7-NB-790

Muskogee, Indian Territory, July 26, 1905.

Sidney Sage,
Talihina, Indian Territory.

Dear Sir:

Receipt is hereby acknowledged of your letter of July 21, 1905, asking if your two children have been approved by the Secretary of the Interior; you also ask the status of the enrollment of your wife Carrie Sage as an intermarried citizen of the Choctaw Nation.

In reply to your letter you are advised that the names of your children Clyde and Claud Sage have been placed upon a schedule of citizens by blood of the Choctaw Nation which has been prepared for forwarding to the Secretary of the Interior and you will be notified when their enrollment is approved by him.

Referring to the application for the enrollment of your wife Carrie Sage as an intermarried citizen of the Choctaw Nation, you are advised that on August 4, 1903, Mrs. Sage was notified that it would be necessary for her to furnish legal evidence of her divorce from her former husband Carl Kilgore. Up to this time this evidence has not been received and until the same is furnished no further consideration can be given the application for her enrollment as an intermarried citizen of the Choctaw Nation.

Respectfully,

Commissioner.

Applications for Enrollment of Choctaw Newborn
Act of 1905 Volume XII

BIRTH AFFIDAVIT.

DEPARTMENT OF THE INTERIOR.
COMMISSION TO THE FIVE CIVILIZED TRIBES.

    IN RE APPLICATION FOR ENROLLMENT, as a citizen of the Choctaw Nation, of Claud Sage , born on the 25 day of Nov , 1904

Name of Father: Sidney Sage   a citizen of the Choctaw Nation.
Name of Mother: Carrie Sage   a citizen of the Choctaw Nation.

Postoffice   Talihina Ind Ter

AFFIDAVIT OF MOTHER.

UNITED STATES OF AMERICA, Indian Territory, }
    Central   DISTRICT. }

    I, Carrie Sage , on oath state that I am 38 years of age and a citizen by intermarriage , of the Choctaw Nation; that I am the lawful wife of Sidney Sage , who is a citizen, by blood of the Choctaw Nation; that a male child was born to me on 25 day of November , 1904; that said child has been named Claud Sage , and was living March 4, 1905.

                        Carrie Sage

Witnesses To Mark:
  {

    Subscribed and sworn to before me this 6 day of June , 1905

                        Sam T Roberts Jr
                        Notary Public.

AFFIDAVIT OF ATTENDING PHYSICIAN OR MID-WIFE.

UNITED STATES OF AMERICA, Indian Territory, }
    Central   DISTRICT. }

    I, W.B. Miller , a Physician , on oath state that I attended on Mrs. Carrie Sage , wife of Sidney Sage on the 25 day of November , 1904; that there was born to her on said date a male child; that said child was living March 4, 1905, and is said to have been named Claud Sage

                        W.B. Miller M.D.

Applications for Enrollment of Choctaw Newborn
Act of 1905   Volume XII

Witnesses To Mark:
{

    Subscribed and sworn to before me this   6   day of   June   , 1905

                                      Sam T Roberts Jr
                                        Notary Public.

Choc New Born 791
       Burton Oran Burks   b.   12-13-02
       Ora Velma Burks   b.   1-24-05

BIRTH AFFIDAVIT.
DEPARTMENT OF THE INTERIOR.
COMMISSION TO THE FIVE CIVILIZED TRIBES.

    IN RE APPLICATION FOR ENROLLMENT, as a citizen of the   Choctaw   Nation, of Burton Oran Burks   , born on the   13   day of   Dec   , 1902

Name of Father: J.M. Burks   a citizen of the   U. S.   ~~Nation~~.
Name of Mother: Lucinda Burks   a citizen of the   Choctaw   Nation.

                    Postoffice   Tupelo, I.T.

AFFIDAVIT OF MOTHER.

UNITED STATES OF AMERICA, Indian Territory, }
    Central   **DISTRICT.**

    I,   Lucinda Burks   , on oath state that I am   30   years of age and a citizen by   Blood   , of the   Choctaw   Nation; that I am the lawful wife of   J. M. Burks   , who is a citizen, ~~by~~ .... of the   U.S.   ~~Nation~~; that a   male   child was born to me on   13   day of   Dec   , 1902; that said child has been named   Burton Oran Burks   , and was living March 4, 1905.

                              Lucinda Burks

Witnesses To Mark:
{

Applications for Enrollment of Choctaw Newborn
Act of 1905   Volume XII

Subscribed and sworn to before me this 7 day of   April   , 1905

(Name Illegible)
Notary Public.

AFFIDAVIT OF ATTENDING PHYSICIAN OR MID-WIFE.

UNITED STATES OF AMERICA, Indian Territory,
   Central   DISTRICT.

I,   Thomas J Allen   , a Physician   , on oath state that I attended on Mrs. Lucinda Burks , wife of   J M Burks   on the 13 day of December , 1902; that there was born to her on said date a   male   child; that said child was living March 4, 1905, and is said to have been named Burton Oran Burks

                            Thomas J Allen M.D.

Witnesses To Mark:
{

Subscribed and sworn to before me this 8 day of   April   , 1905

                            D.D. Brunson
                            Notary Public.

BIRTH AFFIDAVIT.

DEPARTMENT OF THE INTERIOR.
COMMISSION TO THE FIVE CIVILIZED TRIBES.

IN RE APPLICATION FOR ENROLLMENT, as a citizen of the   Choctaw   Nation, of Ora Velma Burks   , born on the 24 day of Jan , 1905

Name of Father: J.M. Burks   a citizen of the U. S. ~~Nation~~.
Name of Mother: Lucinda Burks   a citizen of the   Choctaw   Nation.

                    Postoffice   Tupelo, I.T.

AFFIDAVIT OF MOTHER.

UNITED STATES OF AMERICA, Indian Territory,
   Central   DISTRICT.

I,   Lucinda Burks   , on oath state that I am 30   years of age and a citizen by Blood , of the   Choctaw   Nation; that I am the lawful wife of J. M. Burks , who is a citizen, ~~by~~   ~~of~~   of the   U.S.   ~~Nation~~; that a   Female   child

Applications for Enrollment of Choctaw Newborn
Act of 1905   Volume XII

was born to me on   24   day of   Jan   , 1905; that said child has been named   Ora Velma Burks   , and was living March 4, 1905.

Lucinda Burks

Witnesses To Mark:
{

   Subscribed and sworn to before me this   7th   day of   April   , 1905

(Name Illegible)
Notary Public.

AFFIDAVIT OF ATTENDING PHYSICIAN OR MID-WIFE.

UNITED STATES OF AMERICA, Indian Territory,
   Central   **DISTRICT.**

   I,   W. A. Craigo M.D.   , a   Physician   , on oath state that I attended on Mrs.   Lucinda Burks   , wife of   Joe M Burks   on the   24 day of Jan   , 1905; that there was born to her on said date a   Female   child; that said child was living March 4, 1905, and is said to have been named   Ora Velma Burks

W. A. Craigo M.D.

Witnesses To Mark:
{

   Subscribed and sworn to before me this   4 day of   April   , 1905

(Name Illegible)
Notary Public.

Choc New Born 792
   Ella Davis   b.   2-7-03

Applications for Enrollment of Choctaw Newborn
Act of 1905   Volume XII

Choctaw 2979.

Muskogee, Indian Territory, April 12, 1905.

Rosa Davis (Drake),
    Kinta, Indian Territory.

Dear Madam:

    Receipt is hereby acknowledged of the affidavits of Rosa Drake and Sophie Coley to the birth of Ella Davis, daughter of Tom Davis and Rosa Drake, Indian Territory February 7th, 1903, and the same have been filed with our records as an application for the enrollment of said child.

                  Respectfully,

                                    Commissioner in Charge.

7-N.B. 792.

Muskogee, Indian Territory, May 15, 1905.

Celin Coley,
    Sulphur, Indian Territory.

Dear Sir:

    Receipt is hereby acknowledged of your letter of May 6, asking if application has been received for the enrollment of Eller Davis.

    In reply to your letter you are advised that the affidavits heretofore forwarded to the birth of Ella Davis, daughter of Tom Davis and Rosa Drake, Indian Territory now Davis, have been filed with our records as an application for the enrollment of said child.

                  Respectfully,

                                      Chairman.

Applications for Enrollment of Choctaw Newborn
Act of 1905 Volume XII

BIRTH AFFIDAVIT.

DEPARTMENT OF THE INTERIOR.
COMMISSION TO THE FIVE CIVILIZED TRIBES.

IN RE APPLICATION FOR ENROLLMENT, as a citizen of the Choctaw Nation, of Ella Davis, born on the 7 day of Feby, 1903

Name of Father: Tom Davis   a citizen of the Choctaw Nation.
Name of Mother: Rosa Drake   a citizen of the Choctaw Nation.

Postoffice   Kinta I T

AFFIDAVIT OF MOTHER.

UNITED STATES OF AMERICA, Indian Territory,
     Western   DISTRICT.

I, Rosa Drake, on oath state that I am 36 years of age and a citizen by Blood, of the Choctaw Nation; that I am the lawful wife of Tom Davis, who is a citizen, by Blood of the Choctaw Nation; that a female child was born to me on 7 day of February, 1903; that said child has been named Ella Davis, and was living March 4, 1905.

                                          her
                                 Rosa x Drake
Witnesses To Mark: mark
   { *(Name Illegible)*
   { *(Name Illegible)*

Subscribed and sworn to before me this 8 day of April, 1905

                               L.D. Allen
                                   Notary Public.

AFFIDAVIT OF ATTENDING PHYSICIAN OR MID-WIFE.

UNITED STATES OF AMERICA, Indian Territory,
     Western   DISTRICT.

I, Sophie Coley, a midwife, on oath state that I attended on Mrs. Rosa Drake, wife of Tom Davis deceased on the 7 day of February, 1903; that there was born to her on said date a female child; that said child was living March 4, 1905, and is said to have been named Ella Davis

                                      her
                             Sophie x Coley
                               mark

Applications for Enrollment of Choctaw Newborn
Act of 1905   Volume XII

Witnesses To Mark:
{ *(Name Illegible)*
{ *(Name Illegible)*

Subscribed and sworn to before me this 8 day of   April   , 1905

L.D. Allen
Notary Public.

Choc New Born 793
  Margret Wilkin   b. 6-29-04

Choctaw 2047.

Muskogee, Indian Territory, April 12, 1905.

Levi Wilkin,
  Nashoba, Indian Territory.

Dear Sir:

  Receipt is hereby acknowledged of the affidavits of Lean Wilkin and Delilah Garland to the birth of Margret Wilkin, daughter of Levi Wilkin and Lean Wilkin, June 29th, 1904, and the same have been filed with our records as an application for the enrollment of said child.

      Respectfully,

        Commissioner in Charge.

BIRTH AFFIDAVIT.

DEPARTMENT OF THE INTERIOR.
COMMISSION TO THE FIVE CIVILIZED TRIBES.

IN RE APPLICATION FOR ENROLLMENT, as a citizen of the   Choctaw   Nation, of Margret Wilkin   , born on the 29 day of June , 1904

Name of Father: Levi Wilkin   a citizen of the   Choctaw   Nation.
Name of Mother: Lean Wilkin   a citizen of the   Choctaw   Nation.

      Postoffice   Nashoba Ind Ter

Applications for Enrollment of Choctaw Newborn
Act of 1905   Volume XII

AFFIDAVIT OF MOTHER.

UNITED STATES OF AMERICA, Indian Territory,
Central   DISTRICT.

I, Lean Wilkin, on oath state that I am 20 years of age and a citizen by blood of the Choctaw Nation; that I am the lawful wife of Levi Wilkin, who is a citizen, by blood of the Choctaw Nation; that a Female child was born to me on 29 day of June, 1904; that said child has been named Margret Wilkin, and was living March 4, 1905.

Lean Wilkin

Witnesses To Mark:
- Rachel Garland
- M A Fuller

Subscribed and sworn to before me this 7 day of April, 1905

F.M. Fuller
Notary Public.

AFFIDAVIT OF ATTENDING PHYSICIAN OR MID-WIFE.

UNITED STATES OF AMERICA, Indian Territory,
Central   DISTRICT.

I, Deliah[sic] Garland, a mid wife, on oath state that I attended on Mrs. Lean Wilkin, wife of Levi Wilkin on the 29 day of June, 1904; that there was born to her on said date a Female child; that said child was living March 4, 1905, and is said to have been named Margret Wilkin

Delilah Garland

Witnesses To Mark:
- Rachel Garland
- M A Fuller

Subscribed and sworn to before me this 7 day of April, 1905

F.M. Fuller
Notary Public.

My commishion[sic] expires April 18th 1908

Applications for Enrollment of Choctaw Newborn
Act of 1905   Volume XII

Choc New Born 794
>   Minerva B. Thompson   b. 11-26-03

>   Transferred to Chic NB card #534

>   empty

Choc New Born 795
>   Bengamin[sic] F. Culbertson   b. 1-17-05
>   Ida J. Culbertson   b. 6-23-03

>   Choctaw 4334.

>   Muskogee, Indian Territory, April 12, 1905.

Charles E. Culbertson,
>   Kiowa, Indian Territory.

Dear Sir:

>   Receipt is hereby acknowledged of the affidavits of Sophia A. Culbertson and Dr. L. W. McMorris to the birth of Ida J. Culbertson, daughter of Charles E. Culbertson and Sophia A. Culbertson, June 23rd, 1903; also the affidavits of Sophia A. Culbertson and Dr. L. W. McMorris to the birth of Benjamin F. Culbertson, son of Charles E. Culbertson and Sophia A. Culbertson, January 17th, 1905. These affidavits have been filed with our records as an application for the enrollment of the above named children.

>   Respectfully,

>   Commissioner in Charge.

Applications for Enrollment of Choctaw Newborn
Act of 1905   Volume XII

NEW BORN AFFIDAVIT

No ....

CHOCTAW ENROLLING COMMISSION

IN THE MATTER OF THE APPLICATION FOR ENROLLMENT as a citizen of the Choctaw Nation, of   Bengamon[sic] F. Culbertson   born on the 17th day of   Jany   190 5

Name of father   Charles E Culbertson   a citizen of   Choctaw   Nation, final enrollment No. 412

Name of mother   Sophia A. Culbertson   a citizen of   Choctaw   Nation, final enrollment No.   12120

Kiowa Ind Ter   Postoffice.

AFFIDAVIT OF MOTHER

UNITED STATES OF AMERICA
    INDIAN TERRITORY
DISTRICT   Central

I   Sophia A Culbertson   , on oath state that I am 33   years of age and a citizen by   Blood   of the   Choctaw   Nation, and as such have been placed upon the final roll of the   Choctaw   Nation, by the Honorable Secretary of the Interior my final enrollment number being   12120   ; that I am the lawful wife of Charles E Culbertson   , who is a citizen of the   Choctaw   Nation, and as such has been placed upon the final roll of said Nation by the Honorable Secretary of the Interior, his final enrollment number being   412   and that a   Male   child was born to me on the   17th day of   Jany   190 5; that said child has been named   Bengamon F Culbertson   , and is now living.

Sophia A Culbertson

WITNESSETH:
  Must be two witnesses { Geo W Pound
  who are citizens   { T Colbert

Subscribed and sworn to before me this, the 25th day of   Feby   , 190 5

C.E. Culbertson
Notary Public.

My Commission Expires: Dec 2^d 1905

28

Applications for Enrollment of Choctaw Newborn
Act of 1905   Volume XII

Affidavit of Attending Physician or Midwife

UNITED STATES OF AMERICA,
   INDIAN TERRITORY,
Central   DISTRICT

I, Dr L.W. McMorris   a   Physician on oath state that I attended on Mrs. Sophia A Culbertson   wife of   Charles E Culbertson on the 17th day of Jany , 190 5, that there was born to her on said date a   Male   child, that said child is now living, and is said to have been named   Bengamon F Culbertson

                                        L.W. McMorriet   M. D.

Subscribed and sworn to before me this the   25th day of   Feby   1905

                                      C.E Culbertson
                                          Notary Public.

WITNESSETH:

Must be two witnesses who are citizens and know the child.   { Geo W Pound   T Colbert

We hereby certify that we are well acquainted with   Dr L W McMorris   a   Physician   and know   him   to be reputable and of good standing in the community.

                        Must be two citizen witnesses.   { Geo W Pound   T Colbert

---

BIRTH AFFIDAVIT.

DEPARTMENT OF THE INTERIOR.
COMMISSION TO THE FIVE CIVILIZED TRIBES.

IN RE APPLICATION FOR ENROLLMENT, as a citizen of the   Choctaw   Nation, of Bengamon F. Culbertson   , born on the 17th day of Jany , 1905

Name of Father: Chas E Culbertson   a citizen of the   Choctaw   Nation.
Name of Mother: Sophia A Culbertson   a citizen of the   "   "   Nation.

                                Postoffice

Applications for Enrollment of Choctaw Newborn
Act of 1905   Volume XII

AFFIDAVIT OF MOTHER.

UNITED STATES OF AMERICA, Indian Territory, }
Central   DISTRICT.

   I,   Sophia A. Culbertson   , on oath state that I am   33   years of age and a citizen by   Blood   , of the   Choctaw   Nation; that I am the lawful wife of Chas E Culbertson   , who is a citizen, by   Intermarriage   of the   Choctaw   Nation; that a   Male   child was born to me on   17th day of   January   , 1905; that said child has been named   Bengamon F. Culbertson   , and was living March 4, 1905.

                                     Sophia A Culbertson

Witnesses To Mark:
{

   Subscribed and sworn to before me this   8th day of   April   , 1905

                                     C.E. Culbertson
                                     Notary Public.

AFFIDAVIT OF ATTENDING PHYSICIAN OR MID-WIFE.

UNITED STATES OF AMERICA, Indian Territory, }
Central   DISTRICT.

   I,   Dr L.W. McMorris   , a   Physician   , on oath state that I attended on Mrs.   Sophia A Culbertson   , wife of   Chas E Culbertson   on the   17th day of January   , 1905; that there was born to her on said date a .... child; that said child was living March 4, 1905, and is said to have been named Bengamon F. Culbertson

                                     Lee W McMorriet M.D.

Witnesses To Mark:
{

   Subscribed and sworn to before me this   8th day of   April   , 1905

                                     C.E. Culbertson
                                     Notary Public.

Applications for Enrollment of Choctaw Newborn
Act of 1905   Volume XII

NEW BORN AFFIDAVIT

No ....

CHOCTAW ENROLLING COMMISSION

IN THE MATTER OF THE APPLICATION FOR ENROLLMENT as a citizen of the Choctaw Nation, of   Ida J. Culbertson   born on the   23rd day of   June   190 3

Name of father   Charles E Culbertson   a citizen of   Choctaw   Nation, final enrollment No.   412

Name of mother   Sophia A. Culbertson   a citizen of   Choctaw   Nation, final enrollment No.   12120

Kiowa Ind. Ter.   Postoffice.

AFFIDAVIT OF MOTHER

UNITED STATES OF AMERICA
INDIAN TERRITORY
DISTRICT   Central

I   Sophia A Culbertson   , on oath state that I am   33   years of age and a citizen by   Blood   of the   Choctaw   Nation, and as such have been placed upon the final roll of the   Choctaw   Nation, by the Honorable Secretary of the Interior my final enrollment number being   12120   ; that I am the lawful wife of   Charles E Culbertson   , who is a citizen of the   Choctaw   Nation, and as such has been placed upon the final roll of said Nation by the Honorable Secretary of the Interior, his final enrollment number being   412   and that a   Female   child was born to me on the   23rd day of   June   190 3; that said child has been named   Ida J Culbertson   , and is now living.

Sophia A Culbertson

WITNESSETH:
Must be two witnesses who are citizens   { Geo W Pound
T Colbert

Subscribed and sworn to before me this, the   25th day of   Feby   , 190 5

C.E. Culbertson
Notary Public.

My Commission Expires: Dec 2nd 1905

Applications for Enrollment of Choctaw Newborn
Act of 1905   Volume XII

Affidavit of Attending Physician or Midwife

UNITED STATES OF AMERICA,
   INDIAN TERRITORY,
Central   DISTRICT

I, Dr L.W. McMorris   a   Physician on oath state that I attended on Mrs. Sophia A Culbertson   wife of   Charles E Culbertson on the 23rd day of   June , 190 3, that there was born to her on said date a   Female child, that said child is now living, and is said to have been named   Ida J Culbertson

                                                  L.W. McMorriet   M. D.

Subscribed and sworn to before me this the   25th day of   Feby   1905

                                       C.E Culbertson
                                          Notary Public.

WITNESSETH:
Must be two witnesses who are citizens and know the child.   { Geo W Pound
                     T Colbert

We hereby certify that we are well acquainted with   Dr L W McMorris   a   Physician   and know   him   to be reputable and of good standing in the community.

                     Must be two citizen witnesses.   { Geo W Pound
                                        T Colbert

BIRTH AFFIDAVIT.

DEPARTMENT OF THE INTERIOR.
COMMISSION TO THE FIVE CIVILIZED TRIBES.

IN RE APPLICATION FOR ENROLLMENT, as a citizen of the   Choctaw   Nation, of Ida J. Culbertson   , born on the 23rd day of   June , 1903

Name of Father: Chas E Culbertson   a citizen of the   Choctaw   Nation.
Name of Mother: Sophia A Culbertson   a citizen of the   Choctaw   Nation.

                         Postoffice   Kiowa Ind. Ter.

Applications for Enrollment of Choctaw Newborn
Act of 1905   Volume XII

AFFIDAVIT OF MOTHER.

UNITED STATES OF AMERICA, Indian Territory,
Central   DISTRICT.

I, Sophia A. Culbertson, on oath state that I am 33 years of age and a citizen by Blood, of the Choctaw Nation; that I am the lawful wife of Chas E Culbertson, who is a citizen, by Intermarriage of the Choctaw Nation; that a Female child was born to me on 23rd day of June, 1903; that said child has been named Ida J. Culbertson, and was living March 4, 1905.

Sophia A Culbertson

Witnesses To Mark:

Subscribed and sworn to before me this 8th day of April, 1905

C.E. Culbertson
Notary Public.

AFFIDAVIT OF ATTENDING PHYSICIAN OR MID-WIFE.

UNITED STATES OF AMERICA, Indian Territory,
Central   DISTRICT.

I, Dr L.W. McMorris, a Physician, on oath state that I attended on Mrs. Sophia A Culbertson, wife of Chas E Culbertson on the 23rd day of June, 1903; that there was born to her on said date a .... child; that said child was living March 4, 1905, and is said to have been named Ida J. Culbertson

Lee W McMorriet

Witnesses To Mark:

Subscribed and sworn to before me this 8th day of April, 1905

C.E. Culbertson
Notary Public.

Applications for Enrollment of Choctaw Newborn
Act of 1905   Volume XII

Choc New Born 796
    Moses Holman   b. 9-15-03

(The letter below given, again, without letterhead.)

$W^m O.B.$

COMMISSIONERS: TAMS BIXBY, THOMAS B. NEEDLES, C.R. BRECKINRIDGE. <u>WM. O. BEALL</u> Secretary	**DEPARTMENT OF THE INTERIOR,** **COMMISSIONER TO THE FIVE CIVILIZED TRIBES.**	REFER IN REPLY TO THE FOLLOWING: 7-NB-796.

ADDRESS ONLY THE
COMMISSION TO THE FIVE CIVILIZED TRIBES.

Muskogee, Indian Territory, May 31, 1905.

Alfred Holman,
    Corinne[sic], Indian Territory.

Dear Sir:

    There is enclosed you herewith for execution application for the enrollment of your infant child, Moses Holman, Born September 15, 1903.

    In the affidavits heretofore filed with the Commission filed in this office you executed the one intended for the physician or midwife. If there was no one else in attendance upon your wife at the time of birth of the applicant it will be necessary for you to secure the affidavits of two persons, who have actual knowledge of the facts that the child was born, the date of his birth; that he was living on March 4, 1905, and that Eliza Holman is his mother.

    In having these affidavits executed care should be exercised to see that all names are written in full, as they appear in the body of the affidavit, and in the event that either of the persons signing the affidavit are unable to write, signatures by mark must be attested by two witnesses. Each affidavit must be executed before a Notary Public and the notarial seal and signature of the officer must be attached to each separate affidavit.

                                  Respectfully,
                                    Tams Bixby
VR 31-7.   Chairman.

Applications for Enrollment of Choctaw Newborn
Act of 1905   Volume XII

7 NB 796

Muskogee, Indian Territory, June 16, 1905.

Alfred Holman,
    Corrine, Indian Territory.

Dear Sir:

    Receipt is hereby acknowledged of your affidavit and the affidavits of Eliza Holman, Gilbert Choat and T. Barnett Elapashabbe to the birth of Moses Holman son of Albert and Eliza Holman, September 15, 1903, and the same have been filed with our records in the matter of the enrollment of said child.

Respectfully,

Chairman.

7-NB-796

Muskogee, Indian Territory, July 31, 1905.

Alfred Holman,
    Fort Towson, Indian Territory.

Dear Sir:

    Receipt is hereby acknowledged of your letter of July 1905, asking if you can now file on lands for your infant son Moses Holman.

    In reply to your letter you are advised that the name of your child Moses Holman has been placed upon a schedule of citizens by blood of the Choctaw Nation which has been forwarded the Secretary of the Interior and you will be notified when his enrollment is approved by the Department.

    Pending the approval of his enrollment, however, no selection of allotment could be made in his behalf.

Respectfully,

Commissioner.

Applications for Enrollment of Choctaw Newborn
Act of 1905 Volume XII

BIRTH AFFIDAVIT.

DEPARTMENT OF THE INTERIOR.
COMMISSION TO THE FIVE CIVILIZED TRIBES.

IN RE APPLICATION FOR ENROLLMENT, as a citizen of the Choctaw Nation, of Moses Holman, born on the 15 day of September, 1903

Name of Father: Alferd[sic] Holman   a citizen of the Choctaw Nation.
Name of Mother: Eliza Holman   a citizen of the Choctaw Nation.

Postoffice   Corinne[sic] Ind. Ter.

AFFIDAVIT OF MOTHER.

UNITED STATES OF AMERICA, Indian Territory, }
     Central   DISTRICT. }

I, Eliza Holman, on oath state that I am 28 years of age and a citizen by Blood, of the Choctaw Nation; that I am the lawful wife of Alferd Holman, who is a citizen, by Blood of the Choctaw Nation; that a Male child was born to me on fifteenth day of September, 1903; that said child has been named Moses Holman, and was living March 4, 1905.

                         Eliza Holman

Witnesses To Mark:
   { Barnett * Elapashabbe
   { Columbus Sims

Subscribed and sworn to before me this fourth day of April, 1905

My Commission   Jno E Talbert
Expires Dec 12 1908   Notary Public.

AFFIDAVIT OF ATTENDING PHYSICIAN OR MID-WIFE.

UNITED STATES OF AMERICA, Indian Territory, }
     Central   DISTRICT. }

I, Alferd[sic] Holman, a Acting Midwife, on oath state that I attended on Mrs. My wife Eliza Holman, wife of Alferd Holman on the fifteenth day of September, 1903; that there was born to her on said date a Male child; that said child was living March 4, 1905, and is said to have been named Moses Holman

                         Alfred Holman

Applications for Enrollment of Choctaw Newborn
Act of 1905 Volume XII

Witnesses To Mark:
{ Barnett * Elapashabbe
  Columbus Sims (mark)

Subscribed and sworn to before me this fourth day of April , 1905

My Commission
Expires Dec 12 1908

Jno E Talbert
Notary Public.

United States of America Indian Territory }
    Central District

I Barnett Elapashabbe on oath state that Moses Holman son of Alfred Holman and Eliza Holman was born on 15th day of Sept 1903 and was living on the 4th day of March 1905.

Barnett Elapashabbe

Subscribed and sworn to before me this 10 day of June 1905

John E Talbert
Notary Public

My Com. Expires Dec 12 1908

United States of America Indian Territory }
    Central District

I Gilbert Choat on oath state that Moses Holman son of Alfred Holman and Eliza Holman was born on 15 day of September 1903 and was living on the 4th day of March 1905.

Gilbert Choat

Subscribed and sworn to before me this 10 day of June 1905

John E Talbert
Notary Public

My Com. Expires Dec 12 1908

Applications for Enrollment of Choctaw Newborn
Act of 1905   Volume XII

BIRTH AFFIDAVIT.

DEPARTMENT OF THE INTERIOR.
COMMISSION TO THE FIVE CIVILIZED TRIBES.

IN RE APPLICATION FOR ENROLLMENT, as a citizen of the   Choctaw   Nation, of Moses Holman , born on the 15 day of Sept , 1903

Name of Father: Alfred Holman   a citizen of the   Choctaw   Nation.
Name of Mother: Eliza A Holman   a citizen of the   Choctaw   Nation.

Postoffice   Corinne[sic] Ind T.

AFFIDAVIT OF MOTHER.

UNITED STATES OF AMERICA, Indian Territory, }
Central   DISTRICT.

I,   Eliza Holman , on oath state that I am 28 years of age and a citizen by blood , of the   Choctaw   Nation; that I am the lawful wife of   Alfred Holman , who is a citizen, by Blood   of the   Choctaw   Nation; that a   male   child was born to me on   15   day of   September , 1903; that said child has been named Moses Holman , and was living March 4, 1905.

Eliza Holman

Witnesses To Mark:
{ Joseph P Thompson
{ Solomon Nihka

Subscribed and sworn to before me this 10 day of   June , 1905

My Com exps Dec 12-1908   Jno E Talbert
                                  Notary Public.

AFFIDAVIT OF ATTENDING PHYSICIAN OR MID-WIFE.

UNITED STATES OF AMERICA, Indian Territory, }
Central   DISTRICT.

I,   Alfred Holman , a Acting Midwife , on oath state that I attended on Mrs.   Eliza A Holman , wife of Alfred Holman   on the 15 day of Sept , 1903; that there was born to her on said date a   male   child; that said child was living March 4, 1905, and is said to have been named Moses Holman

Alfred Holman

Applications for Enrollment of Choctaw Newborn
Act of 1905   Volume XII

Witnesses To Mark:
 { Joseph P Thompson
 { Solomon Nihka

    Subscribed and sworn to before me this   10 day of   June   , 1905

My Com exps Dec 12-1908   Jno E Talbert
                                       Notary Public.

Choc New Born 797
    Amanda E. Nicar   b. 5-7-04

                                                Choctaw 4613.

                    Muskogee, Indian Territory, April 21, 1905.

Christy Nicar,
    Corinne[sic], Indian Territory.

Dear Sir:

    Receipt is hereby acknowledged of the affidavits of Ola P. Nicar and Ella Nicar to the birth of Amanda E. Nicar, daughter of Christy Nicar and Ola P. Nicar, May 7th, 1904, and the same have been filed with our records as an application for the enrollment of said child.

                          Respectfully,

                                      Commissioner in Charge.

                                          7-NB-797.

                    Muskogee, Indian Territory, May 31, 1905.

Christy Nicar,
    Citra, Indian Territory.

Dear Sir:

    There is enclosed you herewith for execution application for the enrollment of your infant child, Amanda E. Nicar.

Applications for Enrollment of Choctaw Newborn
Act of 1905   Volume XII

In the affidavits filed in this office on the 14th ultimo the date of the applicant's birth as[sic] May 7, 1904, while in those filed on the 26th ultimo the date is given as April 4, 1904. In the enclosed application the date of birth is left blank. Please insert the correct date and, when the affidavits are properly executed, return them to this office.

In having these affidavits executed care should be exercised to see that all names are written in full, as they appear in the body of the affidavit, and in the event that either of the persons signing the affidavit are unable to write, signatures by mark must be attested by two witnesses. Each affidavit must be executed before a Notary Public and the notarial seal and signature of the officer must be attached to each separate affidavit.

Respectfully,

VR 31-6.

---

7 NB 797

Muskogee, Indian Territory, June 16, 1905.

Christie[sic] Nicar,
    Citra, Indian Territory.

Dear Sir:

Receipt is hereby acknowledged of the affidavits of Ola P. Nicar and Ellia[sic] Nicar to the birth of Amanda E. Nicar, daughter of Christie and Ola P. Nicar, May 7, 1904, and the same have been filed in the matter of the enrollment of said child.

Respectfully,

Chairman.

NEW-BORN AFFIDAVIT.

Number................

...Choctaw Enrolling Commission...

IN THE MATTER OF THE APPLICATION FOR ENROLLMENT, as a citizen of the Choctaw Nation, of Amanda Ellen Nicar

born on the 7 day of __April__ 190 4

Applications for Enrollment of Choctaw Newborn
Act of 1905   Volume XII

Name of father   Christie Nicar   a citizen of   By Marriage
Nation final enrollment No.   12760
Name of mother   Ola P Nicar   a citizen of   Choctaw Nation
Nation final enrollment No.   12760

                                                 Postoffice   Citra I.T.

AFFIDAVIT OF MOTHER.

UNITED STATES OF AMERICA
INDIAN TERRITORY
   Central   DISTRICT

   I   Ola P. Nicar   , on oath state that I am 26 years of age and a citizen by Blood of the Choctaw Nation, and as such have been placed upon the final roll of the Choctaw Nation, by the Honorable Secretary of the Interior my final enrollment number being   12760 ; that I am the lawful wife of   Cristie Nicar , who is a citizen of the   Intermarriage   Nation, and as such has been placed upon the final roll of said Nation by the Honorable Secretary of the Interior, his final enrollment number being   12760   and that a   Female   child was born to me on the   7   day of   April   190 4; that said child has been named   Amanda Ellen Nicar , and is now living.

                                                     Ola P Nicar

Witnesseth.
   Must be two   ⎱ L Impson
   Witnesses who ⎰
   are Citizens.   M Impson

   Subscribed and sworn to before me this   21   day of   Jan   190 5

                                        WH Hudlow
                                           Notary Public.
My commission expires: March 14 1907

AFFIDAVIT OF ATTENDING PHYSICIAN OR MIDWIFE

UNITED STATES OF AMERICA
INDIAN TERRITORY
   Central   DISTRICT

   I,   Ella Nicar   a   is who waited on the lady on oath state that I attended on Mrs.   Ola P Nicar   wife of   Cristie Nicar   on the   7   day of   April   , 190 4, that there was born to her on said date a   Female   child, that said child is now living, and is said to have been named   Amanda Ellen Nicar

                                           mid wife

Applications for Enrollment of Choctaw Newborn
Act of 1905 Volume XII

Subscribed and sworn to before me this, the   21   day of Jan   190 5

WITNESSETH: WH Hudlow   Notary Public.

Must be two witnesses who are citizens { L Impson / M Impson

We hereby certify that we are well acquainted with   Cristie Nicar   and   Ola P Nicar   and know them to be reputable and of good standing in the community.

     L Impson   Ellie Nicar

     M Impson

BIRTH AFFIDAVIT.

DEPARTMENT OF THE INTERIOR.
COMMISSION TO THE FIVE CIVILIZED TRIBES.

IN RE APPLICATION FOR ENROLLMENT, as a citizen of the   Choctaw   Nation, of   Amanda E Nicar   , born on the   7   day of   May , 1904

Name of Father: Christy Nicar   a citizen of the   U.S.   Nation.
Name of Mother: Ola P Nicar   a citizen of the   Choctaw   Nation.

                     Postoffice   Citra Ind. Ter

AFFIDAVIT OF MOTHER.

UNITED STATES OF AMERICA, Indian Territory, }
     Central District   **DISTRICT.**

I,   Ola P Nicar , on oath state that I am   20   years of age and a citizen by blood , of the   Choctaw   Nation; that I am the lawful wife of   Christy Nicar , who is a citizen, by —— of the   United States   Nation; that a   female   child was born to me on   7   day of   May , 1904; that said child has been named   Amanda E Nicar , and was living March 4, 1905.

                                           Ola P Nicar

Witnesses To Mark:
{ L Impson
  Minnie Impson

Applications for Enrollment of Choctaw Newborn
Act of 1905   Volume XII

Subscribed and sworn to before me this 10 day of June , 1905

My Com exp March 14/1907

W.H. Hudlow
Notary Public.

AFFIDAVIT OF ATTENDING PHYSICIAN OR MID-WIFE.

UNITED STATES OF AMERICA, Indian Territory, }
Central   DISTRICT.

I, Ellie Nicar , a midwife , on oath state that I attended on Mrs. Ola P Nicar , wife of Christy Nicar on the 7 day of May , 1904; that there was born to her on said date a female child; that said child was living March 4, 1905, and is said to have been named Amanda E Nicar

Ellie Nicar

Witnesses To Mark:
{ L Impson
{ Minnie Impson

Subscribed and sworn to before me this 10 day of June , 1905

W.H. Hudlow
Notary Public.

My Com exp March 14/1907

BIRTH AFFIDAVIT.

DEPARTMENT OF THE INTERIOR.
COMMISSION TO THE FIVE CIVILIZED TRIBES.

IN RE APPLICATION FOR ENROLLMENT, as a citizen of the Choctaw Nation, of Amanda E Nicar , born on the 7th day of May , 1904

Name of Father: Christy Nicar   ~~a citizen of the~~ Non Citz ~~Nation~~.
Name of Mother: Ola P Nicar   a citizen of the Choctaw Nation.

Postoffice   Citra I.T.

Applications for Enrollment of Choctaw Newborn
Act of 1905   Volume XII

AFFIDAVIT OF MOTHER.

UNITED STATES OF AMERICA, Indian Territory,
Central   DISTRICT.

I, Ola P Nicar, on oath state that I am 20 years of age and a citizen by blood, of the Choctaw Nation; that I am the lawful wife of Christy Nicar, who is a citizen, by ———— of the United States Nation; that a female child was born to me on 7th day of May, 1904; that said child has been named Amanda E Nicar, and was living March 4, 1905.

Ola P Nicar

Witnesses To Mark:

Subscribed and sworn to before me this 5th day of April, 1905

W.H. Angell
Notary Public.

AFFIDAVIT OF ATTENDING PHYSICIAN OR MID-WIFE.

UNITED STATES OF AMERICA, Indian Territory,
Central   DISTRICT.

I, Ella Nicar, a midwife, on oath state that I attended on Mrs. Ola P Nicar, wife of Christy Nicar on the 7th day of May, 1904; that there was born to her on said date a female child; that said child was living March 4, 1905, and is said to have been named Amanda E Nicar

Ellie[sic] Nicar

Witnesses To Mark:
  Joe Finley

Subscribed and sworn to before me this 7 day of April, 1905

W.H. Hudlow
Notary Public.

My Com exp March 14/1907

Applications for Enrollment of Choctaw Newborn
Act of 1905   Volume XII

Choc New Born 798
    Johnson Homer   b. 11-6-04

Choctaw 2023.

Muskogee, Indian Territory, April 12, 1905.

Byington Homer,
    Smithville, Indian Territory.

Dear Sir:

   Receipt is hereby acknowledged of the affidavit of Nicey Homer to the birth of Johnson Homer, son of Byington and Nicey Homer, November 6th, 1904, and the same has been filed with our records as an application for the enrollment of said child.

    Respectfully,

    Commissioner in Charge.

NEW-BORN AFFIDAVIT.

    Number..................

...Choctaw Enrolling Commission...

   IN THE MATTER OF THE APPLICATION FOR ENROLLMENT, as a citizen of the Choctaw   Nation, of   Johnson Homer

born on the   6   day of ___November___ 190 4

Name of father   Byington Homer   a citizen of   Choctaw
Nation final enrollment No.   3821
Name of mother   Nicey Homer   a citizen of   Choctaw
Nation final enrollment No.   5794

                            Postoffice   Smithville I. Ter.

Applications for Enrollment of Choctaw Newborn
Act of 1905 Volume XII

AFFIDAVIT OF MOTHER.

UNITED STATES OF AMERICA
INDIAN TERRITORY
Central   DISTRICT

I   Nicey Harris   , on oath state that I am 27 years of age and a citizen by Blood of the Choctaw Nation, and as such have been placed upon the final roll of the Choctaw Nation, by the Honorable Secretary of the Interior my final enrollment number being   5794 ; that I am the lawful wife of   Byington Homer   , who is a citizen of the   Choctaw   Nation, and as such has been placed upon the final roll of said Nation by the Honorable Secretary of the Interior, his final enrollment number being   3821   and that a   Boy   child was born to me on the 6   day of   November   190 4; that said child has been named   Johnson Homer   , and is now living.

Nicey Harris

Witnesseth.
Must be two Witnesses who are Citizens.   Simpson Wilson

Sallie Wilson

Subscribed and sworn to before me this   11   day of   Feb   190 5

A.W. James
Notary Public.

My commission expires: Dec 8-1906

AFFIDAVIT OF ATTENDING PHYSICIAN OR MIDWIFE

UNITED STATES OF AMERICA
INDIAN TERRITORY
Central   DISTRICT

I,   Lovina Impalumbi   a   woman on oath state that I attended on Mrs.   Nicey Harris wife of   Byington Homer on the   6   day of   Nov   , 190 4 , that there was born to her on said date a   Boy   child, that said child is now living, and is said to have been named   Lovina Impalumbi

Subscribed and sworn to before me this, the   10   day of Feb   190 55

A.W. James   Notary Public.

WITNESSETH:
Must be two witnesses who are citizens   Simpson Wilson

Sallie Wilson

Applications for Enrollment of Choctaw Newborn
Act of 1905   Volume XII

We hereby certify that we are well acquainted with   Nicey Homer   a   Boy[sic]   and know .... to be reputable and of good standing in the community.

    Simpson Wilson   Nicey Harris

    Sallie Wilson   Byington Homer

BIRTH AFFIDAVIT.

DEPARTMENT OF THE INTERIOR.
COMMISSION TO THE FIVE CIVILIZED TRIBES.

IN RE APPLICATION FOR ENROLLMENT, as a citizen of the   Choctaw   Nation, of   Johnson Homer   , born on the 6th   day of   November   , 1904

Name of Father: Byington Homer   a citizen of the   Choctaw   Nation.
Name of Mother: Nicey Homer   a citizen of the   Choctaw   Nation.

                          Postoffice   Smithville, Ind Ter

AFFIDAVIT OF ATTENDING PHYSICIAN OR MID-WIFE.

UNITED STATES OF AMERICA, Indian Territory,
      Central   **DISTRICT.**

I,   Lovina Plumbbi[sic]   , a   mid-wife   , on oath state that I attended on Mrs.   Nicey Homer   , wife of   Byington Homer   on the 6th   day of   November   , 1904; that there was born to her on said date a   male   child; that said child was living March 4, 1905, and is said to have been named Johnson Homer

                                      her
                              Lovina x Plumbbi
Witnesses To Mark: mark
   Robert Anderson
   Vester Rose

      Subscribed and sworn to before me this   5th day of   April   , 1905

                                Wirt Franklin
                                  Notary Public.

Applications for Enrollment of Choctaw Newborn
Act of 1905   Volume XII

BIRTH AFFIDAVIT.

DEPARTMENT OF THE INTERIOR.
COMMISSION TO THE FIVE CIVILIZED TRIBES.

IN RE APPLICATION FOR ENROLLMENT, as a citizen of the Choctaw Nation, of Johnson Homer, born on the 6th day of November, 1904

Name of Father: Byington Homer   a citizen of the Choctaw Nation.
Name of Mother: Nicey Homer   a citizen of the Choctaw Nation.

Postoffice   Smithville, Ind Ter

AFFIDAVIT OF MOTHER.

UNITED STATES OF AMERICA, Indian Territory,
Central   DISTRICT.

I, Nicey Homer, on oath state that I am 21 years of age and a citizen by blood, of the Choctaw Nation; that I am the lawful wife of Byington Homer, who is a citizen, by blood of the Choctaw Nation; that a male child was born to me on 6th day of November, 1904; that said child has been named Johnson Homer, and was living March 4, 1905.

Nicey Homer

Witnesses To Mark:

Subscribed and sworn to before me this 6 day of April, 1905

C.L. Lester
Notary Public.

Choc New Born 799
    Edna May Jones   b. 2-26-03
    Gracie Sybil Jones   b. 11-28-04

Applications for Enrollment of Choctaw Newborn
Act of 1905   Volume XII

Choctaw 5777.

Muskogee, Indian Territory, April 12, 1905.

John F. Jones,
Celestine, Indian Territory.

Dear Sir:

Receipt is hereby acknowledged of the affidavits of Mary Jones and Mary Wilson to the birth of Gracie Sybil Jones, daughter of John F. Jones and Mary Jones, November __, 1904; also the affidavits of Mary Jones, E. M. Devers and Ella Jones to the birth of Edna May Jones, daughter of John F. Jones and Mary Jones, February 25, 1903. The same have been filed with our records as an application for the enrollment of the above named children.

Respectfully,

Commissioner in Charge.

Choctaw N B 799

Muskogee, Indian Territory, June 28, 1905.

John F. Jones,
Celestine, Indian Territory.

Dear Sir:

Receipt is hereby acknowledged of the affidavits of Mary Jones and Denis C. Brady to the birth of Edney[sic] May Jones, daughter of John F. and Mary Jones, February 26, 1903, and the same have been filed with our records in the matter of the enrollment of said child.

Respectfully,

Chairman.

Applications for Enrollment of Choctaw Newborn
Act of 1905   Volume XII

7-NB-799.

Muskogee, Indian Territory, May 31, 1905.

John F. Jones,
    Celestine, Indian Territory.

Dear Sir:

    On the 14th ultimo there was filed in this office, in the matter of the application for the enrollment of your infant child, Gracie Sybil Jones, the affidavits of E. M. Dever and Ellar[sic] Jones. These affidavits show that the child was living on January 27, 1905. It is necessary, for the child to be enrolled, that she was living on March 4, 1905.

    In the affidavits heretofore filed in the matter of the application for the enrollment of Gracie Sybil Jones, the midwife fails to state the date on which the applicant was born. You will please have her affidavit re-executed, using the enclosed blank.

    In having these affidavits executed care should be exercised to see that all names are written in full, as they appear in the body of the affidavit, and in the event that either of the persons signing the affidavit are unable to write, signatures by mark must be attested by two witnesses. Each affidavit must be executed before a Notary Public and the notarial seal and signature of the officer must be attached to each separate affidavit.

Respectfully,

VR 31-5.   Chairman.

---

7 NB 799

Muskogee, Indian Territory, June 13, 1905.

John T[sic]. Jones,
    Celestine, Indian Territory.

Dear Sir:

    Receipt is hereby acknowledged of the affidavits of Mary Jones and Mary Wilson to the birth of Gracie Sybil Jones, daughter of John T[sic]. and Mary Jones, November 28, 1904, and the same have been filed in the matter of the enrollment of said child.

Respectfully,

Chairman.

Applications for Enrollment of Choctaw Newborn
Act of 1905   Volume XII

7-NB-799.

Muskogee, Indian Territory, June 15, 1905.

John F. Jones,
    Celestine, Indian Territory.

Dear Sir:

    There is enclosed herewith for execution the affidavit of the attending physician or midwife in the matter of the enrollment of your infant child, Edney[sic] May Jones.

    The affidavits of E. M. Dever and Ellar[sic] Jones, who attended upon your wife at the time of the birth of the applicant, show that the applicant was living on January 27, 1905. It is necessary for the child to be enrolled that she was living on March 4, 1905.

    In having this affidavit executed care should be exercised to see that all names are written in full as they appear in the body of the affidavit and in the event that the person signing the affidavit is unable to write, signature by mark must be attested by two witnesses. The affidavit must be executed before a Notary Public and his notarial seal and signature attached thereto.

    Please give this matter your immediate attention as no further action can be taken until this affidavit is filed with the Commission.

                  Respectfully,

                                Chairman.

BIRTH AFFIDAVIT.

DEPARTMENT OF THE INTERIOR.
COMMISSION TO THE FIVE CIVILIZED TRIBES.

IN RE APPLICATION FOR ENROLLMENT, as a citizen of the   Choctaw   Nation, of Edna May Jones   , born on the 26th   day of   February   , 1903

Name of Father: John F. Jones   a citizen of the   Choctaw   Nation.
Name of Mother: Mary Jones   a citizen of the   Choctaw   Nation.

                  Postoffice   Celestine, I.T.

Applications for Enrollment of Choctaw Newborn
Act of 1905   Volume XII

AFFIDAVIT OF MOTHER.

UNITED STATES OF AMERICA, Indian Territory,
Central   DISTRICT.

I, Mary Jones, on oath state that I am 30 years of age and a citizen by marriage, of the Choctaw Nation; that I am the lawful wife of John F. Jones, who is a citizen, by blood of the Choctaw Nation; that a female child was born to me on 26th day of February, 1903; that said child has been named Edna May Jones, and was living March 4, 1905.

           Mary Jones

Witnesses To Mark:
{ Mary Wilson
{ Sam Wooley

Subscribed and sworn to before me this 8 day of April, 1905.

           J H Elliott
             Notary Public.

My Com exps July 1908

AFFIDAVIT OF ATTENDING PHYSICIAN OR MID-WIFE.

UNITED STATES OF AMERICA, Indian Territory,
Central   DISTRICT.

I, ~~Mrs Mary Wilson~~, a Mid wife, on oath state that I attended on Mrs. Mary Jones, wife of John F Jones on the 28" day of November, 1905; that there was born to her on said date a Female child; that said child was living March 4, 1905, and is said to have been named Edney May Jones

Witnesses To Mark:

Subscribed and sworn to before me this ____ day of _____, 1905.

             Notary Public.

Applications for Enrollment of Choctaw Newborn
Act of 1905   Volume XII

(The affidavit below typed as given.)

Francis, Ind. Ter. Jan. 27th. 1905.

Being on oath, Mrs. E.M.Devers and Mrs. Ella Jones, deposes and says that they are acquainted with and was at John F Jones on the 26 day of Feb. 1903, and acted as midwife when his wife, Mrs. Mary Jones was confined, and that a girl child was born on said date which is now living and is named Edney May Jones.
They further state that John F Jones is chactaw by blood and his wife Mrs. Mary Jones chactaw by enter marriage.

C M Dever
Ella E Jones

Subscribed and sworn to before me, a notary public, in adf for the southern district, chickasaw Nation, Indian Territory, on this the 27 day of January, 1905.

John I McCoole
Notary Public.

My com. ex. Feb. 11th. 1907.

BIRTH AFFIDAVIT.

DEPARTMENT OF THE INTERIOR.
COMMISSION TO THE FIVE CIVILIZED TRIBES.

IN RE APPLICATION FOR ENROLLMENT, as a citizen of the   Choctaw   Nation, of Edney May Jones   , born on the 26   day of   February   , 1903

Name of Father: John F. Jones   a citizen of the   Choctaw   Nation.
Name of Mother: Mary Jones   a citizen of the   Choctaw   Nation.

Postoffice   Celestine, I.T.

AFFIDAVIT OF MOTHER.

UNITED STATES OF AMERICA, Indian Territory,
   Central   DISTRICT.

I,   Mary Jones   , on oath state that I am   30   years of age and a citizen by intermarried   , of the   Choctaw   Nation; that I am the lawful wife of   John F. Jones   , who is a citizen, by Blood   of the   Choctaw   Nation; that a   female   child was born to me on   26   day of   february[sic]   , 1903; that said child has been named   Edney May Jones   , and was living March 4, 1905.

Mary Jones

Applications for Enrollment of Choctaw Newborn
Act of 1905   Volume XII

Witnesses To Mark:
{

    Subscribed and sworn to before me this   23   day of   June   , 1905

My commission expires   S.S. Aldridge
     March 21 1909   Notary Public.

AFFIDAVIT OF ATTENDING PHYSICIAN OR MID-WIFE.

UNITED STATES OF AMERICA, Indian Territory, }
     Southern   DISTRICT.

    I,   Denis C Brady   , a   Doctor   , on oath state that I attended on Mrs.   Mary Jones   , wife of   John F Jones   on the 26 day of   February   , 1903; that there was born to her on said date a   Female   child; that said child was living March 4, 1905, and is said to have been named   Edney May Jones

                      Denis C. Brady

Witnesses To Mark:
{

    Subscribed and sworn to before me this   21   day of   June   , 1905

                      John I McCoole
                           Notary Public.

MY COMMISSION EXPIRES FEBY. 11TH, 1907

BIRTH AFFIDAVIT.

DEPARTMENT OF THE INTERIOR.
COMMISSION TO THE FIVE CIVILIZED TRIBES.

    IN RE APPLICATION FOR ENROLLMENT, as a citizen of the   Choctaw   Nation, of   Gracie Sybil Jones   , born on the .... day of   November   , 1904

Name of Father: John F. Jones   a citizen of the   Choctaw   Nation.
Name of Mother: Mary Jones   a citizen of the   Choctaw   Nation.

                 Postoffice   Celestine, I.T.

Applications for Enrollment of Choctaw Newborn
Act of 1905   Volume XII

AFFIDAVIT OF MOTHER.

UNITED STATES OF AMERICA, Indian Territory, }
Central   DISTRICT.

I,   Mary Jones   , on oath state that I am   30   years of age and a citizen by marriage   , of the   Choctaw   Nation; that I am the lawful wife of   John F. Jones , who is a citizen, by   blood   of the   Choctaw   Nation; that a   female   child was born to me on   28" day of   November   , 1904; that said child has been named   Gracie Sybil Jones   , and was living March 4, 1905.

                                        Mary Jones

Witnesses To Mark:
{ Sam Wooley
  Turner Daniels

Subscribed and sworn to before me this   8" day of   April   , 1905

                                        J H Elliott
                                                Notary Public.

My Com exp 8 July 1908

AFFIDAVIT OF ATTENDING PHYSICIAN OR MID-WIFE.

UNITED STATES OF AMERICA, Indian Territory, }
Central   DISTRICT.

I,   Mary Wilson   , a   mid-wife   , on oath state that I attended on Mrs.   Mary Jones   , wife of   John F Jones   on the .... day of   November , 1904; that there was born to her on said date a   female   child; that said child was living March 4, 1905, and is said to have been named   Gracie Sybil Jones

                                        Mary Wilson

Witnesses To Mark:
{ Sam Wooley
  Turner Daniels

Subscribed and sworn to before me this   8" day of   April   , 1905

                                        J H Elliott
                                                Notary Public.

My Com exp 8" July 1908

Applications for Enrollment of Choctaw Newborn
Act of 1905   Volume XII

BIRTH AFFIDAVIT.

DEPARTMENT OF THE INTERIOR.
COMMISSION TO THE FIVE CIVILIZED TRIBES.

IN RE APPLICATION FOR ENROLLMENT, as a citizen of the Choctaw Nation, of Gracie Sybil Jones, born on the 28 day of Nov., 1904

Name of Father: John F. Jones   a citizen of the Choctaw Nation.
Name of Mother: Mary Jones   a citizen of the Choctaw Nation.

Postoffice   Celestine, Ind. Ter.

AFFIDAVIT OF MOTHER.

UNITED STATES OF AMERICA, Indian Territory,
Central DISTRICT.

I, Mary Jones, on oath state that I am 30 years of age and a citizen by Intermarried, of the Choctaw Nation; that I am the lawful wife of John F. Jones, who is a citizen, by Blood of the Choctaw Nation; that a Female child was born to me on 28 day of November, 1904; that said child has been named Gracie Sybil Jones, and was living March 4, 1905.

                         Mary Jones

Witnesses To Mark:
{

Subscribed and sworn to before me this 4 day of June, 1905

My commission expires   S.S. Aldridge
March 21 1909   Notary Public.

AFFIDAVIT OF ATTENDING PHYSICIAN OR MID-WIFE.

UNITED STATES OF AMERICA, Indian Territory,
Central Judicial DISTRICT.

I, Mary Wilson, a Midwife, on oath state that I attended on Mrs. Mary Jones, wife of John F Jones on the 28th day of Nov, 1904; that there was born to her on said date a female child; that said child was living March 4, 1905, and is said to have been named Gracie Sybil Jones

                         Mary Wilson

Witnesses To Mark:
{

Applications for Enrollment of Choctaw Newborn
Act of 1905 Volume XII

Subscribed and sworn to before me this 3^d day of June , 1905

                         D S Kennedy
                         Notary Public.

Choc New Born 800
     Roy Ott   b. 10-30-04

COPY

           Muskogee, Indian Territory, May 1, 1905.

Sam Ott,
     Owl, Indian Territory.

Dear Sir:

     Receipt is hereby acknowledged of the affidavits of Rosa Ott and Wicey Wade to the birth of Roy Ott, son of Sam and Rosa Ott, October 30, 1904.

     It is stated in the affidavit of the mother that she is a citizen by blood of the Choctaw Nation. If this is correct you are requested to state the name under which she was enrolled, the names of her parents, and if she has selected an allotment of the lands of the Choctaw or Chickasaw Nation please give her roll number as it appears upon her allotment certificate.

                     Respectfully,
                     SIGNED

                         Tams Bixby
                         Chairman.

BIRTH AFFIDAVIT.

DEPARTMENT OF THE INTERIOR.
COMMISSION TO THE FIVE CIVILIZED TRIBES.

     IN RE APPLICATION FOR ENROLLMENT, as a citizen of the   Choctaw   Nation, of Roy Ott   , born on the   30   day of   October   , 1904

Name of Father: Sam Ott   a citizen of the   Choctaw   Nation.
Name of Mother: Rosa Lawrence   a citizen of the   Choctaw   Nation.

                     Postoffice   Arthur, I.T.

Applications for Enrollment of Choctaw Newborn
Act of 1905   Volume XII

AFFIDAVIT OF MOTHER.

UNITED STATES OF AMERICA, Indian Territory, }
   Southern   DISTRICT. }

    I, Rosa Lawrence , on oath state that I am 20 years of age and a citizen by blood, of the Choctaw Nation; that I am the lawful wife of _____, who is a citizen, by _____ of the _____ Nation; that a male child was born to me on 30th day of October , 1904; that said child has been named Roy Ott , and was living March 4, 1905.

                                        Rosa Lawrence

Witnesses To Mark:
{

    Subscribed and sworn to before me this 6th day of April , 1905

                                        JE Williams
                                                  Notary Public.

BIRTH AFFIDAVIT.
DEPARTMENT OF THE INTERIOR.
COMMISSION TO THE FIVE CIVILIZED TRIBES.

    IN RE APPLICATION FOR ENROLLMENT, as a citizen of the Choctaw Nation, of Roy Ott , born on the 30th day of October , 1904

Name of Father: Sam Ott   a citizen of the Choctaw Nation.
Name of Mother: Rosa Ott   a citizen of the Choctaw Nation.

                              Postoffice   Owl, I.T.

AFFIDAVIT OF MOTHER.

UNITED STATES OF AMERICA, Indian Territory, }
   Central   DISTRICT. }

    I, Rosa Ott , on oath state that I am 20 years of age and a citizen by Blood, of the Choctaw Nation; that I am the lawful wife of Sam Ott , who is a citizen, by Blood of the Choctaw Nation; that a male child was born to me on 30th day of October , 1904; that said child has been named Roy Ott , and was living March 4, 1905.

                                        Rosa Ott

Applications for Enrollment of Choctaw Newborn
Act of 1905 Volume XII

Witnesses To Mark:
{ I.L. Strange
  T.W. Jones

Subscribed and sworn to before me this 27th day of April , 1905

G. E. McGowan
Notary Public.

AFFIDAVIT OF ATTENDING PHYSICIAN OR MID-WIFE.

UNITED STATES OF AMERICA, Indian Territory, }
Southern   DISTRICT.

I, Wicey Wade , a mid-wife , on oath state that I attended on Mrs. Rosa Ott , wife of Sam Ott on the 30th day of October , 1904; that there was born to her on said date a male child; that said child was living March 4, 1905, and is said to have been named Roy Ott

                                her
                          Wicey x Wade
Witnesses To Mark: mark
{ I.L. Strange
  T.W. Jones

Subscribed and sworn to before me this 6th day of April , 1905

G. E. McGowan
Notary Public.

Choc New Born 801
    Eulafay Taylor b. 4-26-03

BIRTH AFFIDAVIT.
DEPARTMENT OF THE INTERIOR.
COMMISSION TO THE FIVE CIVILIZED TRIBES.

    IN RE APPLICATION FOR ENROLLMENT, as a citizen of the Choctaw Nation, of Eulafay Taylor , born on the 26 day of April , 1903

Name of Father: John Taylor   a citizen of the Choctaw Nation.
Name of Mother: Cora Taylor   a citizen of the United States Nation.

Applications for Enrollment of Choctaw Newborn
Act of 1905   Volume XII

Postoffice   Roff ind[sic] Ter

AFFIDAVIT OF MOTHER.

UNITED STATES OF AMERICA, Indian Territory, }
Southern   DISTRICT.

I, Cora Taylor, on oath state that I am 21 years of age and a citizen by ...., of the United States Nation; that I am the lawful wife of John Taylor, who is a citizen, by blood of the Choctaw Nation; that a female child was born to me on 26 day of April, 1903; that said child has been named Eulafay Taylor, and was living March 4, 1905.

Cora Taylor

Witnesses To Mark:
{

Subscribed and sworn to before me this 8th day of April, 1905

Josh Clardy
Notary Public.

AFFIDAVIT OF ATTENDING PHYSICIAN OR MID-WIFE.

UNITED STATES OF AMERICA, Indian Territory, }
Southern   DISTRICT.

I, Alvarado Dilbeck, a mid wife, on oath state that I attended on Mrs. Cora Taylor, wife of John Taylor on the 26 day of April, 1903; that there was born to her on said date a female child; that said child was living March 4, 1905, and is said to have been named Eulafay Taylor

Alvarado Dilbeck

Witnesses To Mark:
{

Subscribed and sworn to before me this 8th day of April, 1905

Josh Clardy
Notary Public.

Applications for Enrollment of Choctaw Newborn
Act of 1905 Volume XII

7 n. B. 801

DEPARTMENT OF THE INTERIOR,
COMMISSION TO THE FIVE CIVILIZED TRIBES.
FILED
JUN 15 1905

Tams Bixby

Certificate of Record of Marriage

UNITED STATES OF AMERICA,
INDIAN TERRITORY,   } sct.
SOUTHERN DISTRICT.

I, C. M. CAMPBELL, Clerk of the United States Court, in the Territory and District aforesaid do hereby certify, that the License for and Certificate of Marriage of

MR.   John Taylor

AND

M   Cora Brandon

were filed in my office in said Territory and District the 24 day of Feb. A.D., 190 2 and duly recorded in Book F. of Marriage Record, Page 259

WITNESS my hand and Seal of said Court, at Ardmore, this 5 day of March A.D. 190 2

C. M. Campbell
CLERK.

☞ Return this License to the United States Clerk at Ardmore, Indian Territory that it may be recorded, when it will be mailed to the proper address.

FILED

Feb 24 1902
FEB 24 1902 3PM

C. M. CAMPBELL Clerk.
Southern Dist. Ind. Ter.

Applications for Enrollment of Choctaw Newborn
Act of 1905   Volume XII

MARKRIAGE LICENSE

UNITED STATES OF AMERICA,
INDIAN TERRITORY,   } ss:
SOUTHERN DISTRICT.

To Any Person Authorized by Law to Solemnize Marriage --- Greeting:

You are hereby commanded to solemnize the Rite and publish the Banns of Matrimony between Mr. John Taylor of Roff, in the Indian Territory, aged 28 years and M Cora Brandon of Roff in the Indian Territory aged 18 years according to law, and do you officially sign and return this License to the parties therein named.

Witness my hand and official seal this 13 day of Feby A.D. 190 2

CM Campbell
Clerk of the United States Court

....Deputy

Certificate of Marriage.

United States of America,
  Indian Territory,   } ss.
  Southern District.

I, C.H. Carleton an Ordained Minister

do hereby certify, that on the 19th day of Feb, A. D. 190 2, I did duly and according to law, as commanded in the foregoing License, solemnize the Rite and publish the Banns of Matrimony between the parties therein named.

Witness my hand, this 19 day of Feb, A. D. 190 2

My credentials are recorded in the office of the Clerk of the United States Court, Indian Territory, Southern District, at Ardmore, Indian Territory Book A, Page 58

NOTE:-The person officiating should fill in the spaces for book and page and sign here

C H Carleton
an Ordained Minister

NOTE (a)-The License and Certificate of Marriage must be returned to the office of the Clerk of the United States Court in the Indian Territory, at Ardmore, within sixty days from the date thereof, or the party to whom the License was issued will be liable in the amount of One Hundred Dollars ($100).

NOTE (b)-No person is authorized to perform the Marriage Ceremony in the Southern District unless the proper credentials have first been recorded in the Clerk's office.

Applications for Enrollment of Choctaw Newborn
Act of 1905 Volume XII

<u>Choc New Born 802</u>
    Nettie Yandell   b. 3-21-03

Choctaw 3643.

Muskogee, Indian Territory, April 12, 1905.

John M. Yandell,
    Boswell, Indian Territory.

Dear Sir:

    Receipt is hereby acknowledged of the affidavits of Dora Yandell and C. B. Smith to the birth of Nettie Yandell, daughter of John M. Yandell and Dora Yandell, March 21, 1903, and the same have been filed with our records as an application for the enrollment of said child.

        Respectfully,

                Commissioner in Charge.

7-NB-802.

Muskogee, Indian Territory, May 29, 1905.

John M. Yandell,
    Boswell, Indian Territory.

Dear Sir:

    There are enclosed herewith the affidavits of Dora Yandell, mother, and C. B. Smith, M.D., to the birth of your infant child, Nettie Yandell, born March 21, 1903, from which the seal of the Notary Public has been omitted.

    You will please have the Notary, before whom these affidavits were executed, attach his seal, which must be an impression and not a scroll, to these affidavits and return them to this office.

        Respectfully,

VR 29-6.   Chairman.

Applications for Enrollment of Choctaw Newborn
Act of 1905 Volume XII

7 N.B. 802.

Muskogee, Indian Territory, June 5, 1905.

John M. Yandell,
    Boswell, Indian Territory.

Dear Sir:

    Receipt is hereby acknowledged of the affidavits of Dora Yandell and C. B. Smith, M. D., to the birth of Nettie Yandell, daughter of John M. and Dora Yandell, March 21, 1903, and the same have been filed with our records in the matter of the enrollment of said child.

                    Respectfully,

                                  Commissioner in Charge.

NEW-BORN AFFIDAVIT.

Number _____

...Choctaw Enrolling Commission...

IN THE MATTER OF THE APPLICATION FOR ENROLLMENT, as a citizen of the Choctaw Nation, of Nettie Yandell

born on the 21 day of March 190 3

Name of father John M Yandell   a citizen of Choctaw
Nation final enrollment No. 10305
Name of mother Dora Yandell   a citizen of Choctaw
Nation final enrollment No. 10304

                    Postoffice   Boswell, I.T.

AFFIDAVIT OF MOTHER.

UNITED STATES OF AMERICA
INDIAN TERRITORY
  Central   DISTRICT

    I Dora Yandell , on oath state that I am 25 years of age and a citizen by blood of the Choctaw Nation, and as such have been placed upon the final roll of the Choctaw Nation, by the Honorable Secretary of the Interior my final enrollment number being 10304 ; that I am the lawful wife of John Yandell , who is a citizen of the Choctaw Nation, and as such has

Applications for Enrollment of Choctaw Newborn
Act of 1905   Volume XII

been placed upon the final roll of said Nation by the Honorable Secretary of the Interior, his final enrollment number being   10305   and that a   Female   child was born to me on the   21   day of   March   190 3; that said child has been named   Nettie Yandell , and is now living.

her
Dora x Yandell
mark

Witnesseth.

   Must be two ⎤ E.T. Dwight
   Witnesses who ⎬
   are Citizens. ⎦ TW Hunter

Subscribed and sworn to before me this   28   day of   Mch   190 5

Thos. W. Hunter
Notary Public.

My commission expires:

AFFIDAVIT OF ATTENDING PHYSICIAN OR MIDWIFE

UNITED STATES OF AMERICA
INDIAN TERRITORY
   Central   DISTRICT

I,   C. B. Smith   a   Physician   on oath state that I attended on Mrs.   Dora Yandell   wife of   John Yandell   on the   21   day of   March   , 190 3 , that there was born to her on said date a   Female   child, that said child is now living, and is said to have been named   Nettie Yandell

C. B. Smith   𝑚.𝒟.

Subscribed and sworn to before me this, the   28   day of   January   190 5

WITNESSETH: Thos. W. Hunter   Notary Public.
   Must be two witnesses ⎰ Allen Leflore
   who are citizens   ⎱
                      R.S. Belvin

We hereby certify that we are well acquainted with   C. B. Smith   a   Physician   and know   him   to be reputable and of good standing in the community.

M. W. Leflore   Thos. W. Hunter

Allen Leflore   E.T. Dwight

Applications for Enrollment of Choctaw Newborn
Act of 1905 Volume XII

BIRTH AFFIDAVIT.

DEPARTMENT OF THE INTERIOR.
COMMISSION TO THE FIVE CIVILIZED TRIBES.

IN RE APPLICATION FOR ENROLLMENT, as a citizen of the Choctaw Nation, of Nettie Yandell, born on the 21st day of March, 1903

Name of Father: John M. Yandell   a citizen of the Choctaw Nation.
Name of Mother: Dora Yandell   a citizen of the Choctaw Nation.

Postoffice   Boswell, Ind. Ter.

AFFIDAVIT OF MOTHER.

UNITED STATES OF AMERICA, Indian Territory,
Central District   DISTRICT.

I, Dora Yandell, on oath state that I am 25 years of age and a citizen by blood, of the Choctaw Nation; that I am the lawful wife of John M. Yandell, who is a citizen, by blood of the Choctaw Nation; that a female child was born to me on 21st day of March, 1903, 1......; that said child has been named Nettie Yandell, and was living March 4, 1905.

                 her
             Dora x Yandell
Witnesses To Mark: mark
   { O A Simmons
   { M. L. Armstrong

Subscribed and sworn to before me this 8th day of April, 1905, 190......

               J.R. Armstrong
                   Notary Public.

AFFIDAVIT OF ATTENDING PHYSICIAN OR MID-WIFE.

UNITED STATES OF AMERICA, Indian Territory,
Central   DISTRICT.

I, C.B. Smith, a M.D., on oath state that I attended on Mrs. Dora Yandell, wife of John M. Yandell on the 21st day of March, 1903, 1......; that there was born to her on said date a female child; that said child was living March 4, 1905, and is said to have been named Nettie Yandell

               C.B. Smith M.D.

Applications for Enrollment of Choctaw Newborn
Act of 1905   Volume XII

Witnesses To Mark:

Subscribed and sworn to before me this 8th day of April, 1905   , 190......

(Seal)

J.R. Armstrong
Notary Public.

Choc New Born 803
    Roy Jackson Mauldin   b. 7-10-03

BIRTH AFFIDAVIT.

DEPARTMENT OF THE INTERIOR.
COMMISSION TO THE FIVE CIVILIZED TRIBES.

IN RE APPLICATION FOR ENROLLMENT, as a citizen of the   Choctaw   Nation, of Roy Jackson Mauldin   , born on the 10th day of July , 1903

Name of Father: Jack Mauldin   a citizen of the United States ~~Nation~~.
Name of Mother: Betsey Mauldin   a citizen of the   Choctaw   Nation.

Postoffice   Elk, Indian Terry

AFFIDAVIT OF MOTHER.

UNITED STATES OF AMERICA, Indian Territory,
    Southern   **DISTRICT.**

I,   Betsey Mauldin   , on oath state that I am   28   years of age and a citizen by   Blood   , of the   Choctaw   Nation; that I am the lawful wife of   Jack Mauldin   , who is a citizen, by .... of the   United States   Nation; that a male   child was born to me on   10th   day of   July   , 1903; that said child has been named   Roy Jackson Mauldin   , and was living March 4, 1905.

                                                       her mark
                              Betsy Mauldin   x

Witnesses To Mark:
    JA Moreson
    G W Cooper

Applications for Enrollment of Choctaw Newborn
Act of 1905 Volume XII

Subscribed and sworn to before me this 27 day of March , 1905

R S Hendon
Notary Public.

AFFIDAVIT OF ATTENDING PHYSICIAN OR MID-WIFE.

UNITED STATES OF AMERICA, Indian Territory, }
    Southern   DISTRICT.

I, J J Chapman , a Physician , on oath state that I attended on Mrs. Betsey Mauldin , wife of Jack Mauldin on the 10th day of July 1903 , +........; that there was born to her on said date a male child; that said child was living March 4, 1905, and is said to have been named Roy Jackson

J. J. Chapman M.D.

Witnesses To Mark:
{

Subscribed and sworn to before me this 1st day of April , 1905

R.S. Hendon
Notary Public.

BIRTH AFFIDAVIT.

DEPARTMENT OF THE INTERIOR.
COMMISSION TO THE FIVE CIVILIZED TRIBES.

IN RE APPLICATION FOR ENROLLMENT, as a citizen of the Choctaw Nation, of Roy Jackson Mauldin , born on the 10 day of July , 1903

Name of Father: Jack Mauldin   a citizen of the   U.S.   Nation.
Name of Mother: Betsie Mauldin   a citizen of the   Choctaw Nation.

Postoffice   Elk, Ind. Ter.

AFFIDAVIT OF MOTHER.

UNITED STATES OF AMERICA, Indian Territory, }
......................................DISTRICT.

I, Betsie Mauldin , on oath state that I am 28 years of age and a citizen by blood , of the Choctaw Nation; that I am the lawful wife of Jack Mauldin , who is a citizen, by ——— of the United States Nation; that a

Applications for Enrollment of Choctaw Newborn
Act of 1905   Volume XII

male   child was born to me on   10   day of   July   , 1903; that said child has been named   Roy Jackson Mauldin   , and was living March 4, 1905.

her mark
Betsie Mauldin   x

Witnesses To Mark:
{ J S Burtan[sic]
{ G W Cooper

Subscribed and sworn to before me this   12 day of   June   , 1905

R S Hendon
Notary Public.

AFFIDAVIT OF ATTENDING PHYSICIAN OR MID-WIFE.

UNITED STATES OF AMERICA, Indian Territory, }
.... DISTRICT. }

I,   John J Chapman   , a   Physician   , on oath state that I attended on Mrs.   Betsie Mauldin   , wife of   Jack Mauldin   on the   10   day of July , 1903; that there was born to her on said date a   male   child; that said child was living March 4, 1905, and is said to have been named   Roy Jackson Mauldin

John J. Chapman M.D.

Witnesses To Mark:
{

Subscribed and sworn to before me this   5   day of   June   , 1905

R.S. Hendon
Notary Public.

7-NB-803.

Muskogee, Indian Territory, May 29, 1905.

Jack Mauldin,
    Elk, Indian Territory.

Dear Sir:

There is enclosed you herewith for execution application for the enrollment of your infant child, Roy Jackson Mauldin, born July 10, 1903.

Applications for Enrollment of Choctaw Newborn
Act of 1905   Volume XII

In the application heretofore filed in this office the seal of the Notary Public was omitted from the mother's affidavit. It will, therefore, be necessary that the enclosed application be executed.

In having these affidavits executed care should be exercised to see that all names are written in full, as they appear in the body of the affidavit, and in the event that either of the persons signing the affidavit are unable to write, signatures by mark must be attested by two witnesses. Each affidavit must be executed before a Notary Public and the notarial seal and signature of the officer must be attached to each separate affidavit.

Respectfully,

VR 29-7.   Chairman.

---

7 NB 803

Muskogee, Indian Territory, June 17, 1905.

Jack Mauldin,
    Elk, Indian Territory.

Dear Sir:

Receipt is hereby acknowledged of the affidavits of Betsie Mauldin and John J. Chapman, to the birth of Roy Jackson Mauldin, son of Jack and Betsie Mauldin, July 10, 1903, and the same have been filed with our records in the matter of the enrollment of said child.

Respectfully,

Chairman.

Choc New Born 804
    Ivey May Johnson   b. 6-23-03

Applications for Enrollment of Choctaw Newborn
Act of 1905   Volume XII

BIRTH AFFIDAVIT.

DEPARTMENT OF THE INTERIOR.
COMMISSION TO THE FIVE CIVILIZED TRIBES.

IN RE APPLICATION FOR ENROLLMENT, as a citizen of the   Choctaw   Nation, of Ivey May Johnson   , born on the 23rd   day of   June   , 1903

Name of Father: Sam Johnson   a citizen of the United States Nation.
Name of Mother: Martha Johnson   a citizen of the   Choctaw   Nation.

Postoffice   Reichert, Ind. Ter.

AFFIDAVIT OF MOTHER.

UNITED STATES OF AMERICA, Indian Territory, }
    Central   DISTRICT.   }

I, Martha Johnson   , on oath state that I am   26   years of age and a citizen by   blood   , of the   Choctaw   Nation; that I am the lawful wife of   Sam Johnson   , who is a citizen, ~~by~~ .... of the   United States   Nation; that a   female   child was born to me on 23rd   day of   June   , 1903; that said child has been named   Ivey May Johnson   , and was living March 4, 1905.

her
Martha x Johnson
mark

Witnesses To Mark:
{ George McClain
{ Leonidas E Merryman

Subscribed and sworn to before me this 30th day of   March   , 1905

Wirt Franklin
Notary Public.

AFFIDAVIT OF ATTENDING PHYSICIAN OR MID-WIFE.

UNITED STATES OF AMERICA, Indian Territory, }
.... DISTRICT. }

I,   Mary Britton   , a   midwife   , on oath state that I attended on Mrs. Martha Johnson   , wife of   Sam Johnson   on the 23^d day of June , 1903; that there was born to her on said date a   female   child; that said child was living March 4, 1905, and is said to have been named Ivey May Johnson

her
Mary x Britton
mark

Applications for Enrollment of Choctaw Newborn
Act of 1905   Volume XII

Witnesses To Mark:
- Sam Johnson
- JH Homer

Subscribed and sworn to before me this 7th day of   April   , 1905

Lacey P. Bobo
Notary Public.

NEW BORN AFFIDAVIT

No ....

CHOCTAW ENROLLING COMMISSION

IN THE MATTER OF THE APPLICATION FOR ENROLLMENT as a citizen of the Choctaw Nation, of   Ivey May Johnson   born on the 23 day of June   190 3

Name of father   Sam Johnson   a citizen of   non   Nation, final enrollment No. ——
Name of mother   Martha Johnson   a citizen of   Choctaw   Nation, final enrollment No. 6g20

Reichert I.T.   Postoffice.

AFFIDAVIT OF MOTHER

UNITED STATES OF AMERICA
INDIAN TERRITORY
DISTRICT   Central

I   Martha Johnson   , on oath state that I am 28 years of age and a citizen by   blood   of the   Choctaw   Nation, and as such have been placed upon the final roll of the   Choctaw   Nation, by the Honorable Secretary of the Interior my final enrollment number being   6g20   ; that I am the lawful wife of   Sam Johnson   , who is a citizen of the   non   Nation, and as such has been placed upon the final roll of said Nation by the Honorable Secretary of the Interior, his final enrollment number being .... and that a   female   child was born to me on the   23   day of   June   190 3; that said child has been named   Ivey May Johnson   , and is now living.

her
Martha x Johnson
mark

Applications for Enrollment of Choctaw Newborn
Act of 1905   Volume XII

WITNESSETH:
Must be two witnesses who are citizens { Samuel R Wilson
David Ward

Subscribed and sworn to before me this, the 16 day of February , 190 5

James Bower
Notary Public.

My Commission Expires:
Sept 23 - 1907

Affidavit of Attending Physician or Midwife

UNITED STATES OF AMERICA,
INDIAN TERRITORY,
Central   DISTRICT

I, Martha Mitchel[sic]   a   midwife on oath state that I attended on Mrs. Martha Johnson   wife of   Sam Johnson on the 23   day of   June , 190 3, that there was born to her on said date a   female   child, that said child is now living, and is said to have been named   Ivey May Johnson

Martha Mitchell   M. D.

Subscribed and sworn to before me this the   3rd day of   Mch   1905

NS Costelow
Notary Public.

WITNESSETH:
Must be two witnesses who are citizens and know the child. { Samuel R Wilson
David Ward

We hereby certify that we are well acquainted with   Martha Mitchell a   midwife   and know   her   to be reputable and of good standing in the community.

Must be two citizen witnesses. { Samuel R Wilson
David Ward

Applications for Enrollment of Choctaw Newborn
Act of 1905   Volume XII

Choc New Born 805
    William L. Truitt   b. 9-7-04

                                                      Choctaw 3437.

                    Muskogee, Indian Territory, April 13, 1905.

William M. Truitt,
    Wapanucka, Indian Territory.

Dear Sir:

    Receipt is hereby acknowledged of the affidavits of Alice Truitt and A. Stephenson to the birth of William L. Truitt, son of William M. and Alice Truitt, September 7, 1904, and the same have been filed with our records as an application for the enrollment of said child.

                          Respectfully,

                                          Commissioner in Charge.

BIRTH AFFIDAVIT.
                          DEPARTMENT OF THE INTERIOR.
            COMMISSION TO THE FIVE CIVILIZED TRIBES.

    IN RE APPLICATION FOR ENROLLMENT, as a citizen of the   Choctaw   Nation, of William L. Truitt   , born on the   7th   day of September   , 1904

Name of Father: William M. Truitt   a citizen of the   Choctaw   Nation.
Name of Mother: Alice Truitt (nee Perkins)   a citizen of the   Choctaw   Nation.

                    Postoffice   Wapanucka I.T.

                    AFFIDAVIT OF MOTHER.

UNITED STATES OF AMERICA, Indian Territory,
    Central   **DISTRICT.**

    I, Alice Truitt (nee Perkins)   , on oath state that I am   22   years of age and a citizen by   blood   , of the   Choctaw   Nation; that I am the lawful wife of William M Truitt   , who is a citizen, by intermarriage   of the   Choctaw Nation; that a   Male   child was born to me on   7th   day of September   , 1904; that said child has been named   William L. Truitt   , and was living March 4, 1905.

                                        Alice Truitt

Applications for Enrollment of Choctaw Newborn
Act of 1905   Volume XII

Witnesses To Mark:
{

Subscribed and sworn to before me this 7th day of April , 1905

WT Richard
Notary Public.

AFFIDAVIT OF ATTENDING PHYSICIAN OR MID-WIFE.

UNITED STATES OF AMERICA, Indian Territory,
Central   DISTRICT.

I, A Stephenson   , a Physician   , on oath state that I attended on Mrs. Alice Truitt (nee Perkins)   , wife of William M Truitt   on the 7th day of September   , 1904; that there was born to her on said date a male   child; that said child was living March 4, 1905, and is said to have been named William L Truitt

A. Stephenson M.D.

Witnesses To Mark:
{

Subscribed and sworn to before me this 7th day of April , 1905

WT Richard
Notary Public.

Choc New Born 806
   Mary Elizabeth Rushing   b. 3-7-03

Choctaw 5381.

Muskogee, Indian Territory, April 13, 1905.

Joe Rushing,
   Ada, Indian Territory.

Dear Sir:

Receipt is hereby acknowledged of the affidavits of Caraline Rushing and N. O. King to the birth of Mary Elizabeth Rushing, daughter of Joe and Caraline Rushing,

Applications for Enrollment of Choctaw Newborn
Act of 1905   Volume XII

March 7, 1903, and the same have been filed with our records as an application for the enrollment of said child.

Respectfully,

Commissioner in Charge.

NEW BORN AFFIDAVIT

No ....

CHOCTAW ENROLLING COMMISSION

IN THE MATTER OF THE APPLICATION FOR ENROLLMENT as a citizen of the Choctaw Nation, of   Mary Elizabeth Rushing   born on the 7th day of   March   190 3

Name of father   Joe Rushing   a citizen of   Choctaw   Nation, final enrollment No.   7-5381
Name of mother   Caraline Rushing   a citizen of   Choctaw   Nation, final enrollment No.   13618

Ada, I.T.   Postoffice.

AFFIDAVIT OF MOTHER

UNITED STATES OF AMERICA
INDIAN TERRITORY
DISTRICT   Southern

I   Caraline Rushing   , on oath state that I am   23   years of age and a citizen by   Blood   of the   Choctaw   Nation, and as such have been placed upon the final roll of the   Choctaw   Nation, by the Honorable Secretary of the Interior my final enrollment number being   13618   ; that I am the lawful wife of   Joe Rushing   , who is a citizen of the   Choctaw   Nation, and as such has been placed upon the final roll of said Nation by the Honorable Secretary of the Interior, his final enrollment number being   7-5381   and that a   Female   child was born to me on the   7th   day of   Mch   190 3; that said child has been named   Mary Elizabeth Rushing   , and is now living.

WITNESSETH: Caraline Rushing
  Must be two witnesses ⎰ J C Walker
  who are citizens   ⎱ W^{m} McDaniel

Applications for Enrollment of Choctaw Newborn
Act of 1905   Volume XII

Subscribed and sworn to before me this, the 28th day of Feb , 190 5

J. F. McKeel
Notary Public.

My Commission Expires: Jan 28th 1907

Affidavit of Attending Physician or Midwife

UNITED STATES OF AMERICA,
INDIAN TERRITORY,
Cent   DISTRICT

I, N. O. King a Midwife on oath state that I attended on Mrs. Caraline Rushing wife of Joe Rushing on the 7th day of March , 190 3, that there was born to her on said date a Female child, that said child is now living, and is said to have been named Mary Elizabeth Rushing

N O King   M. D.

Subscribed and sworn to before me this the 25 day of Feb 1905

R. T. Breedlove
Notary Public.

WITNESSETH:

Must be two witnesses who are citizens and know the child.
{ *(Name Illegible)*
  A P Turner

We hereby certify that we are well acquainted with Mrs. N. O. King a midwife and know her to be reputable and of good standing in the community.

Must be two citizen witnesses.
{ *(Name Illegible)*
  A P Turner

Applications for Enrollment of Choctaw Newborn
Act of 1905 Volume XII

BIRTH AFFIDAVIT.

DEPARTMENT OF THE INTERIOR.
COMMISSION TO THE FIVE CIVILIZED TRIBES.

IN RE APPLICATION FOR ENROLLMENT, as a citizen of the Choctaw Nation, of Mary Elizebeth[sic] Rushing, born on the 7 day of Mch, 1903

Name of Father: Joe Rushing   a citizen of the Choctaw Nation.
Name of Mother: Caraline Rushing   a citizen of the Choctaw Nation.

Postoffice   Ada I.T.

AFFIDAVIT OF MOTHER.

UNITED STATES OF AMERICA, Indian Territory,
Central   DISTRICT.

I, Caraline Rushing, on oath state that I am 23 years of age and a citizen by Blood, of the Choctaw Nation; that I am the lawful wife of Joe Rushing, who is a citizen, by marriage of the Choctaw Nation; that a Female child was born to me on 7 day of March, 1903; that said child has been named Mary Elizebeth Rushing, and was living March 4, 1905.

Caraline Rushing

Witnesses To Mark:
{

Subscribed and sworn to before me this 7 day of April, 1905

R.T. Breedlove
Notary Public.

AFFIDAVIT OF ATTENDING PHYSICIAN OR MID-WIFE.

UNITED STATES OF AMERICA, Indian Territory,
Central   DISTRICT.

I, N. O. King, a midwife, on oath state that I attended on Mrs. Caraline Rushing, wife of Joe Rushing on the 7 day of Mch, 1903; that there was born to her on said date a Female child; that said child was living March 4, 1905, and is said to have been named Mary Elizebeth Rushing

N. O. King

Witnesses To Mark:
{

Applications for Enrollment of Choctaw Newborn
Act of 1905   Volume XII

Subscribed and sworn to before me this 7 day of   April   , 1905

>R.T. Breedlove
>Notary Public.

Choc New Born 807
>Cephus Jefferson   b. 1-29-05

Choctaw 2904.

Muskogee, Indian Territory, April 13, 1905.

Wallace Jefferson,
>Red Oak, Indian Territory.

Dear Sir:

Receipt is hereby acknowledged of the affidavits of Sackey Jefferson and Jno. J. Gill to the birth of Cephus Jefferson, the son of Wallace and Sackey Jefferson, January 29, 1905, and the same have been filed with our records as an application for the enrollment of said child.

>Respectfully,

>Commissioner in Charge.

BIRTH AFFIDAVIT.

DEPARTMENT OF THE INTERIOR.
COMMISSION TO THE FIVE CIVILIZED TRIBES.

IN RE APPLICATION FOR ENROLLMENT, as a citizen of the   Choctaw   Nation, of _____, born on the _____ day of _____, 1____

Name of Father: Wallace Jefferson - roll #10452 a citizen of the Choctaw Nation.
Name of Mother: Sackey Jefferson - roll #8550   a citizen of the Choctaw Nation.

>Postoffice   Red Oak Ind. Ter.

Applications for Enrollment of Choctaw Newborn
Act of 1905   Volume XII

AFFIDAVIT OF MOTHER.

UNITED STATES OF AMERICA, Indian Territory, }
    Central   DISTRICT. }

    I, Sackey Jefferson, on oath state that I am about 39 years of age and a citizen by blood, of the Choctaw Nation; that I am the lawful wife of Wallace Jefferson, who is a citizen, by blood of the Choctaw Nation; that a male child was born to me on 29th day of January, 1905; that said child has been named Cephus Jefferson, and was living March 4, 1905.

                                      Sackey Jefferson

Witnesses To Mark:
{

    Subscribed and sworn to before me this 8th day of April, 1905

                                      Lacey P Bobo
                                      Notary Public.

AFFIDAVIT OF ATTENDING PHYSICIAN OR MID-WIFE.

UNITED STATES OF AMERICA, Indian Territory, }
.... DISTRICT. }

    I, John J Gill, a Physician, on oath state that I attended on Mrs. Sackey Jefferson, wife of Wallace Jefferson on the 29th day of January, 1905; that there was born to her on said date a male child; that said child was living March 4, 1905, and is said to have been named Cephus Jefferson

                                      John J Gill M.D.

Witnesses To Mark:
{

    Subscribed and sworn to before me this 8th day of April, 1905

                                      Lacey P Bobo
                                      Notary Public.

Applications for Enrollment of Choctaw Newborn
Act of 1905 Volume XII

Choc New Born 808
    Mitchell Ellis   b. 3-6-04

                                                            Choctaw 2510.

                          Muskogee, Indian Territory, April 12, 1905.

Floyde Ellis,
        Vireton, Indian Territory.

Dear Sir:

        Receipt is hereby acknowledged of the affidavits of Anna S. Ellis and O. W. Rice to the birth of Mitchell Ellis, son of Floyde and Anna S. Ellis, March 6, 1904, and the same have been filed with our records as an application for the enrollment of said child.

                                      Respectfully,

                                                                  Commissioner in Charge.

BIRTH AFFIDAVIT.
                          DEPARTMENT OF THE INTERIOR.
              COMMISSION TO THE FIVE CIVILIZED TRIBES.

        IN RE APPLICATION FOR ENROLLMENT, as a citizen of the   Choctaw   Nation, of Mitchell Ellis   , born on the 6th day of March   , 1904

Name of Father: Floyde Ellis   a citizen of the United States Nation.
Name of Mother: Anna S. Ellis   a citizen of the   Choctaw   Nation.

                              Postoffice   Vireton I.T.

                               AFFIDAVIT OF MOTHER.

UNITED STATES OF AMERICA, Indian Territory, }
        Central   DISTRICT. }

        I,   Anna S. Ellis   , on oath state that I am 23   years of age and a citizen by Blood   , of the   Choctaw   Nation; that I am the lawful wife of Floyde Ellis   , who is a citizen, by .... of the   United States   ~~Nation~~; that a male   child was born to me on   Sixth   day of   March   , 1904; that said child has been named   Mitchell Ellis   , and was living March 4, 1905.

                                          Anna S Ellis

Applications for Enrollment of Choctaw Newborn
Act of 1905   Volume XII

Witnesses To Mark:
{

    Subscribed and sworn to before me this 6th   day of   April   , 1905

                          W.D. Jolly
                               Notary Public.

AFFIDAVIT OF ATTENDING PHYSICIAN OR MID-WIFE.

UNITED STATES OF AMERICA, Indian Territory, }
    Central   DISTRICT. }

    I,   O. W. Rice   , a   Physician   , on oath state that I attended on Mrs.   Anna S. Ellis   , wife of   Floyde Ellis   on the 6th   day of   March   , 1904; that there was born to her on said date a   male   child; that said child was living March 4, 1905, and is said to have been named   Mitchell Ellis

                             O.W. Rice

Witnesses To Mark:
{

    Subscribed and sworn to before me this 6th   day of   April   , 1905

                               W.D. Jolly
                               Notary Public.

Choc New Born 809
    Minnie Guess   b. 9-14-03

                                        Choctaw 3940.

                  Muskogee, Indian Territory, April 13, 1905.

John M. Guess,
    Massey, Indian Territory.

Dear Sir:

    Receipt is hereby acknowledged of the affidavits of Maud Guess and J. J. Breaker to the birth of Minnie Guess, daughter of John M. and Maud Guess, September 14, 1903,

Applications for Enrollment of Choctaw Newborn
Act of 1905 Volume XII

and the same have been filed with our records as an application for the enrollment of said child.

Respectfully,

Commissioner in Charge.

BIRTH AFFIDAVIT.

DEPARTMENT OF THE INTERIOR.
COMMISSION TO THE FIVE CIVILIZED TRIBES.

IN RE APPLICATION FOR ENROLLMENT, as a citizen of the Choctaw Nation, of Minnie Guess, born on the 14 day of Sept, 1903

Name of Father: John M. Guess   a citizen of the Choctaw Nation.
Name of Mother: Maud Guess   a citizen of the Chotaw[sic] Nation.

Postoffice   Massey, Ind. T.

AFFIDAVIT OF MOTHER.

UNITED STATES OF AMERICA, Indian Territory, }
     Western   DISTRICT.

I, Minnie[sic] Guess, on oath state that I am 29 years of age and a citizen by In=termarriage[sic], of the Choctaw Nation; that I am the lawful wife of John M. Guess, who is a citizen, by blood of the Choctaw Nation; that a Female child was born to me on 14 day of Sept, 1903; that said child has been named Minnie Guess, and was living March 4, 1905.

Maud Guess

Witnesses To Mark:
{

Subscribed and sworn to before me this 5 day of April, 1905

J. M. White
Notary Public.

Applications for Enrollment of Choctaw Newborn
Act of 1905   Volume XII

AFFIDAVIT OF ATTENDING PHYSICIAN OR MID-WIFE.

UNITED STATES OF AMERICA, Indian Territory,
    Central   DISTRICT.

I,   J. J. Breaker   , a   Physician   , on oath state that I attended on Mrs.   Maud Guess   , wife of   John M. Guess   on the 14 day of Sept. , 1903; that there was born to her on said date a   Female   child; that said child was living March 4, 1905, and is said to have been named   Minnie Guess

                                J.J. Breaker M.D.

Witnesses To Mark:
{

Subscribed and sworn to before me this 8 day of   April   , 1905

                                E.W. Frey
                                    Notary Public.

Choc New Born 810
        Mary Ann Wright b. 10-8-03

                                                7 NB 810

                    Muskogee, Indian Territory, June 16, 1905.

Sampson Wright,
    Redoak, Indian Territory.

Dear Sir:

Receipt is hereby acknowledged of the affidavits of Bency Wright and Judith Lewis to the birth of Mary-Ann Wright, daughter of Sampson and Bency Wright, October 8, 1903, and the same have been filed in the matter of the enrollment of said child.
                    Respectfully,

                                            Chairman.

Applications for Enrollment of Choctaw Newborn
Act of 1905   Volume XII

7-NB-810.

Muskogee, Indian Territory, June 6, 1905.

Sampson Wright,
    Redoak, Indian Territory.

Dear Sir:

    There is enclosed you herewith for execution application for the enrollment of your infant child, Mary Ann Wright.

    In the mothers[sic] affidavit of April 8, 1905, she gives the date of the applicant's birth as October 8, 1905, while the midwife in her affidavit of the same date, gives it as October 8, 1903. In the enclosed application the date of birth is left blank. Please insert the correct date and when the affidavits are properly executed return them to this office.

    In having these affidavits executed care should be exercised to see that all names are written in full, as they appear in the body of the affidavit, and in the event that either of the persons signing the affidavit are unable to write, signatures by mark must be attested by two witnesses. Each affidavit must be executed before a Notary Public and the notarial seal and signature of the officer must be attached to each separate affidavit.

                                          Respectfully,

VR 6-5.   Commissioner in Charge.

BIRTH AFFIDAVIT.

DEPARTMENT OF THE INTERIOR.
COMMISSION TO THE FIVE CIVILIZED TRIBES.

    IN RE APPLICATION FOR ENROLLMENT, as a citizen of the   Choctaw   Nation, of Mary Ann Wright   , born on the .... day of ...., 1........

Name of Father: Sampson Wright   a citizen of the   Choctaw   Nation.
Name of Mother: Bency Wright   a citizen of the   Choctaw   Nation.

                                    Postoffice   Red Oak, Ind. Ter.

Applications for Enrollment of Choctaw Newborn
Act of 1905 Volume XII

AFFIDAVIT OF MOTHER.

UNITED STATES OF AMERICA, Indian Territory,
Central DISTRICT.

I, Bency Wright , on oath state that I am 22 years of age and a citizen by blood , of the Choctaw Nation; that I am the lawful wife of Sampson Wright , who is a citizen, by blood of the Choctaw Nation; that a female child was born to me on 8th day of October , 1903; that said child has been named Mary Ann Wright , and was living March 4, 1905.

Bency Wright

Witnesses To Mark:
   Clifford V Peery
   John Hart

Subscribed and sworn to before me this 12th day of June , 1905

Chas. H. Hudson

My Com. expires 1-11-1905[sic]   Notary Public.

AFFIDAVIT OF ATTENDING PHYSICIAN OR MID-WIFE.

UNITED STATES OF AMERICA, Indian Territory,
Central DISTRICT.

I, Judith Lewis , a mid wife , on oath state that I attended on Mrs. Bency Wright , wife of Sampson Wright on the 8 day of October , 1903; that there was born to her on said date a female child; that said child was living March 4, 1905, and is said to have been named Mary Ann Wright

Judith Lewis

Witnesses To Mark:
   Clifford V Peery
   John Hart

Subscribed and sworn to before me this 12th day of June , 1905

Chas. H. Hudson

My Com. expires 1-11-1905[sic]   Notary Public.

Applications for Enrollment of Choctaw Newborn
Act of 1905   Volume XII

BIRTH AFFIDAVIT.

DEPARTMENT OF THE INTERIOR,
COMMISSION TO THE FIVE CIVILIZED TRIBES.

IN RE Application for Enrollment, as a citizen of the   Choctaw   Nation, of   Mary Ann Wright   , born on the   8   day of   Oct   , 1903

Name of Father: Sampson Wright   a citizen of the   Choctaw   Nation.
Name of Mother: Bency Wright   a citizen of the   Choctaw   Nation.

Post-Office: Red Oak

AFFIDAVIT OF MOTHER.

UNITED STATES OF AMERICA, }
  INDIAN TERRITORY.
  Central   District.

I,   Bency Wright   , on oath state that I am   22   years of age and a citizen by   birth   , of the   Choctaw   Nation; that I am the lawful wife of   Sampson Wright   , who is a citizen, by   birth   of the   Choctaw   Nation; that a   girl   child was born to me on   8   day of   Oct   , 1905 , that said child has been named   Mary Ann Wright   , and is now living.

                                        Bency Wright

WITNESSES TO MARK:
{

Subscribed and sworn to before me this   8   *day of*   April   , 1905.

                                        W. W. Ish
                                           NOTARY PUBLIC.

AFFIDAVIT OF ATTENDING PHYSICIAN OR MID-WIFE.

UNITED STATES OF AMERICA, }
  INDIAN TERRITORY.
  Central   District.

I,   Logan Harlin   , a   Nurs   , on oath state that I attended on Mrs.   Bency Wright   , wife of   Sampson Wright   on the   8   day of   Oct   , 1903 ; that there was born to her on said date a   girl   child; that said child is now living and is said to have been named   May Ann Wright

                                        Logan Harlin

Applications for Enrollment of Choctaw Newborn
Act of 1905   Volume XII

WITNESSES TO MARK:
{

    Subscribed and sworn to before me this   8   day of   April   , 1905.

W. W. Ish
NOTARY PUBLIC.

Choc New Born 811
    William W. Tyler   b. 5-16-04

Choctaw 974.

Muskogee, Indian Territory, April 12, 1905.

George W. Tyler,
    Parsons, Indian Territory.

Dear Sir:

    Receipt is hereby acknowledged of the affidavits of Carrie Tyler (Gardner) and E. V. Tate to the birth of William W. Tyler, son of George W. and Carrie Tyler, May 16, 1904, and the same have been filed with our records as an application for the enrollment of said child.

Respectfully,

Commissioner in Charge.

NEW-BORN AFFIDAVIT.

    Number............

...Choctaw Enrolling Commission...

    IN THE MATTER OF THE APPLICATION FOR ENROLLMENT, as a citizen of the Choctaw   Nation, of   William Ward Tyler

born on the 16th day of   May   190 4

Name of father   George Tyler   a citizen of   ———
Nation final enrollment No. ———

Applications for Enrollment of Choctaw Newborn
Act of 1905   Volume XII

Name of mother   Carrie Gardner now Tyler   a citizen of   Choctaw
Nation final enrollment No.   2587

                                            Postoffice   Parsons I.T.

AFFIDAVIT OF MOTHER.

UNITED STATES OF AMERICA
INDIAN TERRITORY
Central   DISTRICT

I   Carrie Gardner - Tyler   , on oath state that I am 18 years of age and a citizen by blood of the   Choctaw   Nation, and as such have been placed upon the final roll of the   Choctaw   Nation, by the Honorable Secretary of the Interior my final enrollment number being   2587 ; that I am the lawful wife of   George Tyler , who is a citizen of the ——— Nation, and as such has been placed upon the final roll of said Nation by the Honorable Secretary of the Interior, his final enrollment number being ——— and that a   Male   child was born to me on the   16th day of   May   190 4; that said child has been named   William Ward Tyler , and is now living.

                                        Carrie Gardner Tyler

Witnesseth.

Must be two Witnesses who are Citizens.   } D A Fowler
                     Edward Gardner

Subscribed and sworn to before me this   24th   day of   Feb   190 5

                                  W.A. Shoney
                                           Notary Public.

My commission expires: Jan 10 1909

AFFIDAVIT OF ATTENDING PHYSICIAN OR MIDWIFE

UNITED STATES OF AMERICA
INDIAN TERRITORY
Central   DISTRICT

I,   E. V. Tate   a   midwife   on oath state that I attended on Mrs. Carrie Gardner-Tyler   wife of George Tyler on the   16th day of   May , 190 4, that there was born to her on said date a   male   child, that said child is now living, and is said to have been named   William Ward Tyler

                                       her
                           E. V. Tate x   M.D.
WITNESSETH: mark

Must be two witnesses who are citizens and know the child.   { D.A. Fowler
                             Edmund Gardner

Applications for Enrollment of Choctaw Newborn
Act of 1905 Volume XII

Subscribed and sworn to before me this, the 24th day of Feb 1905

W. A. Shoney   Notary Public.

We hereby certify that we are well acquainted with E. V. Tate a midwife and know her to be reputable and of good standing in the community.

D. A. Fowler

Edmund Gardner

BIRTH AFFIDAVIT.

DEPARTMENT OF THE INTERIOR.
COMMISSION TO THE FIVE CIVILIZED TRIBES.

IN RE APPLICATION FOR ENROLLMENT, as a citizen of the Choctaw Nation, of William W. Tyler, born on the 16th day of May, 1904

Name of Father: George W. Tyler   a citizen of the United States Nation.
Name of Mother: Carrie Tyler (nee Gardner)   a citizen of the Choctaw Nation.

Postoffice   Parsons I.T.

AFFIDAVIT OF MOTHER.

UNITED STATES OF AMERICA, Indian Territory,
Central DISTRICT.

I, Carrie Tyler (nee Gardner), on oath state that I am 18 years of age and a citizen by Blood, of the Choctaw Nation; that I am the lawful wife of George W. Tyler, who is a citizen, by non citizen of the Choctaw Nation; that a male child was born to me on 16th day of May, 1904; that said child has been named William W. Tyler, and was living March 4, 1905.

Carrie Tyler (nee Gardner)

Witnesses To Mark:

Subscribed and sworn to before me this 8th day of April, 1905

E.J. Gardner
Notary Public.

Applications for Enrollment of Choctaw Newborn
Act of 1905   Volume XII

AFFIDAVIT OF ATTENDING PHYSICIAN OR MID-WIFE.

UNITED STATES OF AMERICA, Indian Territory,
Central   DISTRICT.

I, E. V. Tate   , a midwife   , on oath state that I attended on Mrs. Carrie Tyler   , wife of   George W. Tyler   on the 16th day of May , 1904; that there was born to her on said date a   male   child; that said child was living March 4, 1905, and is said to have been named William W. Tyler

E. V. Tate

Witnesses To Mark:
{

Subscribed and sworn to before me this 8th day of April   , 1905

E.J. Gardner
Notary Public.

Choc New Born 812
   Russell Ray Jones b. 4-3-03
   Acy Louis Jones b. 1-23-05

Choctaw 4786.

Muskogee, Indian Territory, April 13, 1905.

James A. Jones,
   Fitzhugh, Indian Territory.

Dear Sir:

Receipt is hereby acknowledged of the affidavits of Lou Jones and C. S. Wilkinson to the birth of Acy Louis Jones and Russell Ray Jones, children of James A. and Lou Jones, April 3, 1903 and January 23, 1905, respectively, and the same have been filed with our records as applications for the enrollment of said children.

Respectfully,

Commissioner in Charge.

Applications for Enrollment of Choctaw Newborn
Act of 1905 Volume XII

BIRTH AFFIDAVIT.

DEPARTMENT OF THE INTERIOR.
COMMISSION TO THE FIVE CIVILIZED TRIBES.

IN RE APPLICATION FOR ENROLLMENT, as a citizen of the Choctaw Nation, of Russell Ray Jones, born on the 3 day of April, 1903

Name of Father: James A. Jones   a citizen of the Choctaw Nation.
Name of Mother: Lou Jones   a citizen of the Choctaw Nation.

Postoffice Fitzhugh

AFFIDAVIT OF MOTHER.

UNITED STATES OF AMERICA, Indian Territory, }
Sixteenth   DISTRICT.

I, Lou Jones, on oath state that I am 30 years of age and a citizen by Blood, of the Choctaw Nation; that I am the lawful wife of James A Jones, who is a citizen, by Intermarriage of the Choctaw Nation; that a male child was born to me on 3rd day of April, 1903; that said child has been named Russell Ray Jones, and was living March 4, 1905.

                                her
                            Lou x Jones
Witnesses To Mark: mark
  TM Suddath
  Ed Johnston

Subscribed and sworn to before me this 8th day of April, 1905

                            W M Canterbury
My Commission Expires Jan. 20, 1909.   Notary Public.

AFFIDAVIT OF ATTENDING PHYSICIAN OR MID-WIFE.

UNITED STATES OF AMERICA, Indian Territory, }
Sixteenth   DISTRICT.

I, C.S. Wilkinson, a Physician, on oath state that I attended on Mrs. Lou Jones, wife of James A Jones on the 3rd day of April, 1903; that there was born to her on said date a male child; that said child was living March 4, 1905, and is said to have been named Russell Ray Jones

                            CS Wilkinson

Applications for Enrollment of Choctaw Newborn
Act of 1905 Volume XII

Witnesses To Mark:
{

Subscribed and sworn to before me this 8th day of April , 1905

W M Canterbury

My Commission Expires Jan. 20, 1909.   Notary Public.

BIRTH AFFIDAVIT.

DEPARTMENT OF THE INTERIOR.
COMMISSION TO THE FIVE CIVILIZED TRIBES.

IN RE APPLICATION FOR ENROLLMENT, as a citizen of the Choctaw Nation, of Acy Louis Jones , born on the 23 day of Jan , 1905

Name of Father: James A. Jones   a citizen of the Choctaw Nation.
Name of Mother: Lou Jones   a citizen of the Choctaw Nation.

Postoffice   Fitzhugh I.T.

AFFIDAVIT OF MOTHER.

UNITED STATES OF AMERICA, Indian Territory, }
.... DISTRICT. }

I, Lou Jones , on oath state that I am 30 years of age and a citizen by Blood , of the Choctaw Nation; that I am the lawful wife of James A Jones , who is a citizen, by Intermarriage of the Choctaw Nation; that a male child was born to me on 23 day of Jan , 1905; that said child has been named Acy Louis Jones , and was living March 4, 1905.

                                 her
                             Lou x Jones
Witnesses To Mark: mark
{ TM Suddath
  Ed Johnston

Subscribed and sworn to before me this 8th day of April , 1905

W M Canterbury

My Commission Expires Jan. 20, 1909.   Notary Public.

Applications for Enrollment of Choctaw Newborn
Act of 1905   Volume XII

AFFIDAVIT OF ATTENDING PHYSICIAN OR MID-WIFE.

UNITED STATES OF AMERICA, Indian Territory, }
.... DISTRICT. }

I,   C.S. Wilkinson   , a   Physician   , on oath state that I attended on Mrs.   Lou Jones   , wife of   James A Jones   on the 23   day of   Jan   , 1905; that there was born to her on said date a   male   child; that said child was living March 4, 1905, and is said to have been named Acy Louis Jones

CS Wilkinson

Witnesses To Mark:
{

Subscribed and sworn to before me this 8th   day of   April   , 1905

W M Canterbury
Notary Public.

My Commission Expires Jan. 20, 1909.

Choc New Born 813
   Lou LeFlore   b. 4-28-04

Choctaw 3012.

Muskogee, Indian Territory, April 12, 1905.

Mack H. LeFlore,
   Leflore, Indian Territory.

Dear Sir:

Receipt is hereby acknowledged of the affidavits of Bertha LeFlore and Adna[sic] Jones to the birth of Lou LeFlore, daughter of Mack H. and Bertha LeFlore, April 24, 1904, and the same have been filed with our records as an application for the enrollment of said child.

Respectfully,

Commissioner in Charge.

Applications for Enrollment of Choctaw Newborn
Act of 1905　Volume XII

7-NB-813.

Muskogee, Indian Territory, May 29, 1905.

Mack H. LeFlore,
    LeFlore, Indian Territory.

Dear Sir:

There is enclosed you herewith for execution application for the enrollment of your infant child, Lou LeFlore.

In the affidavits of February 21, 1905, heretofore filed in this office, the date of the applicant's birth is given as April 28, 1904, while in these of the 8th ultimo, it is given as April 24, 1904. In the enclosed application the date of birth is left blank. Please insert the correct date and when the affidavits are properly executed return them to this office.

In having these affidavits executed care should be exercised to see that all names are written in full, as they appear in the body of the affidavit, and in the event that either of the persons signing the affidavit are unable to write, signatures by mark must be attested by two witnesses. Each affidavit must be executed before a Notary Public and the notarial seal and signature of the officer must be attached to each separate affidavit.

Respectfully,

VR 29-8.　　　　　　　　　　　　　　　　　　　　　　　　　　　　Chairman.

7-NB-813.

Muskogee, Indian Territory, June 10, 1905.

Mack H. LeFlore,
    Leflore, Indian Territory.

Dear Sir:

Receipt is hereby acknowledged of the affidavits of Bertha LeFlore and Edna Jones to the birth of Lou LeFlore, daughter of Mach[sic] H. and Bertha LeFlore, April 28, 1904, and the same have been filed with our records in the matter of the enrollment of said child.

Respectfully,

Chairman.

Applications for Enrollment of Choctaw Newborn
Act of 1905   Volume XII

BIRTH AFFIDAVIT.

DEPARTMENT OF THE INTERIOR.
COMMISSION TO THE FIVE CIVILIZED TRIBES.

IN RE APPLICATION FOR ENROLLMENT, as a citizen of the Choctaw Nation, of Lou LeFlore, born on the 24[sic] day of April, 1904

Name of Father: Mack H LeFlore   a citizen of the Choctaw Nation.
Name of Mother: Bertha LeFlore   a citizen of the Choctaw Nation.

Postoffice   LeFlore I.T.

AFFIDAVIT OF MOTHER.

UNITED STATES OF AMERICA, Indian Territory, } Central DISTRICT.

I, Bertha LeFlore, on oath state that I am 38 years of age and a citizen by Marriage, of the Choctaw Nation; that I am the lawful wife of Mack H LeFlore, who is a citizen, by blood of the Choctaw Nation; that a female child was born to me on 24 day of April, 1904; that said child has been named Lou LeFlore, and was living March 4, 1905.

Bertha LeFlore

Witnesses To Mark:

Subscribed and sworn to before me this 8 day of April, 1905

Robert E Lee
My Com expires Jan 11-1906   Notary Public.

AFFIDAVIT OF ATTENDING PHYSICIAN OR MID-WIFE.

UNITED STATES OF AMERICA, Indian Territory, } Central DISTRICT.

I, Adna[sic] Jones, a midwife, on oath state that I attended on Mrs. Bertha LeFlore, wife of Mack H. LeFlore on the 24 day of April, 1904; that there was born to her on said date a female child; that said child was living March 4, 1905, and is said to have been named Lou LeFlore

her
Adna x Jones
mark

Applications for Enrollment of Choctaw Newborn
Act of 1905   Volume XII

Witnesses To Mark:
{ Louis Jones
{ Arthur N B Jones

Subscribed and sworn to before me this 8 day of   April   , 1905

                                          Robert E Lee
My Com expires Jan 11-1906   Notary Public.

Final enrollment no of Mack H. LeFlore being No. 8821.
Final enrollment no of Bertha LeFlore being No. 279.

BIRTH AFFIDAVIT.

DEPARTMENT OF THE INTERIOR.
COMMISSION TO THE FIVE CIVILIZED TRIBES.

IN RE APPLICATION FOR ENROLLMENT, as a citizen of the   Choctaw   Nation, of Lou LeFlore   , born on the 28 day of April , 1904

Name of Father: Mack H LeFlore   a citizen of the   Choctaw   Nation.
Name of Mother: Bertha LeFlore   a citizen of the   Choctaw   Nation.

                            Postoffice   LeFlore Ind. Ter.

AFFIDAVIT OF MOTHER.

UNITED STATES OF AMERICA, Indian Territory, }
    Central   **DISTRICT.** }

I, Bertha LeFlore   , on oath state that I am 38   years of age and a citizen by   intermarriage   , of the   Choctaw   Nation; that I am the lawful wife of Mack H LeFlore   , who is a citizen, by blood   of the   Choctaw   Nation; that a   female   child was born to me on 28   day of April   , 1904; that said child has been named   Lou LeFlore   , and was living March 4, 1905.

                                      Bertha LeFlore
Witnesses To Mark:
{

Subscribed and sworn to before me this 6 day of   June   , 1905

                                      W L Harris
My Com exp 7/8/08   Notary Public.

Applications for Enrollment of Choctaw Newborn
Act of 1905   Volume XII

AFFIDAVIT OF ATTENDING PHYSICIAN OR MID-WIFE.

UNITED STATES OF AMERICA, Indian Territory,
Central   DISTRICT.

I, Edna Jones, a midwife, on oath state that I attended on Mrs. Bertha LeFlore, wife of Mack H. LeFlore on the 28 day of April, 1904; that there was born to her on said date a female child; that said child was living March 4, 1905, and is said to have been named Lou LeFlore

                            her
                    Edna x Jones
                            mark

Witnesses To Mark:
  { Louis Jones
  { Arthur N B Jones

Subscribed and sworn to before me this 6 day of June, 1905

                            W L Harris
My Com exp 7/8/08   Notary Public.

NEW BORN AFFIDAVIT

No ....

CHOCTAW ENROLLING COMMISSION

IN THE MATTER OF THE APPLICATION FOR ENROLLMENT as a citizen of the Choctaw Nation, of   Lou LeFlore   born on the 28th day of April   190 4

Name of father   Mack H. LeFlore   a citizen of   Choctaw   Nation,
final enrollment No.   8821   *by Marriage*
Name of mother   Bertha LeFlore   a citizen of   Choctaw   Nation,
final enrollment No.   279

                    LeFlore I.T.   Postoffice.

Applications for Enrollment of Choctaw Newborn
Act of 1905   Volume XII

AFFIDAVIT OF MOTHER

UNITED STATES OF AMERICA
INDIAN TERRITORY
DISTRICT   Central

I   Bertha LeFlore   , on oath state that I am   39   years of age and a citizen by   marriage   of the   Choctaw   Nation, and as such have been placed upon the final roll of the   Choctaw   Nation, by the Honorable Secretary of the Interior my final enrollment number being   279   ; that I am the lawful wife of   Mack H LeFlore   , who is a citizen of the   Choctaw   Nation, and as such has been placed upon the final roll of said Nation by the Honorable Secretary of the Interior, his final enrollment number being   8821   and that a   female   child was born to me on the   28th day of   April   190 4; that said child has been named   Lou LeFlore   , and is now living.

WITNESSETH: Bertha LeFlore
Must be two witnesses { Isaac Durant
who are citizens   Sallie Ward

Subscribed and sworn to before me this, the   21   day of   February   , 190 5

Robert E. Lee
Notary Public.

My Commission Expires: Jan 11 - 1906

Affidavit of Attending Physician or Midwife

UNITED STATES OF AMERICA,
INDIAN TERRITORY,
Central   DISTRICT

I,   Adna Jones   a   midwife on oath state that I attended on Mrs. Bertha LeFlore   wife of   Mack H LeFlore on the   28th day of   April   , 190 4, that there was born to her on said date a   female child, that said child is now living, and is said to have been named   Lou LeFlore

Adna Jones   Midwife

Subscribed and sworn to before me this the   21   day of   February   1905

Robert E. Lee
My com. expires Jan. 11-1906   Notary Public.

WITNESSETH:
Must be two witnesses { Isaac Durant
who are citizens and
know the child.   Sallie Ward

Applications for Enrollment of Choctaw Newborn
Act of 1905   Volume XII

We hereby certify that we are well acquainted with   Adna Jones
a   midwife   and know   her   to be reputable and of good standing in the community.

Must be two citizen ⎰ Isaac Durant
witnesses.   ⎱ Sallie Ward

Choc New Born 814
    Benjamin Baxter Freeny   b. 12-12-04

Choctaw 3897.

Muskogee, Indian Territory, April 12, 1905.

Robert C. Freeny,
    Caddo, Indian Territory.

Dear Sir:

    Receipt is hereby acknowledged of the affidavits of Josephine Freeny and M. J. Harmon to the birth of Benjamin Baxter Freeny, son of Robert C. and Josephine Freeny, December 12, 1904, and the same have been filed with our records as an application for the enrollment of said child.

Respectfully,

Commissioner in Charge.

7 NB 814

Muskogee, Indian Territory, June 16, 1905.

R. C. Freeny,
    Caddo, Indian Territory.

Dear Sir:

    Receipt is hereby acknowledged of your letter of June 10, 1905, enclosing affidavits of Josephine Freeny and Montie Jane Harmon to the birth of Benjamin Baxton[sic] Freeney, son of Robert C. and Josephine Freeny, December 12, 1904, and the same have been filed in the matter of the enrollment of said child.

Applications for Enrollment of Choctaw Newborn
Act of 1905   Volume XII

Respectfully,

Chairman.

7-NB-814.

Muskogee, Indian Territory, June 6, 1905.

Robert C. Freeny,
    Caddo, Indian Territory.

Dear Sir:

    There is enclosed you herewith for execution application for the enrollment of your infant child, Benjamin Baxter Freeny.

    In the affidavits of March 1, 1905, heretofore filed in this office, the mother gives the date of the applicant's birth as December 12, 1905, while the attending physician gives it as December 12, 1904. In the affidavits of April 8, 1905, this date is given as December 12, 1904. In the enclosed application the date of birth is left blank. Please insert the correct date and when the affidavits are properly executed return them to this office.

    In having these affidavits executed care should be exercised to see that all names are written in full, as they appear in the body of the affidavit, and in the event that either of the persons signing the affidavit are unable to write, signatures by mark must be attested by two witnesses. Each affidavit must be executed before a Notary Public and the notarial seal and signature of the officer must be attached to each separate affidavit.

Respectfully,

Commissioner in Charge.

VR 6-4

Applications for Enrollment of Choctaw Newborn
Act of 1905 Volume XII

NEW BORN AFFIDAVIT

No ....

CHOCTAW ENROLLING COMMISSION

IN THE MATTER OF THE APPLICATION FOR ENROLLMENT as a citizen of the Choctaw Nation, of Benjamin B. Freeny born on the Twelvth[sic] day of December 190 5

Name of father Robt C. Freeny a citizen of Choctaw Nation, final enrollment No. 10961
Name of mother Josephine Freeny a citizen of Choctaw Nation, final enrollment No. 359

Caddo, Ind. Ter. Postoffice.

AFFIDAVIT OF MOTHER

UNITED STATES OF AMERICA }
   INDIAN TERRITORY
DISTRICT Central

I Josephine Freeny , on oath state that I am 37 years of age and a citizen by marriage of the Choctaw Nation, and as such have been placed upon the final roll of the Choctaw Nation, by the Honorable Secretary of the Interior my final enrollment number being 359 ; that I am the lawful wife of Robt. C. Freeny , who is a citizen of the Choctaw Nation, and as such has been placed upon the final roll of said Nation by the Honorable Secretary of the Interior, his final enrollment number being .... and that a Male child was born to me on the 12th day of December 190 5; that said child has been named Benjamin Baxter Freeny , and is now living.

WITNESSETH: Josephine Freeny
  Must be two witnesses { *(Name Illegible)*
  who are citizens W.H. Goforth

Subscribed and sworn to before me this, the 1st day of March , 190 5

Sol. J. Homer
Notary Public.
My Commission Expires: Jan. 10, 1907

Applications for Enrollment of Choctaw Newborn
Act of 1905   Volume XII

Affidavit of Attending Physician or Midwife

UNITED STATES OF AMERICA, }
INDIAN TERRITORY,
Central   DISTRICT

I,   W. R. Bowman   a   Practicing Physician   on oath state that I attended on Mrs. Josephine Freeny   wife of Robt. C. Freeny   on the   12th day of December , 190 4, that there was born to her on said date a   male   child, that said child is now living, and is said to have been named   Benjamin B. Freeny

W.R. Bowman   M. D.

Subscribed and sworn to before me this the   12th day of March   1905

Sol. J. Homes
Notary Public.

WITNESSETH:

Must be two witnesses
who are citizens and
know the child.
{ W.H. Goforth
   (Name Illegible)

We hereby certify that we are well acquainted with   W. R. Bowman   a   Practicing Physician   and know   him   to be reputable and of good standing in the community.

Must be two citizen
witnesses.
{ W.H. Goforth
  (Name Illegible)

BIRTH AFFIDAVIT.

DEPARTMENT OF THE INTERIOR.
COMMISSION TO THE FIVE CIVILIZED TRIBES.

IN RE APPLICATION FOR ENROLLMENT, as a citizen of the   Choctaw   Nation, of   Benjamin Baxter Freeny   , born on the   12th day of December , 1904

Name of Father: Robert C. Freeny   a citizen of the   Choctaw   Nation.
Name of Mother: Josephine Freeny   a citizen of the   Choctaw   Nation.

Postoffice   Caddo Ind. Ter.

Applications for Enrollment of Choctaw Newborn
Act of 1905   Volume XII

AFFIDAVIT OF MOTHER.

UNITED STATES OF AMERICA, Indian Territory, }
Central   DISTRICT.

I, Josephine Freeny, on oath state that I am 37 years of age and a citizen by marriage, of the Choctaw Nation; that I am the lawful wife of Robert C. Freeny, who is a citizen, by blood of the Choctaw Nation; that a male child was born to me on 12th day of December, 1904; that said child has been named Benjamin Baxter Freeny, and was living March 4, 1905.

Josephine Freeny

Witnesses To Mark:
{

Subscribed and sworn to before me this 8th day of April, 1905

J L Rappolee
Notary Public.

AFFIDAVIT OF ATTENDING PHYSICIAN OR MID-WIFE.

UNITED STATES OF AMERICA, Indian Territory, }
Central   DISTRICT.

I, M. J. Harmon, a Mid-wife, on oath state that I attended on Mrs. Josephine Freeny, wife of Robert C. Freeny on the 12th day of December, 1904; that there was born to her on said date a male child; that said child was living March 4, 1905, and is said to have been named Benjamin Baxter Freeny

M.J. Harmon

Witnesses To Mark:
{

Subscribed and sworn to before me this 8th day of April, 1905

J L Rappolee
Notary Public.

Applications for Enrollment of Choctaw Newborn
Act of 1905 Volume XII

BIRTH AFFIDAVIT.

DEPARTMENT OF THE INTERIOR.
COMMISSION TO THE FIVE CIVILIZED TRIBES.

IN RE APPLICATION FOR ENROLLMENT, as a citizen of the Choctaw Nation, of Benjamin Baxter Freeny, born on the 12th day of December, 1904

Name of Father: Robert C. Freeny   a citizen of the Choctaw Nation.
Name of Mother: Josephine Freeny   a citizen of the Choctaw Nation.

Postoffice   Caddo Ind. Ter.

AFFIDAVIT OF MOTHER.

UNITED STATES OF AMERICA, Indian Territory, }
     Central   DISTRICT.

I, Josephine Freeny, on oath state that I am 37 years of age and a citizen by intermarriage, of the Choctaw Nation; that I am the lawful wife of Robert C. Freeny, who is a citizen, by blood of the Choctaw Nation; that a male child was born to me on 12th day of December, 1904; that said child has been named Benjamin Baxter Freeny, and was living March 4, 1905.

                                           Josephine Freeny
Witnesses To Mark:
{

Subscribed and sworn to before me this 10th day of June, 1905

                                       A.E. Richey
                                       Notary Public.

AFFIDAVIT OF ATTENDING PHYSICIAN OR MID-WIFE.

UNITED STATES OF AMERICA, Indian Territory, }
     Central   DISTRICT.

I, Montie Jane Harmon, a Mid-wife, on oath state that I attended on Mrs. Josephine Freeny, wife of Robert C. Freeny on the 12th day of December, 1904; that there was born to her on said date a male child; that said child was living March 4, 1905, and is said to have been named Benjamin Baxter Freeny

                                       Montie Jane Harmon
Witnesses To Mark:
{

Applications for Enrollment of Choctaw Newborn
Act of 1905 Volume XII

Subscribed and sworn to before me this 10th day of June, 1905

A.E. Richey
Notary Public.

Com expires May 1" 1909.

Choc New Born 815
    John E. Hekia b. 5-25-04

7-NB-815.

Muskogee, Indian Territory, May 29, 1905.

Sibby Hekia,
    Atoka, Indian Territory.

Dear Madam:

    There is enclosed you herewith for execution application for the enrollment of your infant child, John E. Hekia, born May 25, 1904.

    In the application heretofore filed in this office the seal of the Notary Public was omitted from the physician's affidavit. It will, therefore, be necessary that this affidavit be re-executed.

    In having these affidavits executed care should be exercised to see that all names are written in full, as they appear in the body of the affidavit, and in the event that either of the persons signing the affidavit are unable to write, signatures by mark must be attested by two witnesses. Each affidavit must be executed before a Notary Public and the notarial seal and signature of the officer must be attached to each separate affidavit.

Respectfully,

VR 29-9.   Chairman.

Applications for Enrollment of Choctaw Newborn
Act of 1905   Volume XII

D.J.

REFER IN REPLY TO THE FOLLOWING:
7-NB-815

DEPARTMENT OF THE INTERIOR,
COMMISSIONER TO THE FIVE CIVILIZED TRIBES.

Muskogee, Indian Territory, July 28, 1905.

Sibby Hekia,
    Atoka, Indian Territory.

Dear Madam:

    Your attention is called to a communication addressed to you by the Commission to the Five Civilized Tribes, under date of May 29, 1905, with which there was inclosed for execution application for the enrollment of your infant child, John E. Hekia, born May 25, 1904.

    In said letter you were advised that in the application heretofore filed in this office, the seal of the Notary Public was omitted from the physician's affidavit, and that it was necessary for the enrollment of the child that the application be re-executed. No reply to this letter has been received.

    This matter should receive your immediate attention as no further action can be taken relative to the enrollment of your said child until the application heretofore forwarded you is in due form filed in this office.

                  Respectfully,
                  Tams Bixby
                  Commissioner.

W^mO.B.

REFER IN REPLY TO THE FOLLOWING:
7-NB-815.

DEPARTMENT OF THE INTERIOR,
COMMISSIONER TO THE FIVE CIVILIZED TRIBES.

NOV 1- 1905
Muskogee, Indian Territory, September 27, 1905.

Sibby Hekia,
    Atoka, Indian Territory.

Dear Madam:

    Your attention is called to letters heretofore addressed to you by this office, under date of May 29, 1905 and July 29, 1905, in which you were advised that, in the application heretofore filed for the enrollment of your minor son John E. Hekia, the seal of the notary public was omitted from the physician's affidavit and that it was necessary,

Applications for Enrollment of Choctaw Newborn
Act of 1905   Volume XII

in the matter of the enrollment of said child, that the application be re-executed. No reply to these letters has been received.

You are again advised that it will be necessary for you to furnish this office with proper proof of the birth of your said son and a blank for that purpose which has been filled out is inclosed herewith. In having the same executed be careful to see that the notary public, before whom the affidavits are sworn to, attaches his name and seal to each affidavit. In case any signature is by mark the same must be attested by two disinterested witnesses. Be careful to see that the affiants sign their names to the affidavits as said names appear in the body thereof.

Respectfully,
Tams Bixby
Commissioner.

CTD-2.
Env.

7-NB-815

Muskogee, Indian Territory, March 7, 1906.

C. S. Arnold,
    Attorney Southern Trust Company,
        Atoka, Indian Territory.

Dear Sir:

Receipt is hereby acknowledged of your letter of March 1, 1906, with which you inclose the affidavit of W. E. Dicken to the birth of John E. Hekia, child of Sibby Hekia, May 25, 1904, and the same has been filed with the record in the matter of the enrollment of said child.

In event further evidence is necessary to enable this office to pass upon the right of this child, you will be duly notified.

Respectfully,
Acting Commissioner.

Applications for Enrollment of Choctaw Newborn
Act of 1905   Volume XII

CRB

REFER IN REPLY TO THE FOLLOWING:

DEPARTMENT OF THE INTERIOR,
COMMISSIONER TO THE FIVE CIVILIZED TRIBES.

Muskogee, Indian Territory, March 7, 1906.

Lacey P. Bobo,
    Hugo, Indian Territory.

Dear Sir:

    Referring to Choctaw NB roll card No. 815, John E. Hekia, duplicate of which was furnished you when you went out in the field, you are advised that as the affidavit of the attending physician has been furnished in this case it will not be necessary for you to take further steps to secure the same.

                          Respectfully,

                                    W^m.O.Beall
                                    Acting Commissioner.

AFFIDAVIT OF ATTENDING PHYSICIAN OR MID-WIFE.

~~UNITED STATES OF AMERICA, Indian Territory~~,
Oklahoma Territory   ~~DISTRICT.~~
Oklahoma County

    I,   W.E. Dicken   , a   Physician   , on oath state that I attended on Mrs.   Sibby Hekia   , ~~wife of~~   on the 25th day of   May   , 1904; that there was born to her on said date a   male   child; that said child was living March 4, 1905, and is said to have been named   John E. Hekia

                                    W.E. Dicken, M.D.

Witnesses To Mark:
   { Mrs W.E. Dicken
     Mrs. H. N. Foss

    Subscribed and sworn to before me this   28th day of   Feb   , 1906

                                    Margaret McVean
                                       Notary Public.

My Commission Expires May 20th 1907

Applications for Enrollment of Choctaw Newborn
Act of 1905   Volume XII

BIRTH AFFIDAVIT.

DEPARTMENT OF THE INTERIOR.
COMMISSION TO THE FIVE CIVILIZED TRIBES.

IN RE APPLICATION FOR ENROLLMENT, as a citizen of the   Choctaw   Nation, of John E. Hekia   , born on the 25th day of May   , 1904

Name of Father: ——————————   a citizen of the ————Nation.
Name of Mother: Sibby Hekia   a citizen of the Choctaw   Nation.

Postoffice   Atoka I.T.

AFFIDAVIT OF MOTHER.

UNITED STATES OF AMERICA, Indian Territory,
     Central   DISTRICT.

I, Sibby Hekia   , on oath state that I am 17 years of age and a citizen by blood , of the Choctaw Nation; ~~that I am the lawful wife of~~ ———— ~~, who is a citizen by~~ ———— ~~of the~~ ———— ~~Nation~~; that a male child was born to me on 25th day of May   , 1904; that said child has been named John E. Hekia , and was living March 4, 1905.

Witnesses To Mark:
{ ....
  ....

Subscribed and sworn to before me this .... day of ...., 1.........

Notary Public.

AFFIDAVIT OF ATTENDING PHYSICIAN OR MID-WIFE.

UNITED STATES OF AMERICA, Indian Territory,
     Central   DISTRICT.

I, W. E. Dicken   , a physician , on oath state that I attended on Mrs. Sibby Hekia   , wife of ———————— on the 25th day of May , 1904; that there was born to her on said date a male child; that said child was living March 4, 1905, and is said to have been named John E. Hekia

Witnesses To Mark:
{ ....
  ....

Applications for Enrollment of Choctaw Newborn
Act of 1905   Volume XII

Subscribed and sworn to before me this .... day of ...., 1905.

....
Notary Public.

BIRTH AFFIDAVIT.

DEPARTMENT OF THE INTERIOR.
COMMISSION TO THE FIVE CIVILIZED TRIBES.

    IN RE APPLICATION FOR ENROLLMENT, as a citizen of the   Choctaw   Nation, of John E. Hekia   , born on the 25th day of May , 1904

Name of Father:...a citizen of the .... Nation.
Name of Mother: Sibby Hekia   a citizen of the   Choctaw   Nation.

                    Postoffice   Atoka, Indian Territory.

AFFIDAVIT OF MOTHER.

Oklahoma
UNITED STATES OF AMERICA, ~~Indian~~ **Territory,**
~~Central~~ *Oklahoma County* ~~DISTRICT.~~

    I,   Sibby Hekia   , on oath state that I am   17   years of age and a citizen by blood   , of the   Choctaw   Nation; that I am the lawful wife of ...., who is a citizen, by .... of the .... Nation; that a   male   child was born to me on   25th   day of   May   , 1904; that said child has been named John E. Hekia   , and was living March 4, 1905.

                                          Sibbie Hekia

Witnesses To Mark:
  { Abbie Matthews
   Mrs. N.E. Bond

    Subscribed and sworn to before me this 3rd day of   April   , 1905

                                    Margaret McVean
                                          Notary Public.

Commission expires, May 25th 1907

Applications for Enrollment of Choctaw Newborn
Act of 1905   Volume XII

AFFIDAVIT OF ATTENDING PHYSICIAN OR MID-WIFE.

Oklahoma

UNITED STATES OF AMERICA, ~~Indian~~ Territory,
Oklahoma County, Oklahoma ~~DISTRICT.~~

I, W. E. Dicken , a Physician , on oath state that I attended on ~~Mrs.~~ Sibby Hekia , wife of .... on the 25th day of May , 1904; that there was born to her on said date a male child; that said child was living March 4, 1905, and is said to have been named John E. Hekia

W. E. Dicken
Physician

Witnesses To Mark:
{ W.M. Parrish
{ Allie J. Thomas

Subscribed and sworn to before me this 7th day of April , 1905

Margaret McVean
Notary Public.

Commission expires, May 25th 1907

Choc New Born 816
   William Perry   b. 11-17-03

   Dismissed 11-16-05

7-NB-816.

Muskogee, Indian Territory, May 29, 1905.

Hampton Perry,
   Reichert, Indian Territory.

Dear Sir:

Referring to the application for the enrollment of your infant child, William Perry, born November 17, 1903, it is noted in the affidavits heretofore filed in this office that the applicant died on September 12, 1904.

If this is correct you will please have the enclosed proof of death executed and return to this office.

Applications for Enrollment of Choctaw Newborn
Act of 1905   Volume XII

Respectfully,

Chairman.

Enclosed D-C.

7-NB-816.

Muskogee, Indian Territory, August 18, 1905.

Hampton Perry,
    Reichert, Indian Territory.

Dear Sir:

    Referring to the application for the enrollment of your infant child William Perry, born November 17, 1903, it is noted in the affidavits heretofore filed that the applicant died September 12, 1904. For the purpose of making his death a matter of record there is inclosed herewith blank for proof of death which you are requested to have filled out, executed and returned to this office.

Respectfully,

Acting Commissioner.

D C
Env.

Choctaw NB 816

Muskogee, Indian Territory, November 2, 1905.

Elum McCurtain,
    Houston, Indian Territory.

Dear Sir:

    Receipt is hereby acknowledged of your affidavit and the affidavit of Ruth McCurtain to the death of William Perry, a citizen by blood of the Choctaw Nation, which occurred September 12, 1904, and the same have been filed as evidence of death of the above named person.

Respectfully,

Commissioner.

Applications for Enrollment of Choctaw Newborn
Act of 1905 Volume XII

7-NB-816

Muskogee, Indian Territory, November 18, 1905.

Hampton Perry,
    Reichert, Indian Territory.

Dear Sir:

    You are hereby advised that it appearing from the records of this office that your infant child, William Perry, died prior to March 4, 1905, the Commissioner to the Five Civilized Tribes, on November 16, 1905, dismissed the application for his enrollment as a citizen by blood of the Choctaw Nation.

                Respectfully,

                Wm. O. Beall

                      Acting Commissioner.

BIRTH AFFIDAVIT.

DEPARTMENT OF THE INTERIOR.
COMMISSION TO THE FIVE CIVILIZED TRIBES.

IN RE APPLICATION FOR ENROLLMENT, as a citizen of the Choctaw Nation, of William Perry, born on the 17th day of November, 1903

Name of Father: Hampton Perry   a citizen of the Choctaw Nation.
                  roll #6639
Name of Mother: Emeline Perry nee Taylor   a citizen of the " Nation.

                Postoffice   Reichert Ind Ter

AFFIDAVIT OF MOTHER.

UNITED STATES OF AMERICA, Indian Territory, }
.... DISTRICT. }

    I, Emeline Perry - nee Taylor, on oath state that I am 38 years of age and a citizen by blood, of the Choctaw Nation; that I am the lawful wife of Hampton Perry dec'd, who ~~is~~ was a citizen, by blood of the Choctaw Nation; that a male child was born to me on 17 day of November, 1903; that said child has been named William Perry, and ~~was living March 4, 1905~~.
                                died Sept 12 1904

Applications for Enrollment of Choctaw Newborn
Act of 1905 Volume XII

Witnesses To Mark:
{

Emeline x Perry - nee Taylor
her mark

Subscribed and sworn to before me this 7th day of April , 1905

Lacey P Bobo
Notary Public.

AFFIDAVIT OF ATTENDING PHYSICIAN OR MID-WIFE.

UNITED STATES OF AMERICA, Indian Territory,
.... DISTRICT.

I, Ida Cronister[sic] , a ...., on oath state that I attended on Mrs. Monroe I.T. , wife of .... on the .... day of ...., 1........; that there was born to her on said date a .... child; that said child was living March 4, 1905, and is said to have been named ....

Witnesses To Mark:
{

Subscribed and sworn to before me this .... day of ...., 1905.

Notary Public.

Ida Cronitzer, Monroe, I.T. attended Mrs. Emeline Perry - nee Taylor at the birth of above child

---

DEPARTMENT OF THE INTERIOR.
COMMISSION TO THE FIVE CIVILIZED TRIBES.

In the matter of the death of William Perry a citizen of the Choctaw Nation, who formerly resided at or near Conser , Ind. Ter., and died on the 12 day of September , 1904

Applications for Enrollment of Choctaw Newborn
Act of 1905 Volume XII

AFFIDAVIT OF RELATIVE.

UNITED STATES OF AMERICA, Indian Territory, }
Central DISTRICT.

I, Elum Mc.Curtain , on oath state that I am 49 years of age and a citizen by Blood , of the Choctaw Nation; that my postoffice address is Houston , Ind. Ter.; that I am A first Cousin of William Perry who was a citizen, by Blood , of the Choctaw Nation and that said William Perry died on the 12th day of September , 1904

Elum McCurtain

Witnesses To Mark:
{

Subscribed and sworn to before me this 30th day of October , 1905.

J. M. Young
Notary Public.

My Com. Exp. Mch 1909.

AFFIDAVIT OF ACQUAINTANCE.

UNITED STATES OF AMERICA, Indian Territory, }
Central DISTRICT.

I, Ruth Mc.Curtain , on oath state that I am 21 years of age, and a citizen by Blood of the Choctaw Nation; that my postoffice address is Houston , Ind. Ter.; that I was personally acquainted with William Perry who was a citizen, by Blood , of the Choctaw Nation; and that said William Perry died on the 12th day of September , 1904

Ruth McCurtain

Witnesses To Mark:
{ ~~Ruth McCurtain~~

Subscribed and sworn to before me this 30th day of October , 1905.

J. M. Young
Notary Public.

Applications for Enrollment of Choctaw Newborn
Act of 1905   Volume XII

Choc New Born 817
Johnie F. McGahey   b. 2-13-05

NEW BORN AFFIDAVIT

No ....

CHOCTAW ENROLLING COMMISSION

IN THE MATTER OF THE APPLICATION FOR ENROLLMENT as a citizen of the Choctaw Nation, of   Johnie Franklin McGahey   born on the 13th day of February   190 5

Name of father   Alexander J McGahey   a citizen of   Choctaw   Nation, final enrollment No.   5071   (nee Brown)
Name of mother   Celia McGahey   a citizen of   Choctaw   Nation, final enrollment No.   11145

Atoka, Ind. Ter.   Postoffice.

AFFIDAVIT OF MOTHER

UNITED STATES OF AMERICA
  INDIAN TERRITORY
DISTRICT   Central

I   Celia McGahey   , on oath state that I am   23   years of age and a citizen by   blood   of the   Choctaw   Nation, and as such have been placed upon the final roll of the   Choctaw   Nation, by the Honorable Secretary of the Interior my final enrollment number being   11145   ; that I am the lawful wife of   Alexander J McGahey   , who is a citizen of the   Choctaw   Nation, and as such has been placed upon the final roll of said Nation by the Honorable Secretary of the Interior, his final enrollment number being   5071   and that a   Male   child was born to me on the   13th day of February 190 5; that said child has been named   Johnie Franklin McGahey   , and is now living.

WITNESSETH: Celia McGahey
  Must be two witnesses { B F Rogers
  who are citizens   L.L. McGahey

Subscribed and sworn to before me this, the   24th day of   February   , 190 5

W.F. Rogers
Notary Public.

My Commission Expires: Feb 24-1906

Applications for Enrollment of Choctaw Newborn
Act of 1905 Volume XII

BIRTH AFFIDAVIT.

DEPARTMENT OF THE INTERIOR.
COMMISSION TO THE FIVE CIVILIZED TRIBES.

IN RE APPLICATION FOR ENROLLMENT, as a citizen of the Choctaw Nation, of Johnnie[sic] F. McGahey, born on the 13th day of February, 1905

Name of Father: Alexander J. McGahey   a citizen of the Choctaw Nation.
Name of Mother: Celia McGahey nee Brown   a citizen of the Choctaw Nation.

Postoffice   Atoka, I.T.

AFFIDAVIT OF MOTHER.

UNITED STATES OF AMERICA, Indian Territory, }
Central   DISTRICT.

I, Celia McGahey, on oath state that I am 23 years of age and a citizen by blood, of the Choctaw Nation; that I am the lawful wife of Alexander J. McGahey, who is a citizen, by blood of the Choctaw Nation; that a male child was born to me on 13th day of February, 1905; that said child has been named Johnnie F. McGahey, and was living March 4, 1905.

Celia McGahey

Witnesses To Mark:
{

Subscribed and sworn to before me this 8th day of April, 1905

W.H. Angell
Notary Public.

AFFIDAVIT OF ATTENDING PHYSICIAN OR MID-WIFE.

UNITED STATES OF AMERICA, Indian Territory, }
Central   DISTRICT.

I, T. J. Long, a physician, on oath state that I attended on Mrs. Celia McGahey, wife of Alexander J. McGahey on the 13th day of February, 1905; that there was born to her on said date a male child; that said child was living March 4, 1905, and is said to have been named Johnnie F. McGahey

T. J. Long M.D.

Applications for Enrollment of Choctaw Newborn
Act of 1905 Volume XII

Witnesses To Mark:

{

    Subscribed and sworn to before me this 10th day of April , 1905

                               W.H. Angell
                               Notary Public.

Affidavit of Attending Physician or Midwife

UNITED STATES OF AMERICA, }
    INDIAN TERRITORY,
  Central   DISTRICT

    I, T. J. Long a Physician on oath state that I attended on Mrs. Celia McGahey wife of Alexander J. McGahey on the 13th day of February , 190 5, that there was born to her on said date a male child, that said child is now living, and is said to have been named Johnie Franklin McGahey

                           T. J. Long   M. D.

    Subscribed and sworn to before me this the 25 day of February 1905

                        Jno H Linebaugh
                            Notary Public.

WITNESSETH:
    Must be two witnesses { B.F. Rogers
    who are citizens and
    know the child.   L.L. McGahey

    We hereby certify that we are well acquainted with Dr. T.J. Long a Practicing Physician and know him to be reputable and of good standing in the community.

                    Must be two citizen { B.F. Rogers
                    witnesses.   L. L. McGahey

Applications for Enrollment of Choctaw Newborn
Act of 1905 Volume XII

Choc New Born 818
Zel[sic] Ora Wilson b. 9-12-02

NEW BORN AFFIDAVIT

No _____

CHOCTAW ENROLLING COMMISSION

IN THE MATTER OF THE APPLICATION FOR ENROLLMENT as a citizen of the Choctaw Nation, of   Zell Ora Wilson   born on the 12th day of   September   190 3

Name of father   Lark H Wilson   a citizen of _____ Nation, final enrollment No. _____

Name of mother   Elizabeth Wilson   a citizen of   Choctaw   Nation, final enrollment No. 11701

Atoka I.T.   Postoffice.

AFFIDAVIT OF MOTHER

UNITED STATES OF AMERICA }
INDIAN TERRITORY }
DISTRICT   Central }

I   Elizabeth Wilson   , on oath state that I am   19   years of age and a citizen by   Blood   of the   Choctaw   Nation, and as such have been placed upon the final roll of the   Choctaw   Nation, by the Honorable Secretary of the Interior my final enrollment number being   11701   ; that I am the lawful wife of   Lark H Wilson   , who is a citizen of the _____ Nation, and as such have been placed upon the final roll of said Nation by the Honorable Secretary of the Interior, his final enrollment number being ____ and that a   Female   child was born to me on the 12th day of   September   190 3; that said child has been named   Zell Ora Wilson   , and is now living.

WITNESSETH: Elizabeth Wilson

Must be two witnesses { Myra Hendrix
who are citizens   { Wilburn Thompson

Subscribed and sworn to before me this, the 22^{d} day of   February   , 190 5

A.E. Folsom
Notary Public.

My Commission Expires: Jan 9-1909

Applications for Enrollment of Choctaw Newborn
Act of 1905 Volume XII

Affidavit of Attending Physician or Midwife

UNITED STATES OF AMERICA,
INDIAN TERRITORY,
Central   DISTRICT

I, Myra Hendrix   a   Mid wife on oath state that I attended on Mrs. Elizabeth Wilson   wife of   Lark H Wilson on the   12th day of   September   , 190 3, that there was born to her on said date a Female   child, that said child is now living, and is said to have been named   Zell Ora Wilson

mid wife
Myra Hendrix   ~~M. D.~~

Subscribed and sworn to before me this the   22^d day of   February   1905

A.E. Folsom
Notary Public.

WITNESSETH:
Must be two witnesses who are citizens and know the child. { Wallie Thompson
Wilburn Thompson

We hereby certify that we are well acquainted with   Myra Hendrix a   midwife   and know   her   to be reputable and of good standing in the community.

Must be two citizen witnesses. { Wallie Thompson
Wilburn Thompson

BIRTH AFFIDAVIT.

DEPARTMENT OF THE INTERIOR.
COMMISSION TO THE FIVE CIVILIZED TRIBES.

IN RE APPLICATION FOR ENROLLMENT, as a citizen of the   Choctaw   Nation, of Zel Ora Wilson   , born on the   12th day of   September   , 1903

Name of Father: Lark A. Wilson   a citizen of the United States ~~Nation~~.
Name of Mother: Elizabeth Wilson   a citizen of the   Choctaw   Nation.

Postoffice   Atoka I.T.

Applications for Enrollment of Choctaw Newborn
Act of 1905   Volume XII

AFFIDAVIT OF MOTHER.

UNITED STATES OF AMERICA, Indian Territory, }
    Central   DISTRICT.

    I,   Elizabeth Wilson   , on oath state that I am   19   years of age and a citizen by   blood   , of the   Choctaw   Nation; that I am the lawful wife of   Lark A. Wilson   , who is a citizen, by ——— of the   United States   Nation; that a female   child was born to me on 12th day of   September   , 1903; that said child has been named   Zel Ora Wilson   , and was living March 4, 1905.

                                          Elizabeth Wilson

Witnesses To Mark:
{

    Subscribed and sworn to before me this 10th day of   April   , 1905

                                          W.H. Angell
                                                  Notary Public.

AFFIDAVIT OF ATTENDING PHYSICIAN OR MID-WIFE.

UNITED STATES OF AMERICA, Indian Territory, }
    Central   DISTRICT.

    I,   Myra Hendrix   , a   midwife   , on oath state that I attended on Mrs.   Elizabeth Wilson   , wife of   Lark A. Wilson   on the 12th day of   September   , 1903; that there was born to her on said date a   female   child; that said child was living March 4, 1905, and is said to have been named   Zel Ora Wilson

                                          Myra Hendrix

Witnesses To Mark:
{

    Subscribed and sworn to before me this 10th day of   April   , 1905

                                          W.H. Angell
                                                 Notary Public.

Applications for Enrollment of Choctaw Newborn
Act of 1905   Volume XII

Choc New Born 819
      Gracie Kelly   b. 12-25-02
      Jewel Kelly   b. 9-6-04

7-4389

Muskogee, Indian Territory, April 13, 1905.

W. W. Kelly,
    Pauls Valley, Indian Territory.

Dear Sir:

    Receipt is hereby acknowledged of your letter of April 8, 1905, enclosing affidavits of Mollie Kelly and Martha Halstead to the birth of Jewel Kelly and Gracie Kelly, children of William W. and Mollie Kelly, September 6, 1904, and December 25, 1902, and the same have been filed with our records as an application for the enrollment of said children.

                Respectfully,

                              Commissioner in Charge.

7-NB-819

Muskogee, Indian Territory, July 26, 1905.

William W. Kelly,
    Pauls Valley, Indian Territory.

Dear Sir:

    Receipt is hereby acknowledged of your letter of July 18, 1905, asking if Gracie and Jewell[sic] Kelley[sic] have been approved.

    In reply to your letter you are advised that the names of your children Gracie and Jewel Kelley have been placed upon a schedule of citizens by blood of the Choctaw Nation which has been forwarded the Secretary of the Interior and you will be notified when their enrollment is approved by the Department.

                Respectfully,

                              Commissioner.

Applications for Enrollment of Choctaw Newborn
Act of 1905   Volume XII

BIRTH AFFIDAVIT.

DEPARTMENT OF THE INTERIOR.
COMMISSION TO THE FIVE CIVILIZED TRIBES.

IN RE APPLICATION FOR ENROLLMENT, as a citizen of the Choctaw Nation, of Gracie Kelly, born on the 25th day of December, 1902

Name of Father: William W. Kelly   a citizen of the Choctaw Nation.
Name of Mother: Mollie Kelly   a citizen of the Choctaw Nation.

Postoffice   Pauls Valley, I.T.

AFFIDAVIT OF MOTHER.

UNITED STATES OF AMERICA, Indian Territory,
Southern Judicial   DISTRICT.

I, Mollie Kelly, on oath state that I am 31 years of age and a citizen by intermarriage, of the Choctaw Nation; that I am the lawful wife of William W. Kelly, who is a citizen, by blood of the Choctaw Nation; that a female child was born to me on 25th day of December, 1902; that said child has been named Gracie, and was living March 4, 1905.

Mollie Kelly

Witnesses To Mark:

Subscribed and sworn to before me this 8th day of April, 1905

(Name Illegible)
Notary Public.

AFFIDAVIT OF ATTENDING PHYSICIAN OR MID-WIFE.

UNITED STATES OF AMERICA, Indian Territory,
Southern Judicial   DISTRICT.

I, Mrs Martha Halstead, a midwife, on oath state that I attended on Mrs. Mollie Kelly, wife of William W. Kelly on the 25th day of December, 1902; that there was born to her on said date a female child; that said child was living March 4, 1905, and is said to have been named Gracie

                         her
               Martha Halstead x
                         mark

Applications for Enrollment of Choctaw Newborn
Act of 1905   Volume XII

Witnesses To Mark:
{ *(Name Illegible)*
  R A Thompson

Subscribed and sworn to before me this 29 day of   March   , 1905

                                 Henry Luntz
                                        Notary Public.

BIRTH AFFIDAVIT.

DEPARTMENT OF THE INTERIOR.
COMMISSION TO THE FIVE CIVILIZED TRIBES.

IN RE APPLICATION FOR ENROLLMENT, as a citizen of the   Choctaw   Nation, of Jewel Kelly   , born on the 6th day of September , 1904

Name of Father: William W. Kelly   a citizen of the   Choctaw   Nation.
Name of Mother: Mollie Kelly   a citizen of the   Choctaw   Nation.

                      Postoffice   Pauls Valley, I.T.

AFFIDAVIT OF MOTHER.

UNITED STATES OF AMERICA, Indian Territory, }
Southern Judicial   DISTRICT.

     I, Mollie Kelly   , on oath state that I am 31   years of age and a citizen by intermarriage   , of the   Choctaw   Nation; that I am the lawful wife of   William Kelly   , who is a citizen, by blood   of the   Choctaw   Nation; that a female   child was born to me on 6th day of September   , 1904; that said child has been named Jewel   , and was living March 4, 1905.

                                   Mollie Kelly

Witnesses To Mark:
{

Subscribed and sworn to before me this 8th day of April , 1905

                                (Name Illegible)
                                  Notary Public.

Applications for Enrollment of Choctaw Newborn
Act of 1905   Volume XII

AFFIDAVIT OF ATTENDING PHYSICIAN OR MID-WIFE.

UNITED STATES OF AMERICA, Indian Territory, }
Southern Judicial   DISTRICT.

I,   Mrs Martha Halstead   , a   midwife   , on oath state that I attended on Mrs.   Mollie Kelly   , wife of   William W. Kelly   on the   6th   day of September   , 1902; that there was born to her on said date a   female   child; that said child was living March 4, 1905, and is said to have been named   Jewel

                                         her
                        Martha Halstead   x
                                    mark

Witnesses To Mark:
  { *(Name Illegible)*
     R A Thompson

Subscribed and sworn to before me this 29   day of   March   , 1905

                            Henry Luntz
                            Notary Public.

Choc New Born 820
    Leona Maria[sic] Lewis   b. 2-16-04

                                      7-2144

                Muskogee, Indian Territory, April 13, 1905.

Silas Lewis,
    Nashoba, Indian Territory.

Dear Sir:

    Receipt is hereby acknowledged of your letter of April 7, 1905, enclosing affidavits of Allie Lewis and Emeline Lomar to the birth of Leona Moria Lewis, daughter of Silas and Ollie Lewis, February 16, 1904, and the same have been filed with our records as an application for the enrollment of said child.

                        Respectfully,

                                    Commissioner in Charge.

Applications for Enrollment of Choctaw Newborn
Act of 1905   Volume XII

Choctaw 2144

Muskogee, Indian Territory, April 29, 1905.

Silas Lewis,
    Nashoba, Indian Territory.

Dear Sir:

    Receipt is hereby acknowledged of your letter of April 18, asking if application for the enrollment of your baby has been received and if you can now go to the land office and file on land for yourself and your child.

    In reply to your letter you are advised that it appears from our records that selection of allotment has been made in your behalf. You are advised that the application for the enrollment of your child, Lena[sic] Moria Lewis has been received and field with our records, but no selection of allotment can be made in her behalf until her enrollment has been approved by the Secretary of the Interior.

    Respectfully,

    Chairman.

7-NB-820.

Muskogee, Indian Territory, May 29, 1905.

Silas Lewis,
    Nashoba, Indian Territory.

Dear Sir:

    Referring to the application for the enrollment of your infant child, Leona Moria Lewis, born February 16, 1904, it is noted, from the affidavits heretofore filed in this office, that the applicant claims through you.

    In this event it will be necessary for you to file in this office either the original or a certified copy of the license and certificate of your marriage to the applicant's mother, Ollie Lewis.

    Respectfully,

    Chairman.

Applications for Enrollment of Choctaw Newborn
Act of 1905   Volume XII

7-NB-820.

Muskogee, Indian Territory, June 13, 1905.

Silas Lewis,
    Nashoba, Indian Territory.

Dear Sir:

    Receipt is hereby acknowledged of your letter of June 3, transmitting marriage license and certificate between yourself and Olie[sic] G. Fuller, and the same have been filed with the record in the matter of the enrollment of your child, Moria Leona[sic] Lewis.

        Respectfully,

                Chairman.

7-NB-820

Muskogee, Indian Territory, September 14, 1905.

Silas Lewis,
    Nashoba, Indian Territory.

Dear Sir:

    Replying to your letter of September 9th, you are advised that on August 22, 1905, the Secretary of the Interior approved the enrollment of your minor child, Leona Moria Lewis as a citizen by blood of the Choctaw Nation and her name appears upon the roll of new-born citizens by blood of the Choctaw Nation opposite number 1362.

    The child is now entitled to an allotment and selection thereof should be made without delay at the land office for the nation in which the prospective allotment is located.

        Respectfully,

                Acting Commissioner.

Applications for Enrollment of Choctaw Newborn
Act of 1905 Volume XII

No. 531

Certificate of Record of Marriages.

UNITED STATES OF AMERICA,
INDIAN TERRITORY, } SCT:
Central   DISTRICT.

I,   *E.J. Fannin*   , Clerk of the United States Court in the Indian Territory and District aforesaid, do hereby CERTIFY, that the License for and Certificate of the Marriage of

Mr.   Silas B. Lewis   and

M   Olie G. Fuller   was

filed in my office in said Territory and District the 20 day of Mch A.D., 190 3 and duly recorded in Book .... of Marriage Record, Page 266

WITNESS my hand and seal of said Court, at   Antlers   , this 20 day of   Mch   , A.D. 190 3

E.J. Fannin
Clerk.

By   Jos R Fultz   Deputy.

DEPARTMENT OF THE INTERIOR,
Commission to the Five Civilized Tribes.

FILED

JUN 13 1905

Tams Bixby CHAIRMAN.

Applications for Enrollment of Choctaw Newborn
Act of 1905 Volume XII

No. 531

FORM NO. 598.

MARRIAGE LICENSE.

UNITES STATES OF AMERICA,
THE INDIAN TERRITORY, } ss:
Central   DISTRICT.

To any Person Authorized by Law to Solemnize Marriage—Greeting:

You are hereby commanded to solemnize the Rite and publish the **Banns of Matrimony** *between* Mr.   Silas B Lewis   *of* Tuskahoma *in the Indian Territory, aged* 24 *years, and* Miss Olie G Fuller *of* Tuskahoma *in the Indian Territory, aged* 16 *years, according to law, and do you officially sign and return this License to the parties therein named.*

WITNESS my hand and official seal, this   16th   day of   Jany   A. D. 190 3

E.J. Fannin
Clerk of the United States Court.

Jos R Fultz   *Deputy*

CERTIFICATE OF MARRIAGE.

UNITES STATES OF AMERICA,
THE INDIAN TERRITORY, } ss: I,   Peter J. Hudson
Central   DISTRICT.   *a*   Minister of the Gospel

do hereby CERTIFY, that on the   21st   day of   Jan   A, D. 190 3 ; I did duly and according to law, as commanded in the foregoing License, solemnize the Rite and publish the BANNS OF MATRIMONY between the parties therein named.

Witness my hand this 21st   day of   Jan   , A. D. 190 3

My credentials are recorded in the office of the Clerk of the United States Court in the Indian Territory, Central District, Book   A   Page   157

Peter J Hudson
a   Minister of the Gospel

Applications for Enrollment of Choctaw Newborn
Act of 1905   Volume XII

NEW-BORN AFFIDAVIT.

Number..................

...Choctaw Enrolling Commission...

IN THE MATTER OF THE APPLICATION FOR ENROLLMENT, as a citizen of the Choctaw Nation, of Leona Moria Lewis

born on the 16 day of February 190 4

Name of father Silas Lewis   a citizen of Choctaw Nation final enrollment No. 6191
Name of mother Ollie G Lewis   a citizen of..
Nation final enrollment No.........................

Postoffice Nashoba I T

AFFIDAVIT OF MOTHER.

UNITED STATES OF AMERICA
INDIAN TERRITORY
  Central   DISTRICT

I Ollie G Lewis , on oath state that I am 16 years of age and a citizen by intermarriage of the .... Nation, and as such have been placed upon the final roll of the .... Nation, by the Honorable Secretary of the Interior my final enrollment number being ....; that I am the lawful wife of Silas Lewis , who is a citizen of the Choctaw Nation, and as such has been placed upon the final roll of said Nation by the Honorable Secretary of the Interior, his final enrollment number being 6191 and that a Female child was born to me on the 16 day of February 190 4; that said child has been named Leona Moria Lewis , and is now living.

Ollie G Lewis

Witnesseth.
  Must be two } (Name Illegible)
  Witnesses who
  are Citizens.   (Name Illegible)

Subscribed and sworn to before me this 8 day of February 190 5

F. M. Fuller
Notary Public.

My commission expires: April 18th 1908

Applications for Enrollment of Choctaw Newborn
Act of 1905   Volume XII

AFFIDAVIT OF ATTENDING PHYSICIAN OR MIDWIFE

UNITED STATES OF AMERICA
INDIAN TERRITORY
   Central   DISTRICT

I,   Emeline Loman   a   mid wife on oath state that I attended on Mrs.   Ollie G Lewis   wife of   Silas Lewis on the 16th day of February , 190 4, that there was born to her on said date a   Female child, that said child is now living, and is said to have been named   Leona Moria Lewis

               her
             Emeline x Loman   MiDwife
WITNESSETH: mark

Must be two witnesses who are citizens and know the child.
{ Sampson Tom
  Washington Hardy

      Subscribed and sworn to before me this, the   9   day of February   190 5

             F.M. Fuller   Notary Public.

   We hereby certify that we are well acquainted with   Emeline Loman a   Choctaw   and know   her   to be reputable and of good standing in the community.

           { Sampson Tom
             Washington Hardy

BIRTH AFFIDAVIT.

DEPARTMENT OF THE INTERIOR.
COMMISSION TO THE FIVE CIVILIZED TRIBES.

IN RE APPLICATION FOR ENROLLMENT, as a citizen of the   Choctaw   Nation, of Leona Moria Lewis   , born on the 16   day of   February , 1904

Name of Father: Silas Lewis   a citizen of the   Choctaw   Nation.
Name of Mother: Ollie Lewis   a citizen of the   Choctaw   Nation.
by intermarriage

          Postoffice   Nashoba, I.T.

Applications for Enrollment of Choctaw Newborn
Act of 1905   Volume XII

AFFIDAVIT OF MOTHER.

UNITED STATES OF AMERICA, Indian Territory, }
Central   DISTRICT. }

I, Ollie Lewis , on oath state that I am 17 years of age and a citizen by intermarriage , of the Choctaw Nation; that I am the lawful wife of Silas Lewis , who is a citizen, by blood of the Choctaw Nation; that a Female child was born to me on the 16 day of February , 1904; that said child has been named Leona Moria Lewis , and was living March 4, 1905.

Ollie Lewis

Witnesses To Mark:
{ (Name Illegible)
{ Butte Tyler

Subscribed and sworn to before me this 3 day of April , 1905

F.M. Fuller
Notary Public.

AFFIDAVIT OF ATTENDING PHYSICIAN OR MID-WIFE.

UNITED STATES OF AMERICA, Indian Territory, }
Central   DISTRICT. }

I, Emeline Loman , a mid wife , on oath state that I attended on Mrs. Ollie Lewis , wife of Silas Lewis on the 16 day of February , 1904; that there was born to her on said date a Female child; that said child was living March 4, 1905, and is said to have been named Leona Moria Lewis

her
Emeline x Loman
mark

Witnesses To Mark:
{ (Name Illegible)
{ Butte Tyler

Subscribed and sworn to before me this 3 day of April , 1905

F.M. Fuller
Notary Public.

My commission expires April 18th 1908

Applications for Enrollment of Choctaw Newborn
Act of 1905 Volume XII

Choc New Born 821
    Myrtle Susie Cowen b. 7-21-04

7-1800

Muskogee, Indian Territory, April 13, 1905.

J. R. Cowen,
    Durant, Indian Territory.

Dear Sir:

    Receipt is hereby acknowledged of your letter of April 7, 1905, enclosing affidavits of Francis Cowen and M. A. Troutt to the birth of Myrtle Susie Cowen, daughter of J. R. and Francis Cowen, July 21, 1904, and the same have been filed with our records as an application for the enrollment of said child.

                Respectfully,

                Commissioner in Charge.

Affidavit of Attending Physician or Midwife

UNITED STATES OF AMERICA,
    INDIAN TERRITORY,
  Central   DISTRICT

    I, Mary E[sic] Troutt   a   U. S. Citizen
on oath state that I attended on Mrs. Frances[sic] Cowen   wife of J. R. Cowen
on the 21st day of July , 190 4, that there was born to her on said date a   Female
child, that said child is now living, and is said to have been named Myrtle Susie Cowen

                Mary A. Troutt
                    ~~M. D.~~
                Midwife

Subscribed and sworn to before me this the 27th day of February   1905

              T.M. Hensley
                Notary Public.
/My commission expires Dec. 5th. 1906/   Cent. Dist, I.T.

WITNESSETH:
  Must be two witnesses   *(Name Illegible)*
  who are citizens and
  know the child.   *(Name Illegible)*

Applications for Enrollment of Choctaw Newborn
Act of 1905   Volume XII

We hereby certify that we are well acquainted with Mary A Troutt
a   U. S. Citizen   and know   her   to be reputable and of good standing in the community.

Must be two citizen { E.E. Dyer
witnesses. { A Frank Ross

NEW-BORN AFFIDAVIT.

Number..............

Choctaw Enrolling Commission.

IN THE MATTER OF THE APPLICATION FOR ENROLLMENT, as a citizen of the Choctaw   Nation, of   Myrtle Susie Cowen

born on the   21st   day of   July, A. D.   1904

Name of father   J. R. Cowen   a citizen of Choctaw Nation, by inter-marriage
Nation final enrollment No ....
Name of mother   Frances Cowen   a citizen of   Choctaw Nation
Nation final enrollment No   6100

Postoffice   Durant, Indian Territory

AFFIDAVIT OF MOTHER.

UNITED STATES OF AMERICA,
INDIAN TERRITORY,
Central   DISTRICT

I   Frances Cowen   on oath state that I am   21   years of age and a citizen by   blood   of the   Choctaw   Nation, and as such have been placed upon the final roll of the   Choctaw   Nation, by the Honorable Secretary of the Interior my final enrollment number being.............. ; that I am the lawful wife of   J. R. Cowen   , who is a citizen of the   Choctaw   Nation, *by intermarriage* and as such has been placed upon the final roll of said Nation by the Honorable Secretary of the Interior, his final enrollment number being.............. and that a   Female   child was born to me on the   21st   day of   July, A. D.   190 4; that said child has been named   Myrtle Susie Cowen   , and is now living.

Frances Cowen

WITNESSETH:
Must be two Witnesses who are Citizens.   } William M Harkins
Victor M Johnson

Applications for Enrollment of Choctaw Newborn
Act of 1905   Volume XII

Subscribed and sworn to before me this 27- day of February A.D. 1905

(Name Illegible)
Notary Public.

My commission expires 12- 6- 1906.

BIRTH AFFIDAVIT.

DEPARTMENT OF THE INTERIOR.
COMMISSION TO THE FIVE CIVILIZED TRIBES.

IN RE APPLICATION FOR ENROLLMENT, as a citizen of the Choctaw Nation, of Myrtle Susie Cowen , born on the 21st day of July , 1904

Name of Father: J.R. Cowen   a citizen of the Choctaw   Nation.
Name of Mother: Francis Cowen   a citizen of the Choctaw   Nation.

Postoffice   Durant, Indian Territory.

AFFIDAVIT OF MOTHER.

UNITED STATES OF AMERICA, Indian Territory,
Central   DISTRICT.

I, Francis Cowen , on oath state that I am 21 years of age and a citizen by blood , of the Choctaw Nation; that I am the lawful wife of J. R. Cowen , who is a citizen, by Intermarriage of the Choctaw(nation)[sic] Nation; that a Female child was born to me on 21st day of July , 1904; that said child has been named Myrtle Susie Cowen , and was living March 4, 1905.

Francis Cowen

Witnesses To Mark:

Subscribed and sworn to before me this 7th day of April , 1905

T.M. Hinsley
Notary Public.
My commission expires   Central District, Indian Territory
12- 5- 1906.

Applications for Enrollment of Choctaw Newborn
Act of 1905   Volume XII

AFFIDAVIT OF ATTENDING PHYSICIAN OR MID-WIFE.

UNITED STATES OF AMERICA, Indian Territory, ⎫
    Central   DISTRICT. ⎬

    I, Mrs. M. A. Troutt , a Female , on oath state that I attended on Mrs. Francis Cowen , wife of J. R. Cowen on the 21st day of July , 1904; that there was born to her on said date a Female child; that said child was living March 4, 1905, and is said to have been named Myrtle Susie Cowen

                                              M. A. Troutt

Witnesses To Mark:
{

    Subscribed and sworn to before me this 7th day of   April   , 1905

                                              T.M. Hinsley
                                              Notary Public.
My commission expires   Central District, Indian Territory
12- 5- 1906.

Choc New Born 822
        Bonnie B. Foster   b. 11-27-03

                                                              7-5715

                            Muskogee, Indian Territory, April 13, 1905.

A. S. Taylor,
        Minco, Indian Territory.

Dear Sir:

    Receipt is hereby acknowledged of your letter of April 8, 1905, enclosing affidavits of Mary A. Foster and W. E. Brown to the birth of Bonnie B. Foster, daughter of William F. and Mary A. Foster, November 27, 1903, and the same have been filed with our records as an application for the enrollment of said child.

                                         Respectfully,

                                      Commissioner in Charge.

Applications for Enrollment of Choctaw Newborn
Act of 1905   Volume XII

BIRTH AFFIDAVIT.

DEPARTMENT OF THE INTERIOR.
COMMISSION TO THE FIVE CIVILIZED TRIBES.

IN RE APPLICATION FOR ENROLLMENT, as a citizen of the   Choctaw   Nation, of Bonnie B. Foster   , born on the   27   day of   Nov , 1903

Name of Father: William F. Foster   a citizen of the   Choctaw   Nation.
Name of Mother: Mary A Foster   a citizen of the   Choctaw   Nation.

Postoffice   Minco Ind. Terr.

AFFIDAVIT OF MOTHER.

UNITED STATES OF AMERICA, Indian Territory, }
    Southern   DISTRICT.

    I,   Mary A. Foster   , on oath state that I am 42   years of age and a citizen by   Int. Marriage   , of the   Choctaw   Nation; that I am the lawful wife of William F. Foster   , who is a citizen, by blood   of the   Choctaw   Nation; that a   Female   child was born to me on   27   day of   November   , 1903; that said child has been named   Bonnie B. Foster   , and was living March 4, 1905.

                                  Mary A Foster

Witnesses To Mark:
{

    Subscribed and sworn to before me this 30   day of   March   , 1905

My commision[sic] expires 8/4/1908   A.S. Taylor
                                       Notary Public.

AFFIDAVIT OF ATTENDING PHYSICIAN OR MID-WIFE.

UNITED STATES OF AMERICA, Indian Territory, }
    Central   DISTRICT.

    I,   W.E. Brown   , a   Physician   , on oath state that I attended on Mrs.   Mary A Foster   , wife of   W. F. Foster   on the 27   day of   November   , 1903; that there was born to her on said date a   Female   child; that said child was living March 4, 1905, and is said to have been named Bonnie B. Foster

                                  W.E. Brown

Witnesses To Mark:
{

Applications for Enrollment of Choctaw Newborn
Act of 1905   Volume XII

Subscribed and sworn to before me this 3rd day of April , 1905

                                    John Remise

My Commission expires Feb. 17th, 190 7   Notary Public.

<u>Choc New Born 823</u>
    Jincy James b. 7-9-03

                                            7-3695

                    Muskogee, Indian Territory, April 13, 1905.

Johnnie N. James,
    Boswell, Indian Territory.

Dear Sir:

    Receipt is hereby acknowledged of the affidavits of Laura A. James and Francis Beckwith to the birth of Jincy James daughter of Johnie[sic] N. and Laura A. James July 9, 1903, and the same have been filed with our records as an application for the enrollment of said child.

                  Respectfully,

                  Commissioner in Charge.

BIRTH AFFIDAVIT.

DEPARTMENT OF THE INTERIOR,
COMMISSION TO THE FIVE CIVILIZED TRIBES.

    In Re Application for Enrollment, as a citizen of the   Choctaw   Nation, of   Jincy James   , born on the   9   day of   July   , 1903

Name of Father: Johnie N. james[sic]   a citizen of the Choctaw Nation.
Name of Mother: Laura A. James   a citizen of the Choctaw Nation.

                  Post-office   Boswell, I.T.

Applications for Enrollment of Choctaw Newborn
Act of 1905   Volume XII

AFFIDAVIT OF MOTHER.

UNITED STATES OF AMERICA,
   INDIAN TERRITORY,
   Central   District.

    I, Laura A. James , on oath state that I am 30 years of age and a citizen by Blood , of the Choctaw Nation; that I am the lawful wife of Johnie N. James , who is a citizen, by Adopsion[sic] of the Choctaw Nation; that a Female child was born to me on 9 day of July , 1903 , that said child has been named Jincy James , and is now living.

                                              her
                                      Laura A x James
WITNESSES TO MARK: mark
   { Oliver Beckwith
     J M Harris

    Subscribed and sworn to before me this 10   day of   Apr , 1905.

                                        Perry M Clark
                                            NOTARY PUBLIC.

AFFIDAVIT OF ATTENDING PHYSICIAN OR MID-WIFE.

UNITED STATES OF AMERICA,
   INDIAN TERRITORY,
   Cent   District.

    I, Francis Beckwith , a Mid-Wife , on oath state that I attended on Mrs. Laura A James , wife of Johnie N. James on the 9 day of July , 1903 ; that there was born to her on said date a Female child; that said child is now living and is said to have been named Jincy James

                                              her
                                      Francis x Beckwith
WITNESSES TO MARK: mark
   { Oliver Beckwith
     J M Harris

    Subscribed and sworn to before me this 10   day of   Apr , 1905.

                                        Perry M Clark
                                            NOTARY PUBLIC.

Applications for Enrollment of Choctaw Newborn
Act of 1905   Volume XII

Choc New Born 824
Lula Sam   b. 9-2-04

(Copy) DEPARTMENT OF THE INTERIOR.
COMMISSION TO THE FIVE CIVILIZED TRIBES.

In the matter of the death of   Lula Sam   a citizen of the   Choctaw Nation, who formerly resided at or near   Red Oak   , Ind. Ter., and died on the   2th[sic] day of   March   , 1905

AFFIDAVIT OF RELATIVE.

UNITED STATES OF AMERICA, Indian Territory,
Central   DISTRICT.

I,   Stanford Sam   , on oath state that I am   38   years of age and a citizen by blood   , of the Choctaw   Nation; that my postoffice address is   Red Oak   , Ind. Ter.; that I am   the father   of   Lula Sam   who was a citizen, by   blood   , of the Choctaw   Nation and that said   Lula Sam   died on the   2nd   day of   March   , 1905

(signed)   STANFORD SAM .

Witnesses To Mark:
{

Subscribed and sworn to before me this   5th   day of   February   , 1906

(SEAL)   (signed)   LACEY P. BOBO.
Notary Public.

AFFIDAVIT OF ACQUAINTANCE.

UNITED STATES OF AMERICA, Indian Territory,
Central   DISTRICT.

I,   Sam Jefferson   , on oath state that I am   36   years of age, and a citizen by blood   of the Choctaw   Nation; that my postoffice address is   Red Oak   , Ind. Ter.; that I was personally acquainted with   Lula Sam   who was a citizen, by   blood   , of the Choctaw Nation; and that said   Lula Sam   died on the   2nd   day of   March   , 1905

(signed)   SAM JEFFERSON

Witnesses To Mark:
{

Applications for Enrollment of Choctaw Newborn
Act of 1905   Volume XII

Subscribed and sworn to before me this 5th   day of   February   , 1906

(SEAL)   (signed)   LACEY P. BOBO.

DEPARTMENT OF THE INTERIOR.
COMMISSION TO THE FIVE CIVILIZED TRIBES.

(Copy)

In the matter of the death of   Lula Sam   a citizen of the   Choctaw (Pending enrollment and approval   Nation, who formerly resided at or near   Red Oak   , Ind. Ter., and died on the 9th   day of   March   , 1905

AFFIDAVIT OF RELATIVE.

UNITED STATES OF AMERICA, Indian Territory,
Central   DISTRICT.

I,   Susan Sam   , on oath state that I am   about 22   years of age and a citizen by blood   , of the Choctaw   Nation; that my postoffice address is   Red Oak   , Ind. Ter.; that I am   the mother   of   Lula Sam   who was a citizen, by blood   , of the Choctaw   Nation and that said   Lula Sam   died on the   9th   day of   March   , 1905

(signed)   SUSAN SAM

Witnesses To Mark:
{

Subscribed and sworn to before me this 8th   day of   April   , 1906

(SEAL)   (signed)   LACEY P. BOBO.
                                                       Notary Public.

AFFIDAVIT OF ACQUAINTANCE.

UNITED STATES OF AMERICA, Indian Territory,
Central   DISTRICT.

I,   Lucy Anderson   , on oath state that I am   about 40   years of age, and a citizen by blood   of the Choctaw   Nation; that my postoffice address is   Red Oak   , Ind. Ter.; that I was personally acquainted with   Lula Sam   who was a citizen, by blood   , of the Choctaw   Nation; and that said   Lula Sam   died on the   9th   day of   March   , 1905

(signed)   LUCY her x mark ANDERSON

Witnesses To Mark:
{ J. W. Homer
  A. J. Gardenhire

Applications for Enrollment of Choctaw Newborn
Act of 1905 Volume XII

Subscribed and sworn to before me this 8th day of April , 1906

(SEAL) (signed) LACEY P. BOBO.
Notary Public.

BIRTH AFFIDAVIT.
(Copy) DEPARTMENT OF THE INTERIOR.
COMMISSION TO THE FIVE CIVILIZED TRIBES.

IN RE APPLICATION FOR ENROLLMENT, as a citizen of the Choctaw Nation, of Lula Sam , born on the 2nd day of September , 1904

Name of Father: Stanford Sam--roll #8716   a citizen of the Choctaw Nation.
Name of Mother: Susan Sam--   8717   a citizen of the Choctaw Nation.

Postoffice   Red Oak, Ind. Ter.

AFFIDAVIT OF MOTHER.

UNITED STATES OF AMERICA, Indian Territory, }
     Central   **DISTRICT.** }

I, Susan Sam , on oath state that I am about 22 years of age and a citizen by blood , of the Choctaw Nation; that I am the lawful wife of Stanford Sam , who is a citizen, by blood of the Choctaw Nation; that a female child was born to me on 2nd day of September , 1904; that said child has been named Lula Sam , and was living March 4, 1905. died March 9, 1905

(signed) SUSAN SAM

Witnesses To Mark:
{

Subscribed and sworn to before me this 8th day of April , 1906

(SEAL) (signed) LACEY P. BOBO.
Notary Public.

Applications for Enrollment of Choctaw Newborn
Act of 1905   Volume XII

AFFIDAVIT OF ATTENDING PHYSICIAN OR MID-WIFE.

UNITED STATES OF AMERICA, Indian Territory, }
    Central   DISTRICT. }

I, Lucy Anderson , a mid-wife , on oath state that I attended on Mrs. Susan Sam , wife of Stanford Sam on the 2nd day of September , 1904; that there was born to her on said date a female child; that said child was living March 4, 1905, and is said to have been named Lula Sam

(signed) LUCY her x mark ANDERSON

Witnesses To Mark:
  { J. W. Homer
    A. J. Gardenhire

Subscribed and sworn to before me this 8th day of April , 1906

(SEAL)   (signed)   LACEY P. BOBO.
                                      Notary Public.

DEPARTMENT OF THE INTERIOR,
COMMISSIONER TO THE FIVE CIVILIZED TRIBES.
CHOCTAW-CHICKASAW DIVISION.
Talihina, Indian Territory, February 9, 1906.

666

In the matter of the enrollment of Lula Sam, Choctaw by blood, daughter of Stanford Sam, Choctaw by Blood, Roll Number 8716, and Susan Sam, Choctaw by blood, Roll Number 8717.

Testimony taken at Red Oak, Indian Territory, February 3, 1906:

Jacob Homer, Interpreter.

EXAMINATION BY THE COMMISSIONER:

Q What is your name? A Stanford Sam.
Q How old are you, Stanford? A About 38.
Q What is your post office? A Red Oak, I. T.
Q What is your wife's name? A Susan Sam.
Q Did you have a child born between September 25, 1902, and March 4, 1905: if so, what was the name of that child?
A Yes; Lula Sam.

Applications for Enrollment of Choctaw Newborn
Act of 1905   Volume XII

Q When was Lula Sam Born[sic]
A September 2, 1904.
Q Is the shild[sic] now living?
A It is not--it's dead.
Q When did Lula Sam die:
A The 2nd of March 1905.
Q The records of the Commission to the Five Civilized Tribes show that the mother Susan Sam and mid-wife, Lucy Anderson, made affidavit on the _____ day of April 1905 that the said Lula Sam died March 9, 1905: Were they mistaken as regards [sic] the date of Lula Sam's death?
A Yes, they were mistaken; I will be honest about it; I studied a long time about it and it was March 2, 1905.
Q Have you a record of the birth and death of Lula Sam?
A Yes, I have it on my book.
Q And your record shows that Lula Sam died March 2, 1905? A Yes
Q Can you read and write? A Yes.
Q Did you put the date of birth and date of death on your book?
A Yes, sir.
Q You were present when your wife, Susan Sam, and midwife, Lucy Anderson made affidavit before me, Lacey P. Bobo, affirming that Lula Sam was born September 2, 1904, and was living on March 4, 1905, and in response to my persistent inquiries about the exact date of death you stated very positively that the child died March 9, 1905: Were you mistaken then as to the date of the child's death? A Yes.
Q What afterwards convinced you of you mistake as to that affidavit?
A Every man is this way: when the family has died they always cant[sic] think of anything at all, but after a while they then remember when it died, and I was the same way; I just could not remember things at all, because my child had died not very long since when I appeared before you and I never remembered the date exactly, but afterwards I counted up when that child was born and then I found out exactly the date when it died.
Q You state upon oath that your daughter, Lula Sam, died March 2, 1905, and not on March 9, 1905? A Yes.
Q What day of the week was it that your child Lula Sam died?
A The first Thursday in March,

Witness   Excused.

Testimony taken at Red Oak, Indian Territory, on February 3, 1906: through Jacob Homer, Interpreter.

WATSON HAMPTON, being first duly sworn, testified as follows:

EXAMINATION BY THE COMMISSIONER:

Q What is your name? A Watson Hampton.

Applications for Enrollment of Choctaw Newborn
Act of 1905 Volume XII

Q What is your post office address? A Red Oak, I. T.
Q How old are you? A 41.
Q Are you a citizen by blood of the Choctaw Nation? A Yes.
Q Are you personally acquainted with Susan Sam, wife of Stanford Sam? A Yes.
Q Do you know the name of the little child of Stanford Sam's that died? A No, sir.
Q Do you know whether it was a boy or girl?
A No.
Q Did Susan Sam give birth to a child between September 25, 1902 and March 4, 1905?
A Yes, sir.
Q Did Susan Sam give birth to more than one child that time?
A I think not.
Q Is the child that you mention Susan Sam gave birth to now living? A Dead.
Q When did the child die?
A It was on the morning of the 2nd day of March; I do not know what day of the week.
Q In what year? A 1905.
Q Did you know the name of that child?
A No, I never heard its name until to-day.
Q Do you know the child you mention to be the last child that Susan Sam has given birth to? A Yes, sir.
Q How do you fix in your mind March 2, 1905 as the date of the death of Susan Sam's little child?
A I know it because there was a man sick over here about three miles from here and I was tending to that sick man and that man died on the 2nd of March, in the morning about 4 o'clock and I heard that child died the same hour of the same morning; that the reason I know it died on the 2nd, therefore I remember it.
Q What was the name of that man you mention that died?
A Wallace Jefferson.
Q Was he a Choctaw by blood? A Yes, sir.
Q Were they buried the next day, both of them?
A Yes, I guess so.

Witness   Excused.

Testimony taken four miles West of Red Oak, Indian Territory, February 5, 1906: through Jacob Homer, Interpreter.

SUSAN SAM, being first duly sworn, testified as follows:

<u>EXAMINATION BY THE COMMISSIONER</u>:

Q What is your name? A Susan Sam.
Q How old are you? A About 24.
Q Are you a citizen by blood of the Choctaw Nation? A Yes, sir.
Q What is your post office address? A Red Oak, I. T.
Q Are you the wife of Stanford Sam? A Yes.

Applications for Enrollment of Choctaw Newborn
Act of 1905   Volume XII

Q Did you give birth to a child between September 25, 1902 and March 4, 1905?
A I had a child born in 1904.
Q Was the child a male or female, and what was its name:
A Girl--Lula Sam.
Q When was Lula Sam born?
A September 2, 1904.
Q Is Lula Sam living or dead? A Dead?[sic]
Q When did she die?
A She died the 2nd day of March, about 7 or 8 o'clock at night, 1905.
Q On what day of the week was this?
A Thursday.
Q Have you a record of the birth and death of this child?
A Yes, sir.
The record is here exhibited, showing that Lula Sam was born September 2, 1904 and died March 2, 1905.
Q The records of the Commission to the Five Civilized Tribes show that on April _____ 1905, you made affidavit that Lula Sam was born September 2, 1904 and was living March 4, 1905: At the time you made that affidavit, did you think the child died after March 4, 1905?
A The child was dead before March 4, 1905.
Q At that time did you know the child was dead before March 4, 1905[sic]
A No, I did not remember at that time.
Q Do you state upon oath that your daughter, Lula Sam, died March 2 1905?
A Yes, sir, I am swearing the truth.

Witness   Excused.

Testimony taken four miles west of Red Oak, Indian Territory, February 5, 1905.

SAM JEFFERSON, being first duly sworn, testified, through, Interpreter Jacob Honer[sic], as follows:
EXAMINATION BY THE COMMISSIONER:

Q What is your name? A Sam Jefferson.
Q How old are you? A About 36.
Q What is your post office address? A Red Oak, I. T.
Q Are you a citizen by blood of the Choctaw Nation? A Yes, sir.
Q Were you acquainted with Lula Sam, daughter of Stanford Sam and Susan Sam?
A Yes, sir.
Q Were you present at the time Lula Sam died? A Yes, sir.
Q When did Lula Sam die?
A The 2nd day of March, 1905.
Q Do you remember what day of the week it was?
A Thursday night.

Applications for Enrollment of Choctaw Newborn
Act of 1905   Volume XII

Q How do you fix in your mind Thursday night, March 2, 1905, as being the date of the death of this child?
A I set up with the sick child, and also when that child died I made the coffin for it. Also Wallace Jefferson, a friend of mine, died on the same day.

Witness Excused.

W. P. Covington, being first duly sworn, states that the above and foregoing is a full, true and correct transcript of his stenographic notes taken in said case on said date.

W.P. Covington

Subscribed and sworn to before me, this   10th   day of Feb   1906.

Lacey P. Bobo
Notary Public.

7-NB-824

Muskogee, Indian Territory, February 8, 1906.

Lacey P. Bobo,
    Red Oak, Indian Territory.

Dear Sir:

    Receipt is hereby acknowledged of your letter of February 3, 1906, in which you state you think you can secure evidence that Lula Sam Choctaw new born roll 773 died prior to March 4, 1905.

    In reply to your letter you are advised that the Choctaw and Chickasaw Land Offices have been directed to take no further action looking to an allotment to this citizen until an investigation has been made as to the date of her death, and you are directed to secure such evidence as practicable in this matter.

Respectfully,

Acting Commissioner.

Applications for Enrollment of Choctaw Newborn
Act of 1905   Volume XII

7-NB-824

Muskogee, Indian Territory, February 8, 1906.

Chief Clerk,
      Chickasaw Land Office,
            Ardmore, Indian Territory.

Dear Sir:

    It appearing from information recently forwarded this office that Lula Sam, Choctaw new born roll 773, died prior to March 4, 1905, you are directed to take no further action relative to an allotment to this person until otherwise further advised.

                  Respectfully,

                                  Acting Commissioner.

7-NB-824

Muskogee, Indian Territory, February 8, 1906.

Chief Clerk,
      Choctaw Land Office,
            Atoka, Indian Territory.

Dear Sir:

    It appearing from information recently forwarded this office that Lula Sam, Choctaw new born roll 773, died prior to March 4, 1905, you are directed to take no further action relative to an allotment to this person until otherwise further advised.

                  Respectfully,

                                  Acting Commissioner.

Applications for Enrollment of Choctaw Newborn
Act of 1905   Volume XII

Muskogee, Indian Territory, March 6, 1906.

The Honorable,
    The Secretary of the Interior.

Sir:

On June 23, 1906[sic], the Commission to the Five Civilized Tribes had the honor to transmit for Departmental consideration a schedule constituting part of the final roll of new born citizens of the Choctaw Nation Nos. 717 to 904 inclusive, copies of which have been heretofore returned approved by the Secretary of the Interior, July 22, 1906.

I now have the honor to report that information having been received at this office to the effect that Lula Sam, whose name appears at No. 773 upon said schedule, had died prior to March 4, 1905. I caused an investigation to be made by an enrolling party in the field and from the testimony of Stanford Sam and Susan Sam, the parents of Lula Sam, and Watson Hampton and Sam Jefferson, it is evident that this citizen died March 2, 1905.

There is inclosed herewith for the information of the Department copies of the affidavits and testimony relative to the birth and death of Lula Sam.

I have therefore the honor to recommend that inasmuch so Lula Sam died prior to March 4, 1905, her enrollment at No. 773 upon the approved roll of new born citizens of the Choctaw Nation be cancelled upon the schedules and letter of transmittal of June 23, 1905, in the possession of the Indian Office and the Department and that this office be authorized to make like cancellation upon the schedules and letter of transmittal in its possession.

                        Respectfully,

                                      Acting Commissioner.

Through the Commissioner
    of Indian Affairs.

Applications for Enrollment of Choctaw Newborn
Act of 1905   Volume XII

Muskogee, Indian Territory, April 6, 1906.

Chief Clerk,
    Choctaw Land Office,
        Atoka, Indian Territory.

Dear Sir:
    There is inclosed herewith for the information of your office copy of letter of March 6, 1906, recommending the cancellation of the enrollment of Lula Sam opposite No. 775 upon the schedule of new born citizens of the Choctaw Nation.

    You will be notified when this office has been advised of Departmental action on this recommendation.

Respectfully,

Acting Commissioner.

LM 1/5

Muskogee, Indian Territory, April 6, 1906.

Chief Clerk,
    Chickasaw Land Office,
        Ardmore, Indian Territory.

Dear Sir:
    There is inclosed herewith for the information of your office copy of letter of March 6, 1906, recommending the cancellation of the enrollment of Lula Sam opposite No. 775 upon the schedule of new born citizens of the Choctaw Nation.

    You will be notified when this office has been advised of Departmental action on this recommendation.

Respectfully,

Acting Commissioner.

LM 1/5

Applications for Enrollment of Choctaw Newborn
Act of 1905   Volume XII

DEPARTMENT OF THE INTERIOR,   Y.P.
WASHINGTON.   FHE

D.C.   13944-1906.   April 16, 1906.
I.T.D. 6190-1906.

LRS

The Commissioner to the Five Civilized Tribes,
    Muskogee, Indian Territory.

Sir:

       It is shown by your letter of March 6, 1906, and the papers received therewith, that Lula Sam, whose name appears on the roll of new born citizens of the Choctaw Nation opposite No. 773, died prior to March 4, 1905.

       The Indian Office, reporting in the matter April 11, 1906, concurs in your recommendation that the name of Lula Sam be stricken from said roll, which was approved July 22, 1905, and the letter of transmittal of June 23, 1905.

       The Department also concurring, said name has been stricken from the roll and said letter of transmittal, and you are authorized to take like action relative to said roll in your possession. A copy of the Indian Office letter is inclosed.

                                      Respectfully,

                                      Thos. Ryan,
1 inclosure.   First Assistant Secretary.

(COPY)
DEPARTMENT OF THE INTERIOR,
OFFICE OF INDIAN AFFAIRS,

Land.   WASHINGTON.   April 11, 1906.
23356-1906.

The Honorable,
    The Secretary of the Interior.

Sir:

       There is enclosed a report from the Commissioner to the Five Civilized Tribes, dated March 6, 1906, reporting that he received information to the effect that Lula Sam, whose name appears on a Choctaw schedule of newborn children, at No. 773, died prior to March 4, 1905; that he caused an investigation to be made by an enrolling party in the field; that from the testimony of Stanford Sam and Susan Sam, parents o Lula Sam, and Watson Hampton, and Sam Jefferson, it is evident that Lula Sam died on March 2, 1905.

Applications for Enrollment of Choctaw Newborn
Act of 1905 Volume XII

He enclosed, for the information of the Department, copies of the affidavit and testimony relative to the birth and death of Lula Sam, and recommends that authority be granted for the cancellation of her name on all parts of the approved roll, and that the proper correction be made in his letter transmitting the roll.

From the papers transmitted by Mr. Bixby, it is evident that Lula Sam died on March 2, 1905, wand she is not, under the provisions of the Act of March 3, 1905 (33 Stats., 1048), entitled to enrollment as a citizen of the Choctaw Nation, and the Office concurs in the Commissioner's recommendation, that authority for the cancellation of her name on all parts of the roll and the correction of his letter transmitting the roll be granted.

Very respectfully,

C. F. Larrabee,
Acting Commissioner.

GAW-GH.

7-NB-824

Muskogee, Indian Territory, May 5, 1906.

Chief Clerk,
    Chickasaw Land Office,
        Ardmore, Indian Territory.

Dear Sir:

Referring to Choctaw roll card NB 824, Lula Sam, you are advised that a red line has been drawn through the name of Lula Sam at No. 1 upon said card and the following notation in red ink placed thereon:

> "Enrollment of No. 773 canceled[sic] under Depart-
> mental authority of April 16, 1906 (I.T.D. 6190-
> 1906) D. C. 13944-1906."

You are therefore directed to make duplicate Choctaw roll card in your possession conform to this information.

Respectfully,

Acting Commissioner.

Applications for Enrollment of Choctaw Newborn
Act of 1905   Volume XII

7-NB-824

Muskogee, Indian Territory, May 5, 1906.

Chief Clerk,
    Choctaw Land Office,
        Atoka, Indian Territory.

Dear Sir:

    Referring to Choctaw roll card NB 824, Lula Sam, you are advised that a red line has been drawn through the name of Lula Sam at No. 1 upon said card and the following notation in red ink placed thereon:

> "Enrollment of No. 773 canceled[sic] under Departmental authority of April 16, 1906 (I.T.D. 6190-1906) D. C. 13944-1906."

    You are therefore directed to make duplicate Choctaw roll card in your possession conform to this information.

Respectfully,

Acting Commissioner.

DEPARTMENT OF THE INTERIOR,   Y.P.
WASHINGTON.   FHE

D.C.   13944-1906.   April 16, 1906.
I.T.D. 6190-1906.

LRS

The Commissioner to the Five Civilized Tribes,
    Muskogee, Indian Territory.

Sir:

    It is shown by your letter of March 6, 1906, and the papers received therewith, that Lula Sam, whose name appears on the roll of new born citizens of the Choctaw Nation opposite No. 773, died prior to March 4, 1905.

    The Indian Office, reporting in the matter April 11, 1906, concurs in your recommendation that the name of Lula Sam be stricken from said roll, which was approved July 22, 1905, and the letter of transmittal of June 23, 1905.

Applications for Enrollment of Choctaw Newborn
Act of 1905 Volume XII

The Department also concurring, said name has been stricken from the roll and said letter of transmittal, and you are authorized to take like action relative to said roll in your possession. A copy of the Indian Office letter is inclosed.

Respectfully,

1 inclosure.

Thos. Ryan,
First Assistant Secretary.

(COPY)
DEPARTMENT OF THE INTERIOR,
OFFICE OF INDIAN AFFAIRS,
WASHINGTON.   April 11, 1906.

Land.
23356-1906.

The Honorable,
    The Secretary of the Interior.

Sir:

There is enclosed a report from the Commissioner to the Five Civilized Tribes, dated March 6, 1906, reporting that he received information to the effect that Lula Sam, whose name appears on a Choctaw schedule of newborn children, at No. 773, died prior to March 4, 1905; that he caused an investigation to be made by an enrolling party in the field; that from the testimony of Stanford Sam and Susan Sam, parents o Lula Sam, and Watson Hampton, and Sam Jefferson, it is evident that Lula Sam died on March 2, 1905.

He enclosed, for the information of the Department, copies of the affidavit and testimony relative to the birth and death of Lula Sam, and recommends that authority be granted for the cancellation of her name on all parts of the approved roll, and that the proper correction be made in his letter transmitting the roll.

From the papers transmitted by Mr. Bixby, it is evident that Lula Sam died on March 2, 1905, wand she is not, under the provisions of the Act of March 3, 1905 (33 Stats., 1048), entitled to enrollment as a citizen of the Choctaw Nation, and the Office concurs in the Commissioner's recommendation, that authority for the cancellation of her name on all parts of the roll and the correction of his letter transmitting the roll be granted.

Very respectfully,

C. F. Larrabee,
Acting Commissioner.

GAW-GH.

Applications for Enrollment of Choctaw Newborn
Act of 1905   Volume XII

Choc New Born 825
   Elma May Wall   b. 7-2-04

7-5724

BIRTH AFFIDAVIT.

DEPARTMENT OF THE INTERIOR.
COMMISSION TO THE FIVE CIVILIZED TRIBES.

IN RE APPLICATION FOR ENROLLMENT, as a citizen of the   Choctaw   Nation, of Elma May Wall   , born on the   2   day of   July   , 1904

Name of Father: Tandy Wall   a citizen of the   Choctaw   Nation.
Name of Mother: Phoebe A Wall   a citizen of the   Choctaw   Nation.

                    Postoffice   Tuskahoma I.T.

AFFIDAVIT OF MOTHER.

UNITED STATES OF AMERICA, Indian Territory, }
   Central   DISTRICT.

I,   Phoebe A. Wall   , on oath state that I am   27   years of age and a citizen by blood   , of the   Choctaw   Nation; that I am the lawful wife of   Tandy Wall   , who is a citizen, by blood   of the   Choctaw   Nation; that a   female   child was born to me on   2   day of   July   , 1904; that said child has been named   Elma May Wall   , and was living March 4, 1905.

                    Phoebe A Wall

Witnesses To Mark:
{

Subscribed and sworn to before me this   10   day of   April   , 1905

                    OL Johnson
                         Notary Public.

AFFIDAVIT OF ATTENDING PHYSICIAN OR MID-WIFE.

UNITED STATES OF AMERICA, Indian Territory, }
   Central   DISTRICT.

I,   Emaline Bohanon   , a   midwife   , on oath state that I attended on Mrs.   Phoebe A Wall   , wife of   Tandy Wall   on the   2   day of   July   , 1904;

Applications for Enrollment of Choctaw Newborn
Act of 1905 Volume XII

that there was born to her on said date a   female   child; that said child was living March 4, 1905, and is said to have been named Elma May Wall

her
Emaline x Bohanon
mark

Witnesses To Mark:
{ Chas T Difendafer
{ OL Johnson

Subscribed and sworn to before me this   10   day of   April   , 1905

OL Johnson
Notary Public.

Choc New Born 826
    Matilda Bohanan[sic]   b.   11-23-03

BIRTH AFFIDAVIT.
DEPARTMENT OF THE INTERIOR.
COMMISSION TO THE FIVE CIVILIZED TRIBES.

    IN RE APPLICATION FOR ENROLLMENT, as a citizen of the   Choctaw   Nation, of Matilda Bohanon   , born on the   23   day of   November   , 1903

Name of Father: Ellis Bohanon   a citizen of the   Choctaw   Nation.
Name of Mother: Susan Bohanon   a citizen of the   Choctaw   Nation.

Postoffice   Tuskahoma I.T.

AFFIDAVIT OF MOTHER.

UNITED STATES OF AMERICA, Indian Territory, }
    Central   **DISTRICT.** }

    I,   Susan Bohanon   , on oath state that I am   45   years of age and a citizen by   blood   , of the   Choctaw   Nation; that I am the lawful wife of   Ellis Bohanon   , who is a citizen, by blood   of the   Choctaw   Nation; that a female   child was born to me on   23   day of   November   , 1903; that said child has been named   Matilda Bohanon   , and was living March 4, 1905.

Susan Bohanon

Applications for Enrollment of Choctaw Newborn
Act of 1905   Volume XII

Witnesses To Mark:

  Subscribed and sworn to before me this 10 day of   April   , 1905

                              OL Johnson
                                   Notary Public.

AFFIDAVIT OF ATTENDING PHYSICIAN OR MID-WIFE.

UNITED STATES OF AMERICA, Indian Territory,
  Central   DISTRICT.

  I,   Elsie A Bohanon   , a   midwife   , on oath state that I attended on Mrs.   Susan Bohanon   , wife of   Ellis Bohanon   on the 23 day of November   , 1903; that there was born to her on said date a   female   child; that said child was living March 4, 1905, and is said to have been named Matilda Bohanon

                         Elsie A Bohanon

Witnesses To Mark:

  Subscribed and sworn to before me this 10 day of   April   , 1905

                              OL Johnson
                                   Notary Public.

Choc New Born 827
    Andrew Bohanan   b. 2-27-05

7-760   7-5494

BIRTH AFFIDAVIT.

DEPARTMENT OF THE INTERIOR.
COMMISSION TO THE FIVE CIVILIZED TRIBES.

  IN RE APPLICATION FOR ENROLLMENT, as a citizen of the   Choctaw   Nation, of   Andrew Bohanon   , born on the 27 day of February , 1905

Name of Father: Robert Bohanon   a citizen of the   Choctaw   Nation.
Name of Mother: Elsie A Bohanon nee Bell a citizen of the   Choctaw   Nation.

Applications for Enrollment of Choctaw Newborn
Act of 1905 Volume XII

Postoffice   Tuskahoma I.T.

AFFIDAVIT OF MOTHER.

UNITED STATES OF AMERICA, Indian Territory,
Central   DISTRICT.

I,   Elsie A Bohanon   , on oath state that I am   24   years of age and a citizen by   blood   , of the   Choctaw   Nation; that I am the lawful wife of   Robert Bohanon   , who is a citizen, by   blood   of the   Choctaw   Nation; that a   male   child was born to me on   27   day of   February   , 1905; that said child has been named   Andrew Bohanon   , and was living March 4, 1905.

Elsie A Bohanon

Witnesses To Mark:
{

Subscribed and sworn to before me this   10   day of   April   , 1905

OL Johnson
Notary Public.

AFFIDAVIT OF ATTENDING PHYSICIAN OR MID-WIFE.

UNITED STATES OF AMERICA, Indian Territory,
Central   DISTRICT.

I,   Susan Bohanon   , a   midwife   , on oath state that I attended on Mrs.   Elsie A Bohanon   , wife of   Robert Bohanon   on the   27   day of   February   , 1905; that there was born to her on said date a   male   child; that said child was living March 4, 1905, and is said to have been named   Andrew Bohanon

Susan Bohanon

Witnesses To Mark:
{

Subscribed and sworn to before me this   10   day of   April   , 1905

OL Johnson
Notary Public.

Applications for Enrollment of Choctaw Newborn
Act of 1905   Volume XII

Choc New Born 828
    Allie Lorennie Berry   b. 7-30-04

Choctaw N B 828

Muskogee, Indian Territory, May 20, 1905.

Rebecca Berry,
    Purcell, Indian Territory.

Dear Madam:

    Receipt is hereby acknowledged of your letter of May 13, asking if your child, Allie Lorennie Berry, has been approved and in reply you are advised that the affidavits heretofore forwarded to the birth of your child, Allie Lorennie Berry, have been filed with our records as an application for her enrollment, but her name has not yet been placed upon a schedule of citizens by blood of the Choctaw Nation prepared for forwarding to the Secretary of the Interior.

    Respectfully,

    Chairman.

7-NB-828

Muskogee, Indian Territory, July 11, 1905.

Rebecca Berry,
    Purcell, Indian Territory.

Dear Madam:

    Receipt is hereby acknowledged of your letter of July 3, 1905, asking if the name of your child Allie Lorennie Berry has been sent up to the Secretary of the Interior for approval.

    In reply to your letter you are advised that the name of your child Allie Lorennie Berry has been placed upon a schedule of citizens by blood of the Choctaw Nation which has been forwarded the Secretary of the Interior. You will be notified when her enrollment is approved.

    Respectfully,

    Commissioner.

Applications for Enrollment of Choctaw Newborn
Act of 1905   Volume XII

BIRTH AFFIDAVIT.   *no 33*

DEPARTMENT OF THE INTERIOR,
COMMISSION TO THE FIVE CIVILIZED TRIBES.

IN RE Application for Enrollment, as a citizen of the   Choctaw   Nation, of   Allie Lorennie Berry   , born on the   30   day of   July   , 1904

Name of Father: H H Berry   a citizen of the United States ~~Nation~~.
Name of Mother: Rebecca Berry nee Buckholts   a citizen of the   Choctaw   Nation.
by blood

Post-Office: Purcell, Indian Territory

AFFIDAVIT OF MOTHER.

UNITED STATES OF AMERICA, }
   INDIAN TERRITORY.
   Southern   District.

I,   Rebecca Berry   , on oath state that I am   29   years of age and a citizen by   blood   , of the   Choctaw   Nation; that I am the lawful wife of   H. H. Berry   , who is a citizen, by   birth   of the United States; that a   female   child was born to me on   30   day of   July   , 1904 , that said child has been named   Allie Lorennie Berry   , and is now living.

Rebecca Berry

WITNESSES TO MARK:
{

Subscribed and sworn to before me this   2nd day of   November   , 190 4

Emra C Brown
   NOTARY PUBLIC.

AFFIDAVIT OF ATTENDING PHYSICIAN OR MID-WIFE.

UNITED STATES OF AMERICA, }
   INDIAN TERRITORY.
   Southern   District.

I,   J B Maples   , a   physician   , on oath state that I attended on Mrs.   Rebecca Berry   , wife of   H H Berry   on the   30   day of   July   , 1904 ; that there was born to her on said date a   female   child; that said child is now living and is said to have been named   Allie Lorennie Berry

Applications for Enrollment of Choctaw Newborn
Act of 1905   Volume XII

JB Maples M.D.

WITNESSES TO MARK:

{

Subscribed and sworn to before me this   17   day of   November   , 1904

E.F. Williams
NOTARY PUBLIC.

Indian Territory   )
)
Southern District,   )   A F F I D A V I T.
)
At Purcell.   )

I, Frank Maples of lawful age and being first duly sworn, say that I am the son of Dr. J. B. Maples, and reside in the town of Paoli, I.T. that my father left Paoli on or about the 28th day of November 1904 for the Republic of Mexico and he has not returned to this Territory since. Affiant further says that if said Dr. J. B. Maples was living at Paoli, I.T. he would make affidavit that he attended Mrs. Rebecca Berry, nee Buckholts when her child was born.

M.F. Maples

Subscribed and sworn to before me this
4th day of April 1905.
    AS Kelley
      Notary Public.
My Commission Expires Mch 12-1908.

BIRTH AFFIDAVIT.

DEPARTMENT OF THE INTERIOR.
COMMISSION TO THE FIVE CIVILIZED TRIBES.

IN RE APPLICATION FOR ENROLLMENT, as a citizen of the   Choctaw   Nation, of Allie Lorennie Berry   , born on the   30   day of   July   , 1904

Name of Father: H.H. Berry   a citizen of the   Choctaw   Nation.
Name of Mother: Rebecca Berry nee Buckholts   a citizen of the   Choctaw   Nation.

      Postoffice   Purcell I.T.

Applications for Enrollment of Choctaw Newborn
Act of 1905   Volume XII

AFFIDAVIT OF MOTHER.

UNITED STATES OF AMERICA, Indian Territory,　⎱
　　Southern　　　　　　DISTRICT.　⎰

I, Rebecca Berry nee Buckholts , on oath state that I am 30 years of age and a citizen by blood , of the Choctaw Nation; that I am the lawful wife of H.H. Berry , who is a citizen, ~~by~~ ~~blood~~ of the ~~U. S.~~ ~~Nation~~; that a female child was born to me on 30 day of July , 1904; that said child has been named Allie Lorennie Berry , and was living March 4, 1905.

　　　　　　　　　　　　　　　　　　　Rebecca Berry

Witnesses To Mark:
　⎰
　⎱

　　Subscribed and sworn to before me this 28" day of March , 1905

　　　　　　　　　　　　　　(Name Illegible)
　　　　　　　　　　　　　　Notary Public.

AFFIDAVIT OF ATTENDING PHYSICIAN OR MID-WIFE.

UNITED STATES OF AMERICA, Indian Territory,　⎱
　　Southern　　　　　　DISTRICT.　⎰

I, Jennette Buckholts , a ~~midwife~~ , on oath state that I attended on Mrs. Rebecca Berry , wife of H. H. Berry on the 30" day of July , 1904; that there was born to her on said date a female child; that said child was living March 4, 1905, and is said to have been named Allie Lorennie Berry

　　　　　　　　　　　　　　　　　　Jennette Buckholts

Witnesses To Mark:
　⎰
　⎱

　　Subscribed and sworn to before me this 4th day of April , 1905

　　　　　　　　　　　　　　Geo W Miller
　　　　　　　　　　　　　　Notary Public.

Applications for Enrollment of Choctaw Newborn
Act of 1905 Volume XII

<u>Choc New Born 829</u>
    Sarah Margaret Mackey   b. 1-8-03

---

7 NB 829

Muskogee, Indian Territory, June 30, 1905

E. M. Mackey,
    Wynnewood, Indian Territory.

Dear Sir:

    Receipt is hereby acknowledged of your letter of June 26, 1905, asking if the name of your daughter Sarah Margaret Mackey has been approved.

    In reply to your letter you are advised that the name of your daughter Sarah Margaret Mackey has been placed upon a schedule of citizens by blood of the Choctaw Nation prepared for forwarding to the Secretary of the Interior, but her enrollment has not yet been approved by the Department.

    You will be notified when her enrollment is approved by the Secretary of the Interior.

                                         Respectfully,

                                                    Chairman.

BIRTH AFFIDAVIT.

DEPARTMENT OF THE INTERIOR.
COMMISSION TO THE FIVE CIVILIZED TRIBES.

    IN RE APPLICATION FOR ENROLLMENT, as a citizen of the   Choctaw   Nation, of Sarah Margaret Mackey   , born on the 8th   day of   Jan.   , 1903

Name of Father: E. M. Mackey   a citizen of the   Choctaw   Nation.
Name of Mother: Wayne Lee Mackey   a citizen of the .... Nation.

                          Postoffice   Wynnewood, Ind. Ter.

Applications for Enrollment of Choctaw Newborn
Act of 1905 Volume XII

AFFIDAVIT OF MOTHER.

UNITED STATES OF AMERICA, Indian Territory, ⎫
Southern   DISTRICT.   ⎬

I,   Wayne Lee Mackey   , on oath state that I am   35   years of age and a citizen by   Intermarriage   , of the   Choctaw   Nation; that I am the lawful wife of   E. M. Mackey   , who is a citizen, by   Blood   of the   Choctaw   Nation; that a   Female   child was born to me on 8th   day of   January 1903. , 1........; that said child has been named   Sarah Margaret Mackey   , and was living March 4, 1905.

Wayne Lee Mackey

Witnesses To Mark:
{

Subscribed and sworn to before me this   27th   day of   March   , 1905

(Name Illegible)
Notary Public.

AFFIDAVIT OF ATTENDING PHYSICIAN OR MID-WIFE.

UNITED STATES OF AMERICA, Indian Territory, ⎫
Southern   DISTRICT.   ⎬

I,   A. J. Hoover   , a physician   , on oath state that I attended on Mrs.   Wayne Lee Mackey   , wife of   E. M. Mackey   on the   8th day of January 1903   , 1........; that there was born to her on said date a   female   child; that said child was living March 4, 1905, and is said to have been named Sarah Margaret Mackey

Andrew J. Hoover M.D.

Witnesses To Mark:
{

Subscribed and sworn to before me this   27th   day of   March   , 1905

(Name Illegible)
Notary Public.

Applications for Enrollment of Choctaw Newborn
Act of 1905 Volume XII

Choc New Born 830
    Samuel Oliver Richardson b. 1-21-03
    Mattie C. Richardson b. 2-24-04

7-NB-830

Muskogee, Indian Territory, July 12, 1905.

S. O. Richardson,
    Wynnewood, Indian Territory.

Dear Sir:

    Receipt is hereby acknowledged of your letter of July 8, 1905, asking if your two children Samuel Oliver and Mattie Codelia Richardson have been approved.

    In reply to your letter you are advised that the names of your children Samuel Oliver and Mattie Codelia Richardson have been placed upon a schedule of citizens by blood of the Choctaw Nation which has been forwarded the Secretary of the Interior, and you will be notified when their enrollment is approved.

                  Respectfully,

                                    Commissioner.

BIRTH AFFIDAVIT.

    IN RE-APPLICATION FOR ENROLLMENT, as a citizen of the   Choctaw   Nation, of Mattie C. Richardson, born on the 24   day of   Feby , 190 4

Name of Father: Samuel O. Richardson   a citizen of the   Choctaw   Nation.
Name of Mother: Lucinda C. Richardson   a citizen of the   Choctaw   Nation.

                  Postoffice   Wynnewood I.T.

                  AFFIDAVIT OF MOTHER.

UNITED STATES OF AMERICA, INDIAN TERRITORY, }
    Southern   District.

    I, Lucinda C Richardson , on oath state that I am thirty-three   years of age and a citizen by   blood   , of the   Choctaw   Nation; that I am the lawful wife of   S O Richardson , who is a citizen, by   Intermarriage   of the   Choctaw   Nation; that a female   child was born to me on 24   day of   Feby , 1904 , that said child has been named Mattie C. Richardson   , and is now living.

Applications for Enrollment of Choctaw Newborn
Act of 1905 Volume XII

Lucinda C Richardson

Witnesses To Mark:
{

Subscribed and sworn to before me this 20th day of March , 1905.

JS Wheeler
Notary Public.

AFFIDAVIT OF ATTENDING PHYSICIAN OR MID-WIFE.

UNITED STATES OF AMERICA, INDIAN TERRITORY, }
Southern   District.

I, Andrew J Hoover , a Practicing Physician , on oath state that I attended on Mrs. Lucinda C Richardson , wife of S O Richardson on the 24th day of Feby , 190 4; that there was born to her on said date a female child; that said child is now living and is said to have been named Mattie C Richardson

Andrew J Hoover M.D.

Witnesses To Mark:
{

Subscribed and sworn to before me this 21 day of March , 1905.

JS Wheeler
Notary Public.

BIRTH AFFIDAVIT.

IN RE-APPLICATION FOR ENROLLMENT, as a citizen of the Choctaw Nation, of Samuel Oliver Richardson, born on the 21st day of January , 190 3

Name of Father: Samuel O. Richardson   a citizen of the Choctaw Nation.
Name of Mother: Lucinda C. Richardson   a citizen of the Choctaw Nation.

Postoffice   Wynnewood I.T.

AFFIDAVIT OF MOTHER.

UNITED STATES OF AMERICA, INDIAN TERRITORY, }
Southern District   District.

I, Lucinda C Richardson , on oath state that I am Thirty-Three years of age and a citizen by blood , of the Choctaw Nation; that I am the lawful wife of S. O. Richardson , who is a citizen, by Intermarriage of the Choctaw Nation; that a

Applications for Enrollment of Choctaw Newborn
Act of 1905   Volume XII

male   child was born to me on 21st day of   January , 1903 , that said child has been named Samuel Oliver Richardson   , and is now living.

Lucinda C Richardson

Witnesses To Mark:

{

Subscribed and sworn to before me this   20th day of   March   , 1905.

JS Wheeler
Notary Public.

AFFIDAVIT OF ATTENDING PHYSICIAN OR MID-WIFE.

UNITED STATES OF AMERICA, INDIAN TERRITORY, }
Southern   District. }

I,   Andrew J Hoover   , a Practicing Physician , on oath state that I attended on Mrs. Lucinda C Richardson   , wife of   S O Richardson   on the   21   day of January , 190 3; that there was born to her on said date a   male   child; that said child is now living and is said to have been named Samuel Oliver Richardson

Andrew J Hoover M.D.

Witnesses To Mark:

{

Subscribed and sworn to before me this   21   day of   March   , 1905.

JS Wheeler
Notary Public.

Choc New Born 831
    Jimmie Carnes   b. 10-7-03

BIRTH AFFIDAVIT.

DEPARTMENT OF THE INTERIOR.
COMMISSION TO THE FIVE CIVILIZED TRIBES.

IN RE APPLICATION FOR ENROLLMENT, as a citizen of the   Choctaw   Nation, of Jimmie Carnes   , born on the 7th   day of   October , 1903

Name of Father: Buster Spring   a citizen of the   Choctaw   Nation.
Name of Mother: Molsie Carnes   a citizen of the   Choctaw   Nation.

Applications for Enrollment of Choctaw Newborn
Act of 1905   Volume XII

Postoffice   Tuskahoma, Ind. Ter.

AFFIDAVIT OF MOTHER.

UNITED STATES OF AMERICA, Indian Territory,
Central   DISTRICT.

I, Molsie Carnes, on oath state that I am 19 years of age and a citizen by blood, of the Choctaw Nation; that I am *not* the lawful wife of Buster Spring, who is a citizen, by blood of the Choctaw Nation; that a male child was born to me on 7th day of October, 1903; that said child has been named Jimmie Carnes, and was living March 4, 1905.

Molsie Carnes

Witnesses To Mark:

Subscribed and sworn to before me this 10th day of April, 1905

OL Johnson
Notary Public.

AFFIDAVIT OF ATTENDING PHYSICIAN OR MID-WIFE.

UNITED STATES OF AMERICA, Indian Territory,
Central   DISTRICT.

I, Lizzie Bond, a midwife, on oath state that I attended on ~~Mrs.~~ Miss Molsie Carnes, wife of Buster Spring on the 7th day of October, 1903; that there was born to her on said date a male child; that said child was living March 4, 1905, and is said to have been named Jimmie Carnes

Lizzie x Bond (her mark)

Witnesses To Mark:
Chas T. Difendafer
OL Johnson

Subscribed and sworn to before me this 10th day of April, 1905

OL Johnson
Notary Public.

Applications for Enrollment of Choctaw Newborn
Act of 1905   Volume XII

Choc New Born 832
   Muley[sic] Walls   b. 12-27-03

DEPARTMENT OF THE INTERIOR,
COMMISSION TO THE FIVE CIVILIZED TRIBES.
TUSKAHOMA, IND. TER.,   APRIL 10, 1905.

In the matter of the application for the enrollment of Mulcy Walls as a citizen by blood of the Choctaw Nation.

Mary Morris being first duly sworn testifies as follows:

S. B. McKinney interpreter:

EXAMINATION BY THE COMMISSION:

Q What is your name? A Mary Morris.
Q What is your age? A Thirty-one.
Q What is your post office address? A Tuskahoma.
Q Are you a citizen by blood of the Choctaw Nation? A Chickasaw and Choctaw.
Q Where did you elect to be finally enrolled? A Chickasaw
Q You are a citizen by blood of the Chickasaw Nation? A Yes, sir.
Q What was your name on September 25, 1902? A McCann.
Q You have this day appeared and made application for Mulcy Walls; why didn't the mother of this child appear? A Dead.
Q When did she die? A Last March year ago.
Q March 1904? A Yes, sir.
Q Have you got charge of this child now? A Yes, sir.
Q Who is the mother of Mulcy Walls? A Sibby.
Q Who is the father? A Sam Walls.
Q Is Sam Walls living? A Yes, sir.
Q Did he give you charge of this child? A Yes, sir.
Q When was Mulcy Walls born? A 27th of December 1903.
Q How long have you had charge of this child? A Ever since July 1904.
Q This is the child here (indicating)? A Yes, sir.

Witness excused.

Will Morris being first duly sworn testifies as follows:

EXAMINATION BY THE COMMISSION:

Q What is your name? A Will Morris.
Q What is your age? A Thirty-eight.
Q Post office address? A Tuskahoma.
Q Are you a citizen by blood of the Choctaw Nation? A Yes, sir.

Applications for Enrollment of Choctaw Newborn
Act of 1905   Volume XII

Q Your wife Mary Morris has this day made application for the enrollment of Mulcy Walls who is her ward, when was this Mulcy Ward[sic] born? A 27th of December, 1903.
Q Who is the mother of this child? A Sibby Walls.
Q Who is the father? A Sam Walls.
Q What is the reason that the mother of this child does not appear herself and make application for Mulcy Walls? A Dead.
Q This child is living today? A Yes, sir.

Witness excused.

Chas. T. Difendafer being first duly sworn states that the above and foregoing is a full, true and correct transcript of his stenographic notes taken in said cause on said date.

Chas. T. Difendafer

Subscribed and sworn to before me this 10th day of April 1905.

OL Johnson
Notary Public.

DEPARTMENT OF THE INTERIOR,
COMMISSION TO THE FIVE CIVILIZED TRIBES.
TUSKAHOMA, IND. TER.,   APRIL 10, 1905.

In the matter of the application for the enrollment of Mulcy Walls as a citizen by blood of the Choctaw Nation.

Sam Walls being first duly sworn testifies as follows:

EXAMINATION BY THE COMMISSION:

Q What is your name? A Sam Walls.
Q What is your age? A About thirty-one I guess.
Q What is your post office address? A Tuskahoma.
Q Are you a citizen by blood of the Choctaw Nation? A yes, sir.
Q Are you the father of Mulcy Walls for whom Mary Morris has this day made application? A Yes, sir.
Q When was that child born? A December 24[sic], 1902[sic].
Q Who is the mother of Mulcy Walls? A Sibbl[sic].
Q How is Sibbl spelled? A S-i-b-b-l.
Q Is your wife Sibbl Walls living? A She is dead.
Q When did she die? A She died year ago I think, yes, yes, it was a year ago.
Q Mary Morris now has charge of that child? A Long as she lived she was to take care of it then if she was to die I was to take the child back.
Q Mulcy Walls is living? A Yes, sir.

Applications for Enrollment of Choctaw Newborn
Act of 1905   Volume XII

Witness excused.

Chas. T. Difendafer being first duly sworn states that the above and foregoing is a full, true and correct transcript of his stenographic notes taken in said cause on said date.

Chas T. Difendafer

Subscribed and sworn to before me this 10th day of April 1905.

OL Johnson
Notary Public.

BIRTH AFFIDAVIT.

DEPARTMENT OF THE INTERIOR.
COMMISSION TO THE FIVE CIVILIZED TRIBES.

IN RE APPLICATION FOR ENROLLMENT, as a citizen of the   Choctaw   Nation, of Mulcy Walls   , born on the 27   day of   December   , 1903

Name of Father: Sam Walls   a citizen of the   Choctaw   Nation.
Name of Mother: Sibby Walls   a citizen of the   Choctaw   Nation.

Postoffice   Tuskahoma I.T.

AFFIDAVIT OF MOTHER.

UNITED STATES OF AMERICA, Indian Territory,
.... DISTRICT.

I, ..., on oath state that I am .... years of age and a citizen by ...., of the .... Nation; that I am the lawful wife of ...., who is a citizen, b*See Testimony*he .... Nation; that a .... child was born to me on .... day of ...., 1...., that said child has been named ...., and was living March 4, 1905.

....

Witnesses To Mark:
{ ....
....

Subscribed and sworn to before me this ...... day of ...., 1905.

....
Notary Public.

172

Applications for Enrollment of Choctaw Newborn
Act of 1905   Volume XII

AFFIDAVIT OF ATTENDING PHYSICIAN OR MID-WIFE.

UNITED STATES OF AMERICA, Indian Territory, }
.... DISTRICT. }

   I,   Mary Morris   , a midwife   , on oath state that I attended on Mrs.   Sibby Walls   , wife of   Sam Walls   on the 27   day of   December   , 1903; that there was born to her on said date a   female   child; that said child was living March 4, 1905, and is said to have been named Mulcy Walls

her
Mary x Morris
mark

Witnesses To Mark:
{ Chas T. Difendafer
{ OL Johnson

   Subscribed and sworn to before me this 10 day of   April   , 1905

   OL Johnson
   Notary Public.

7-NB-832.

Muskogee, Indian Territory, May 29, 1905.

Mary Morris,
   Tuskahoma, Indian Territory.

Dear Madam:

   Referring to the application for the enrollment of Mulcy Walls, it is noted from the testimony taken on the 10th ultimo that the mother of the applicant is dead.

   In this event it will be necessary for you to file with the Commission the evidence of two persons, who are disinterested and not related to the applicant, who have actual knowledge of the facts that the child was born, the date of her birth; that she was living on March 4, 1905, and that Sibby Walls was her mother.

   In the testimony above referred to you and your husband, Will Morris, give the date of the child's birth as December 27, 1903, while the father of the applicant, in his testimony taken on the same date, gives the date of birth as December 24, 1902. Before this case can be finally determined it will be necessary for you, your husband and the father of the applicant to make affidavits as to the correct date of the child's birth. These affidavits and the affidavits of the two disinterested parties, above referred to, should be filed in this office as soon as possible.

   Respectfully,
   Chairman.

Applications for Enrollment of Choctaw Newborn
Act of 1905   Volume XII

Choc New Born 833
    Annie Colbert   b. 8-11-03

7 NB 833

Muskogee, Indian Territory, June 7, 1905.

Ellis Colbert,
    Tuskahoma, Indian Territory.

Dear Sir:

    Receipt is hereby acknowledged of the joint affidavit of Wesley Anderson and Rufus Allen to the birth of your child Annie Colbert and the same has been filed in the matter of the enrollment of said child.

    Respectfully,

    Chairman.

7-NB-833:

Muskogee, Indian Territory, May 29, 1905.

Ellis Colbert,
    Tushkahoma[sic], Indian Territory.

Dear Sir:

    Referring to the application for the enrollment of your infant child, Annie Colbert, born August 11, 1903, it is noted, from the testimony taken on April 10, 1905, that you were the only one in attendance upon your wife at the time of birth of the applicant.

    If this is correct it will be necessary for you to file in this office the affidavits of two persons, who are disinterested and not related to the applicant, who have actual knowledge of the facts that the child was born, the date of her birth; that she was living on March 4, 1905, and that Temelius Colbert is her mother.

    In having these affidavits executed care should be exercised to see that all names are written in full, as they appear in the body of the affidavit, and in the event that either of the persons signing the affidavit are unable to write, signatures by mark must be attested by two witnesses. Each affidavit must be executed before a Notary Public and the notarial seal and signature of the officer must be attached to each separate affidavit.

Applications for Enrollment of Choctaw Newborn
Act of 1905   Volume XII

Respectfully,

VR 29-10.   Chairman.

NEW-BORN AFFIDAVIT.

Number............

...Choctaw Enrolling Commission...

IN THE MATTER OF THE APPLICATION FOR ENROLLMENT, as a citizen of the Choctaw Nation, of   Annie Colbert

born on the   11th day of   August   190 3

Name of father   Ellis Colbert   a citizen of   Choctaw
Nation final enrollment No.   5641
Name of mother   Temelius Colbert   a citizen of   Choctaw
Nation final enrollment No.   11655

Postoffice   Tushkahoma[sic] I.T.

AFFIDAVIT OF MOTHER.

UNITED STATES OF AMERICA
INDIAN TERRITORY
   Central   DISTRICT

I   Temelius Colbert   , on oath state that I am 23   years of age and a citizen by   Blood   of the   Choctaw   Nation, and as such have been placed upon the final roll of the   Choctaw   Nation, by the Honorable Secretary of the Interior my final enrollment number being   11655 ; that I am the lawful wife of   Ellis Colbert   , who is a citizen of the   Choctaw   Nation, and as such has been placed upon the final roll of said Nation by the Honorable Secretary of the Interior, his final enrollment number being   5641   and that a   Female   child was born to me on the   11   day of   August   190 3; that said child has been named   Annie Colbert   , and is now living.

                                        her
                                Temelius x Colbert
Witnesseth.   mark
   Must be two ⎱ *(Name Illegible)*
   Witnesses who ⎰
   are Citizens.   W.E. Colbert

Applications for Enrollment of Choctaw Newborn
Act of 1905   Volume XII

Subscribed and sworn to before me this   10   day of   Feby   190 5

Peter W Hudson
Notary Public.

My Commission Expires Feb. 24, 1906.
My commission expires:

DEPARTMENT OF THE INTERIOR,
COMMISSION TO THE FIVE CIVILIZED TRIBES.
TUSKAHOMA, IND. TER.,   APRIL 10, 1905.

In the matter of the application for the enrollment of Annie Colbert as a citizen by blood of the Choctaw Nation.

Ellis Colbert being first duly sworn testifies as follows:

EXAMINATION BY THE COMMISSION:

Q What is your name? A Ellis Colbert.
Q What is your age? A Thirty-four.
Q What is your post office address? A Tuskahoma.
Q What is your wife's name? A Temelius Colbert.
Q Your wife Temelius Colbert has this day made application for the enrollment of your child Annie Colbert as a citizen by blood of the Choctaw Nation. When was Annie born? A 11th of August, 1903.
Q Who attended your wife when Annie was born? A Me.
Q No one else there but yourself? A No, sir.
Q Is Annie Colbert living today? A Yes, sir.

Witness excused.

Alexander Colbert being first duly sworn testifies as follows:

EXAMINATION BY THE COMMISSION:

Q What is your name? A Alexander Colbert.
Q What is your age? A Twenty-eight.
Q What is your post office address? A Tuskahoma.
Q Are you a citizen by blood of the Choctaw Nation? A Yes, sir.
Q Are you acquainted with Temelius Colbert and her husband Ellis Colbert? A Yes, sir.
Q How far do you live from them? A Me? About six miles.
Q Temelius Colbert has this day made application for the enrollment of her minor child Annie Colbert as a citizen of the Choctaw Nation; do you know when Annie Colbert was born? A I don't know the day but I know the time.
Q What year? A 1903
Q What month in 1903? A I think it was in August.
Q You don't recollect the day of the month? A No.

Applications for Enrollment of Choctaw Newborn
Act of 1905   Volume XII

Q Is Annie Colbert living today? A Yes, sir.

Witness excused.

Temelius Colbert being first duly sworn through interpreter Ellis Colbert testifies as follows:

EXAMINATION BY THE COMMISSION:

Q What is your name? A Temelius Colbert.
Q How old are you? A Twenty-three.
Q What is your post office address? A Tuskahoma.
Q You have this day made application for the enrollment of your minor child Annie Colbert as a citizen of the Choctaw Nation? A Yes, sir.
Q When was this child born? A August 11, 1903.
Q Who attended you when this child was born? A My husband.
Q No woman or doctor? A No, sir.
Q Is this the child here? (indicating) A Yes, sir.

Witness excused.

Chas. T. Difendafer being first duly sworn states that the above and foregoing is a full, true and correct transcript of his stenographic notes taken in said cause on said date.

Chas T. Difendafer

Subscribed and sworn to before me this 10th day of April, 1905

OL Johnson
Notary Public.

(The affidavit below typed as given.)

United States of America,
   Indian Teritory
Central District

We Wesley Anderson and Rufus Allen, on oath stated they are acquinted with Annie Colbert that she was born August 11th 1903 and that she was living on March-4-1905 and that Temelius Colbert is her mother.

Wesley Anderson
Rufus Allen

Applications for Enrollment of Choctaw Newborn
Act of 1905   Volume XII

Subscribed & sworn to before me this 3 day of June 1905

                                          PW Hudson
                                              Notary Public.

My Com expires 2/24/06

7-11655   7-5641

BIRTH AFFIDAVIT.

DEPARTMENT OF THE INTERIOR.
COMMISSION TO THE FIVE CIVILIZED TRIBES.

IN RE APPLICATION FOR ENROLLMENT, as a citizen of the   Choctaw   Nation, of Annie Colbert   , born on the   11th   day of   August   , 1903

Name of Father: Ellis Colbert   a citizen of the   Choctaw   Nation.
Name of Mother: Temelius Colbert (nee Morris) a citizen of the   Choctaw   Nation.

                                    Postoffice   Tuskahoma, Ind. Ter.

AFFIDAVIT OF MOTHER.

UNITED STATES OF AMERICA, Indian Territory,
   Central   **DISTRICT.**

    I,   Temelius Colbert   , on oath state that I am   23   years of age and a citizen by   blood   , of the   Choctaw   Nation; that I am the lawful wife of   Ellis Colbert   , who is a citizen, by   blood   of the   Choctaw   Nation; that a   female   child was born to me on   11th   day of   August   , 1903; that said child has been named   Annie Colbert   , and was living March 4, 1905.

                                              her
                                Temelius x Colbert
Witnesses To Mark: mark
   Chas T. Difendafer
   Ellis Colbert

    Subscribed and sworn to before me this   10th   day of   April   , 1905

                                    OL Johnson
                                      Notary Public.

Applications for Enrollment of Choctaw Newborn
Act of 1905   Volume XII

Choc New Born 834
    Allie Daney b. 11-16-03

BIRTH AFFIDAVIT.

DEPARTMENT OF THE INTERIOR,
COMMISSION TO THE FIVE CIVILIZED TRIBES.

IN RE Application for Enrollment, as a citizen of the Choctaw Nation, of Allie Dany[sic], born on the 16 day of November, 1903

Name of Father: Solomon Dany   a citizen of the Choctaw Nation.
Name of Mother: Adaline (Johnson) Dany   a citizen of the Choctaw Nation.

Post-Office: Talihina I.T.

AFFIDAVIT OF MOTHER.

UNITED STATES OF AMERICA, }
    INDIAN TERRITORY.
    .... District.

I, ..., on oath state that I am ...... years of age and a citizen by ......, of ......, *Mother Dead Died April 1-1905* that I am the lawful wife of ......, who is ...... *See Death Affidavit attached* the ...... Nation; that a ...... child was born to me on ...... day of ......, 1......, that said child has been named ...., and is now living.

WITNESSES TO MARK:
{ ....
{ ....

Subscribed and sworn to before me this .... day of ...., 190....

....
                                           NOTARY PUBLIC.

Applications for Enrollment of Choctaw Newborn
Act of 1905   Volume XII

AFFIDAVIT OF ATTENDING PHYSICIAN OR MID-WIFE.

UNITED STATES OF AMERICA,
   INDIAN TERRITORY.
  Central   District.

We, Robert King & Leviney Anderson ,on oath state that We attended on Mrs. Adaline Johnson Dany , wife of Solomon Daney on the 16 day of November , 1903 ; that there was born to her on said date a Female child; that said child is now living and is said to have been named Allie Dany

                                        her
                                 Leviney x Anderson
WITNESSES TO MARK: his mark
{ Dan Bryant   Robert x King
  D. Thomas   mark

Subscribed and sworn to before me this 8 *day of* April , 1905.

                                                Sam T Roberts Jr
                                                   NOTARY PUBLIC.

(The affidavit below typed as given.)

United States of America)
Central District Ind Ter.   )

          Charles Billy being first Sworn deposes and says. My name is Charles Billy,I am Thirty nine years old,reside near Talihina, that I am no relation to either Adaline Johnson Daney,deceased, or her husband Solomon Daney.I futher certify that I know that there was born to Adaline Johnson Daney and her husband Solomon Daney A FEMALE child on Novemember 16th 1903 and that said child was named Allie Daney and that said child was living on the 4th day of March 1905 and is alive today.I futher know that said Adaline Johnson Daney was her Mother.That I am of no relation or have any interest in the prosecution of this claim.

                                                 Charles Billy

Subscribed and sworn to before me this 22nd day June 1905.

My commission expires March 30th 1905.   Jno J Thomas

Applications for Enrollment of Choctaw Newborn
Act of 1905   Volume XII

(The affidavit below typed as given.)

United States of America) ss.
Central District, Ind Ter.   )

    H D Anderson being duly sworn deposes and says.My name is H D Anderson,age Foxty six,my Post Office is Talihina I T.I am acquainted with Solomon Daney and also was acquainted with his deceased wife,Adaline Johnson Daney,and know that there was born to them to November 16th 1903,a Female child and that said child was named Allie Daney and that said child is now alive and was alive on March 4th 1905.

    I futher declare that I am not interested in this claim,nor concerned in it in any manner.

                H D Anderson

Subscribed and sworn to before me this the 10th July 1905.

                Jno J Thomas

My commission expires March 30th 1909.

                    7-NB-834.

         Muskogee, Indian Territory, May 29, 1905.

Solomon Daney,
   Talihina, Indian Territory.

Dear Sir:

    Referring to the application for the enrollment of your infant child, Allie Daney, it is noted from the affidavits heretofore filed in this office that the mother of the applicant is dead.

    In this event it will be necessary for you to file in this oocice[sic] the affidavits of two persons, who are disinterested and not related to the applicant, who have actual knowledge of the facts that the child was born, the date of her birth; that she was living on March 4, 1905, and that Adaline Daney was her mother.

              Respectfully,

                    Chairman.

Applications for Enrollment of Choctaw Newborn
Act of 1905   Volume XII

COMMISSIONERS:
TAMS BIXBY,
THOMAS B. NEEDLES,
C.R. BRECKINBRIDGE.

WM. O. BEALL
Secretary

DEPARTMENT OF THE INTERIOR,
COMMISSIONER TO THE FIVE CIVILIZED TRIBES.

$W^m O.B.$

REFER IN REPLY TO THE FOLLOWING:

7 NB 834.

ADDRESS ONLY THE
COMMISSION TO THE FIVE CIVILIZED TRIBES.

Muskogee, Indian Territory, June 29, 1905.

Solomon Daney,
    Talihina, Indian Territory.

Dear Sir:

    Receipt is hereby acknowledged of the affidavit of Charley Billy to the birth of Allie Daney, daughter of Solomon and Adaline Johnson Daney, November 16, 1903, and the same has been filed with our records in the matter of the enrollment of said child.

    The affidavit of H. D. Anderson which was also enclosed is herewith returned for the reason that he make affidavit of the birth of Adaline Daney, the mother of Allie Daney, instead of to the birth of the child. Before further consideration can be given the application for the enrollment of Allie Daney it will be necessary for you to forward an affidavit similar to that of Charley Billy already filed in this case.

                  Respectfully,

                              Tams Bixby
                                  Chairman.

NB 1-26

(The above letter was given again without letterhead.)

                                         7-NB-834

Muskogee, Indian Territory, July 14, 1905.

Soloman[sic] Daney,
    Talihina, Indian Territory.

Dear Sir:

    Receipt is hereby acknowledged of the affidavit of H. D. Anderson to the birth of Allie Daney, daughter of Solomon and Adaline Johnson Daney, November 16, 1903, and the same has been filed in the matter of the enrollment of said child.

Applications for Enrollment of Choctaw Newborn
Act of 1905   Volume XII

Respectfully,

Commissioner.

———————

Choctaw New
Born 834.

Muskogee, Oklahoma, July 20, 1909.

Subject:

Enrollment of
Allie Daney as a
Newborn Choctaw.

The Honorable,
　　The Secretary of the Interior,

Sir:

　　July 28, 1905, there was transmitted for the consideration of the Department copies of a schedule of new born citizens of the Choctaw Nation enrolled under the Act of Congress approved March 3, 1905, Numbers 1263 to 1480, inclusive, which were approved by the Secretary of the Interior August 22, 1905.

　　In this letter Allie Daney at Number 1365 upon said schedule, was identified as the daughter of Adeline Daney, enrolled as Adeline Johnson, Choctaw by blood roll number 3795.

　　I now have the honor to report that it has subsequently developed that the said Allie Daney is the child of Adeline Daney, enrolled as Adeline Johnson, Choctaw by blood roll number 6207, and the records of this office have been corrected in accordance with this information.

　　This identification does not appear upon the roll proper and I have the honor to recommend that the entry under "Remarks". in office letter of July 28, 1905, be corrected to show that Adeline Johnson, Choctaw Roll Number 6207 is the mother of Adeline[sic] Daney, approved roll of new born Choctaw Number 1365.

Respectfully,

Commissioner.

AB
Through the Commissioner
　　of Indian Affairs.

Applications for Enrollment of Choctaw Newborn
Act of 1905   Volume XII

Choc New Born 835
      Arthur Lee Daney   b. 7-9-04

7-6198   7-6199
BIRTH AFFIDAVIT.

DEPARTMENT OF THE INTERIOR.
COMMISSION TO THE FIVE CIVILIZED TRIBES.

IN RE APPLICATION FOR ENROLLMENT, as a citizen of the Choctaw Nation, of Arthur Lee Daney, born on the 9th day of July, 1904

Name of Father: Daniel Daney   a citizen of the Choctaw Nation.
Name of Mother: Rebecca Daney   a citizen of the Choctaw Nation.

          Postoffice   Talihina, Ind. Ter.

AFFIDAVIT OF MOTHER.

UNITED STATES OF AMERICA, Indian Territory,
   Central   DISTRICT.

    I, Rebecca Daney, on oath state that I am 28 years of age and a citizen by blood, of the Choctaw Nation; that I am the lawful wife of Daniel Daney, who is a citizen, by blood of the Choctaw Nation; that a male child was born to me on 9th day of July, 1904; that said child has been named Arthur Lee Daney, and was living March 4, 1905.

                                  her
                        Rebecca x Daney
Witnesses To Mark: mark
  Daniel Daney
  Chas T. Difendafer

    Subscribed and sworn to before me this 10th day of April, 1905

                            OL Johnson
                              Notary Public.

Applications for Enrollment of Choctaw Newborn
Act of 1905   Volume XII

AFFIDAVIT OF ATTENDING PHYSICIAN OR MID-WIFE.

UNITED STATES OF AMERICA, Indian Territory, }
    Central   DISTRICT.

I, Levina Anderson, a midwife, on oath state that I attended on Mrs. Rebecca Daney, wife of Daniel Daney on the 9th day of July, 1904; that there was born to her on said date a male child; that said child was living March 4, 1905, and is said to have been named Arthur Lee Daney

                      her
                      Levina x Anderson
Witnesses To Mark: mark
  { Daniel Daney
    Chas T. Difendafer

Subscribed and sworn to before me this 10th day of April, 1905

                      OL Johnson
                          Notary Public.

Choc New Born 836
    Wilkin Doctor b. 10-21-04

7-9350 - 19- 3856 freedman

BIRTH AFFIDAVIT.
DEPARTMENT OF THE INTERIOR.
COMMISSION TO THE FIVE CIVILIZED TRIBES.

IN RE APPLICATION FOR ENROLLMENT, as a citizen of the Choctaw Nation, of Wilkin Doctor, born on the 21 day of October, 1904

Name of Father: James Doctor   a citizen of the Chickasaw Nation.
Name of Mother: Levina Doctor   a citizen of the Choctaw Nation.

                Postoffice   Ti I.T.

Applications for Enrollment of Choctaw Newborn
Act of 1905   Volume XII

AFFIDAVIT OF MOTHER.

UNITED STATES OF AMERICA, Indian Territory, }
    Central   DISTRICT. }

I, Levina Doctor, on oath state that I am 25 years of age and a citizen by blood, of the Choctaw Nation; that I am the lawful wife of James Doctor, who is a citizen, by freedman of the Chickasaw Nation; that a male child was born to me on 21 day of October, 1904; that said child has been named Wilkin Doctor, and was living March 4, 1905.

                                    her
                             Levina x Doctor
Witnesses To Mark: mark
  { Chas T Difendafer
    OL Johnson

Subscribed and sworn to before me this 10 day of April, 1905

                            OL Johnson
                            Notary Public.

AFFIDAVIT OF ATTENDING PHYSICIAN OR MID-WIFE.

UNITED STATES OF AMERICA, Indian Territory, }
    Central   DISTRICT. }

I, Jincy Clay, a midwife, on oath state that I attended on Mrs. Levina Doctor, wife of James Doctor on the 21 day of October, 1904; that there was born to her on said date a male child; that said child was living March 4, 1905, and is said to have been named Wilkin Doctor

                                    her
                             Jincy x Clay
Witnesses To Mark: mark
  { Chas T Difendafer
    OL Johnson

Subscribed and sworn to before me this 10 day of April, 1905

                            OL Johnson
                            Notary Public.

Applications for Enrollment of Choctaw Newborn
Act of 1905   Volume XII

Choc New Born 837
    Cleo Inez Hammons   b. 1-17-04

7-NB-837.

Muskogee, Indian Territory, May 29, 1905.

John Hammons,
    Crowder, Indian Territory.

Dear Sir:

    There is enclosed herewith application for the enrollment of your infant child, Cleo Inez Hammons, born January 17, 1905, in which the seal of the Notary Public has been omitted from the physician's affidavit.

    Please have the Notary, before whom this affidavit was made, to attach his seal to the same and then return the application to this office.

Respectfully,

Chairman.

VR 29-10.

---

7 N.B. 837.

Muskogee, Indian Territory, June 7, 1905.

John Hammons,
    Crowder, Indian Territory.

Dear Sir:

    Receipt is hereby acknowledged of the application for the enrollment of Cleo Inez Hammons corrected by having the Notary Public affix his seal to the affidavit of the physician.

Respectfully,

Commissioner in Charge.

Applications for Enrollment of Choctaw Newborn
Act of 1905 Volume XII

7-NB-837

Muskogee, Indian Territory, July 23, 1905.

John Hammons,
    Crowder, Indian Territory.

Dear Sir:

There is inclosed you herewith an affidavit to be executed by W. P. Lewallen the physician in attendance upon your wife at the time of the birth of your infant child, Cleo Inez Hammons, born January 17, 1903[sic], in the matter of the enrollment of said child.

In the affidavits heretofore filed in this case, the affidavit of the mother, executed January 21, 1905, and April 6, 1905, the date of birth is given as January 17, 1904, while the affidavit of the physician, executed April 10, 1905, gives the date of birth as January 17, 1905.

The former date is apparently correct, and you are therefore requested to have the inclosed affidavit properly executed and return to this office immediately as no further action can be taken relative to the enrollment of your said child, until the evidence requested is supplied.

Respectfully,

LM 8/28

Commissioner.

7-NB-837

Muskogee, Indian Territory, August 8, 1905.

John Hammons,
    Crowder, Indian Territory.

Dear Sir:

Receipt is hereby acknowledged of the affidavit of W. P. Lewallen to the birth of Cleo Inez Hammons, daughter of John and Lizzie Hammons, January 17, 1904, and the same has been filed with the records of this office in the matter of the enrollment of said child.

Respectfully,

Commissioner.

Applications for Enrollment of Choctaw Newborn
Act of 1905 Volume XII

AFFIDAVIT OF ATTENDING PHYSICIAN OR MIDWIFE

UNITED STATES OF AMERICA
INDIAN TERRITORY
Western DISTRICT

I, W. P. Lewallen a Physician on oath state that I attended on Mrs. Lizzie Hammons wife of John W Hammons on the 17 day of January, 1904, that there was born to her on said date a Female child, that said child is now living, and is said to have been named Cleo Inez Hammons

W.P. Lewallen *M.D.*

Subscribed and sworn to before me this, the 21 day of January 1905

WITNESSETH: JD Browder   Notary Public.

Must be two witnesses who are citizens { Melvin Priddy
Jno OToole

We hereby certify that we are well acquainted with John W Hammons a Lizzie Hammons and know them to be reputable and of good standing in the community.

Melvin Priddy

Jno OToole

NEW-BORN AFFIDAVIT.

Number

...Choctaw Enrolling Commission...

IN THE MATTER OF THE APPLICATION FOR ENROLLMENT, as a citizen of the Choctaw Nation, of Cleo Inez Hammons

born on the 17 day of __January__ 1904

Name of father John W Hammons   a citizen of United States
Nation final enrollment No.
Name of mother Lizzie Hammons   a citizen of Choctaw
Nation final enrollment No. 13275

Postoffice   Crowder Ind Tery

Applications for Enrollment of Choctaw Newborn
Act of 1905 Volume XII

AFFIDAVIT OF MOTHER.

UNITED STATES OF AMERICA
INDIAN TERRITORY
Western DISTRICT

I Lizzie Hammons , on oath state that I am 21 years of age and a citizen by blood of the Choctaw Nation, and as such have been placed upon the final roll of the Choctaw Nation, by the Honorable Secretary of the Interior my final enrollment number being 13275 ; that I am the lawful wife of John W Hammons , who is a citizen of the United States Nation, and as such has been placed upon the final roll of said Nation by the Honorable Secretary of the Interior, his final enrollment number being .... and that a Female child was born to me on the 17 day of January 190 4; that said child has been named Cleo Inez Hammons , and is now living.

Lizzie Hammons

Witnesseth.

Must be two Witnesses who are Citizens. } Melvin Priddy

Jno OToole

Subscribed and sworn to before me this 21 day of Jan 190 5

JD Browder
Notary Public.

My commission expires: Dec 22-1907.

BIRTH AFFIDAVIT.

DEPARTMENT OF THE INTERIOR.
COMMISSION TO THE FIVE CIVILIZED TRIBES.

IN RE APPLICATION FOR ENROLLMENT, as a citizen of the Choctaw Nation, of Cleo Inez Hammons , born on the 17th day of January , 1904

Name of Father: John Hammons a citizen of the United States ~~Nation~~.
Name of Mother: Lizzie Hammons a citizen of the Choctaw Nation.

Postoffice Crowder, I.T.

AFFIDAVIT OF MOTHER.

UNITED STATES OF AMERICA, Indian Territory, }
Central DISTRICT.

I, Lizzie Hammons , on oath state that I am 21 years of age and a citizen by blood , of the Choctaw Nation; that I am the lawful wife of John Hammons , who is a citizen, ~~by~~ ——— of the United States ~~Nation~~; that a

Applications for Enrollment of Choctaw Newborn
Act of 1905   Volume XII

female   child was born to me on   17th   day of   January   , 1904; that said child has been named   Cleo Inez Hammons   , and was living March 4, 1905.

            Lizzie Hammons

Witnesses To Mark:
{

  Subscribed and sworn to before me this   8th   day of   April   , 1905

            W.H. Angell
              Notary Public.

AFFIDAVIT OF ATTENDING PHYSICIAN OR MID-WIFE.

UNITED STATES OF AMERICA, Indian Territory, }
 Western   DISTRICT.

  I,   W P Lewallen   , a physician   , on oath state that I attended on Mrs.   Lizzie Hammons   , wife of   John Hammons   on the   17th   day of Jany , 1905; that there was born to her on said date a   female   child; that said child was living March 4, 1905, and is said to have been named   Cleo Inez Hammons

            W.P. Lewallen M.D.

Witnesses To Mark:
{

  Subscribed and sworn to before me this   10th   day of   April   , 1905

            Milton Heistein
              Notary Public.

BIRTH AFFIDAVIT.   7-NB 837

DEPARTMENT OF THE INTERIOR.
COMMISSION TO THE FIVE CIVILIZED TRIBES.

  IN RE APPLICATION FOR ENROLLMENT, as a citizen of the   Choctaw   Nation, of   Cleo Inez Hammons   , born on the   17   day of   Jany   , 1904

Name of Father: John Hammons a citizen of the   U.S.   ~~Nation~~.
Name of Mother: Lizzie Hammons a citizen of the   Choctaw   Nation.

      Postoffice   Crowder

Applications for Enrollment of Choctaw Newborn
Act of 1905   Volume XII

AFFIDAVIT OF ATTENDING PHYSICIAN OR MID-WIFE.

UNITED STATES OF AMERICA, Indian Territory, }
    Central   DISTRICT. }

I, W.P. Lewallen, a physician, on oath state that I attended on Mrs. Lizzie Hammons, wife of John Hammons on the 17 day of Jany, 1904; that there was born to her on said date a female child; that said child was living March 4, 1905, and is said to have been named Cleo Inez Hammons

                              W.P. Lewallen M.D.

Witnesses To Mark:
  { Robt F Turner
    Jno OToole

Subscribed and sworn to before me this 4th day of Aug, 1905

                              Milton Heistein
                              Notary Public.

<u>Choc New Born 838</u>
      John Thomas Cartlidge b. 9-11-04

                                        7-4819

              Muskogee, Indian Territory, April 14, 1905.

Albert Cartledge[sic]:
    McAlester, Indian Territory.

Dear Sir:

Receipt is hereby acknowledged of the affidavits of Nancy Cartledge and George N. Fleming to the birth of John Thomas Cartledge son of Albert and Nancy Cartledge, September 11, 1904, and the same have been filed with our records as an application for the enrollment of said child.
                        Respectfully,

                                      Chairman.

Applications for Enrollment of Choctaw Newborn
Act of 1905   Volume XII

NEW-BORN AFFIDAVIT.

Number..........

...Choctaw Enrolling Commission...

IN THE MATTER OF THE APPLICATION FOR ENROLLMENT, as a citizen of the Choctaw Nation, of   John Thomas Cartlidge

born on the 11th day of __Sept__ 190 4

Name of father   Albert Cartlidge   ^ not a citizen of ....
~~Nation final enrollment No.~~ ....
Name of mother   Nancy Cartlidge   a citizen of   Choctaw
Nation final enrollment No. 13293

Postoffice   McAlester I.T.

AFFIDAVIT OF MOTHER.

UNITED STATES OF AMERICA
INDIAN TERRITORY
  Central   DISTRICT

I Nancy Cartlidge   , on oath state that I am 27 years of age and a citizen by blood of the Choctaw Nation, and as such have been placed upon the final roll of the Choctaw Nation, by the Honorable Secretary of the Interior my final enrollment number being   13293 ; that I am the lawful wife of Albert Cartlidge   , who is not a citizen of the Choctaw Nation, ~~and as such has been placed upon the final roll of said Nation by the Honorable Secretary of the Interior, his final enrollment number being~~ and that a Male child was born to me on the 11th day of   Sept   190 4; that said child has been named   John Thomas Cartlidge , and is now living.

                                    Nancy Cartlidge
Witnesseth.   her x mark

Must be two ⎱ James N Reed
Witnesses who ⎰
are Citizens.   JP Wright

Subscribed and sworn to before me this 23^d day of Jany   190 5

                              DW Hopkins
                                    Notary Public.

My commission expires: Dec 15" 1905

Applications for Enrollment of Choctaw Newborn
Act of 1905   Volume XII

AFFIDAVIT OF ATTENDING PHYSICIAN OR MIDWIFE

UNITED STATES OF AMERICA
INDIAN TERRITORY
  Central   DISTRICT

I,   Geo N Fleming   a   Physician   on oath state that I attended on Mrs. Nancy Cartlidge   wife of   Albert Cartlidge   on the   11th   day of   Sept   , 190 4, that there was born to her on said date a   Male   child, that said child is now living, and is said to have been named   John Thomas Cartlidge

                                                Geo N Fleming   *M.D.*

Subscribed and sworn to before me this, the   23   day of   Jany   190 5

WITNESSETH: DW Hopkins   Notary Public.
  Must be two witnesses   { James N Reed
  who are citizens   JP Wright

We hereby certify that we are well acquainted with   Albert Cartlidge   a   Nancy Cartlidge   and know   them   to be reputable and of good standing in the community.

  James N Reed   J P Wright

BIRTH AFFIDAVIT.

DEPARTMENT OF THE INTERIOR.
COMMISSION TO THE FIVE CIVILIZED TRIBES.

IN RE APPLICATION FOR ENROLLMENT, as a citizen of the   Choctaw   Nation, of   John Thomas Cartlidge   , born on the 11th   day of Sept   , 1904

Name of Father: Albert Cartlidge   a citizen of the United States ~~Nation~~.
Name of Mother: Nancy Cartlidge   a citizen of the   Choctaw   Nation.

Postoffice   McAlester Ind. Ter.

Applications for Enrollment of Choctaw Newborn
Act of 1905   Volume XII

AFFIDAVIT OF MOTHER.

UNITED STATES OF AMERICA, Indian Territory, }
    Central   DISTRICT.

I, Nancy Cartlidge, on oath state that I am 26 years of age and a citizen by blood, of the Choctaw Nation; that I am the lawful wife of Albert Cartlidge, who is a citizen, ~~by~~ .... of the United States ~~Nation~~; that a Male child was born to me on 11th day of September, 1904; that said child has been named John Thomas Cartlidge, and was living March 4, 1905.

                            Nancy Cartlidge
Witnesses To Mark: her x mark
  { Otto Siler
    J.V. Cochran

Subscribed and sworn to before me this 10th day of April, 1905

                            D.W. Hopkins
                                Notary Public.

AFFIDAVIT OF ATTENDING PHYSICIAN OR MID-WIFE.

UNITED STATES OF AMERICA, Indian Territory, }
    Central   DISTRICT.

I, Geo N Fleming, a Physician, on oath state that I attended on Mrs. Nancy Cartlidge, wife of Albert Cartlidge on the 11th day of September, 1904; that there was born to her on said date a Male child; that said child was living March 4, 1905, and is said to have been named John Thomas Cartlidge

                            Geo N Fleming M.D.
Witnesses To Mark:
  {

Subscribed and sworn to before me this 10th day of April, 1905

                            D.W. Hopkins
                                Notary Public.

Applications for Enrollment of Choctaw Newborn
Act of 1905   Volume XII

Choc New Born 839
    Amelia May Jones   b. 5-19-04

7-2189.

Muskogee, Indian Territory, April 13, 1905.

Enoch Needham,
    Hugo, Indian Territory.

Dear Sir:

    Receipt is hereby acknowledged of the affidavits of Lizzie Jones and Melinda Jones to the birth of Amelia May Jones, daughter of Ellis and Lizzie Jones, May 19, 1904, and the same have been filed with our records as an application for the enrollment of said child.

                  Respectfully,

                  Commissioner in Charge.

BIRTH AFFIDAVIT.

DEPARTMENT OF THE INTERIOR.
COMMISSION TO THE FIVE CIVILIZED TRIBES.

    IN RE APPLICATION FOR ENROLLMENT, as a citizen of the   Choctaw   Nation, of   Amelia May Jones   , born on the   19th   day of   May   , 1904

Name of Father: Ellis Jones   a citizen of the   Choctaw   Nation.
                          Smallwood
Name of Mother: Lizzie Jones nee Lizzie   a citizen of the   Choctaw   Nation.

                Postoffice   Bennington I.T.

AFFIDAVIT OF MOTHER.

UNITED STATES OF AMERICA, Indian Territory,
    Central   **DISTRICT.**

    I,   Lizzie Jones   , on oath state that I am   24   years of age and a citizen by Blood   , of the   Choctaw   Nation; that I am the lawful wife of   Ellis Jones   , who is a citizen, by Blood   of the   Choctaw   Nation; that a   Female   child was born to me on   the 19th   day of   May   , 1904; that said child has been named Amelia May Jones   , and was living March 4, 1905.

Applications for Enrollment of Choctaw Newborn
Act of 1905   Volume XII

Lizzie Jones

Witnesses To Mark:
{

Subscribed and sworn to before me this 8th day of April , 1905

CC McClard
Notary Public.

AFFIDAVIT OF ATTENDING PHYSICIAN OR MID-WIFE.

UNITED STATES OF AMERICA, Indian Territory, }
Central   DISTRICT. }

I, Melinda Jones , a midwife , on oath state that I attended on Mrs. Lizzie Jones , wife of Ellis Jones on the 19th day of May , 1904; that there was born to her on said date a Female child; that said child was living March 4, 1905, and is said to have been named Amelia May Jones

her
Melinda x Jones
mark

Witnesses To Mark:
{ Mattie McKinney
{ *(Name Illegible)*

Subscribed and sworn to before me this 8th day of April , 1905

C.C. McClard
Notary Public.

New-Born Affidavit

Number..................

Choctaw Enrolling Commission.

IN THE MATTER OF THE APPLICATION FOR ENROLLMENT, as a citizen of the Choctaw Nation, of Amelia Mae[sic] Jones

born on the 19th day of May 190 4

Name of father Ellis Jones   a citizen of   Choctaw
Nation final enrollment No 10381
Name of mother   Lizzie Jones   a citizen of   Choctaw
Nation final enrollment No 13588

Postoffice   Bennington I.T.

Applications for Enrollment of Choctaw Newborn
Act of 1905   Volume XII

AFFIDAVIT OF MOTHER.

UNITED STATES OF AMERICA,
    INDIAN TERRITORY,
Central   DISTRICT

I   Lizzie Jones (nee Smallwood)   on oath state that I am   24   years of age and a citizen by   blood   of the   Choctaw   Nation, and as such have been placed upon the final roll of the   Choctaw   Nation, by the Honorable Secretary of the Interior my final enrollment number being   13588   ; that I am the lawful wife of   Ellis Jones   , who is a citizen of the   Choctaw   Nation, and as such has been placed upon the final roll of said Nation by the Honorable Secretary of the Interior, his final enrollment number being   10381   and that a   Female   child was born to me on the   19th day of   May   190 4 ; that said child has been named   Amelia Mae Jones   , and is now living.

Lizzie Jones

WITNESSETH:
    Must be two Witnesses who are Citizens.   David Gude
    J.N. Jones

Subscribed and sworn to before me this   31   day of   Jan   190 5

BW Williams
Notary Public.

My commission expires   Oct 16th 1907

Affidavit of Attending Physician or Midwife.

UNITED STATES OF AMERICA
INDIAN TERRITORY
Central   DISTRICT

I,   Malinda Jones   a   Midwife   on oath state that I attended on Mrs.   Lizzie Smallwood "nee" Jones   wife of   Ellis Jones   on the   19th day of   May   , 190 4 , that there was born to her on said date a   Female   child, that said child is now living, and is said to have been named   Amelia Mae Jones

Witness to mark
David Gude

                    her
Malinda Jones x   M.D.
                    mark

Subscribed and sworn to before me this, the   31   day of   Jan   190 5

B.W. Williams
Notary Public.

Applications for Enrollment of Choctaw Newborn
Act of 1905   Volume XII

WITNESSETH:

Must be two witnesses who are citizens and know the child.
{ David Gude
J.N. Jones

We hereby certify that we are well acquainted with Malinda Jones a Midwife and know her to be reputable and of good standing in the community.

{ David Gude
J N Jones

Choc New Born 840
    Helen Needham   b. 4-7-03
    Herbert Enoch Needham   b. 1-26-05

7-2189

Muskogee, Indian Territory, April 14, 1905.

Enoch Needham,
    Hugo, Indian Territory.

Dear Sir:

Receipt is hereby acknowledged of the affidavits of Nettie H. Needham and G. B. Green to the birth of Helen Needham daughter of Enoch and Nettie H. Needham, April 7, 1903; also affidavits of Nettie H. Needham and H. H. White to the birth of Herbert Enoch Needham, son of Enoch and Nettie H. Needham, January 26, 1905, and the same have been filed with our records as applications for the enrollment of said children.

Respectfully,

Chairman.

Applications for Enrollment of Choctaw Newborn
Act of 1905   Volume XII

NEW-BORN AFFIDAVIT.

Number..................

Choctaw Enrolling Commission.

IN THE MATTER OF THE APPLICATION FOR ENROLLMENT, as a citizen of the Choctaw   Nation, of   Helen Needham

born on the   7   day of   April   190 3

Name of father   Enoch Needham   a citizen of   Choctaw
Nation final enrollment No   B 767
Name of mother   Nettie H Needham   a citizen of   Choctaw
Nation final enrollment No   6340

Postoffice   Hugo I.T.

AFFIDAVIT OF MOTHER.

UNITED STATES OF AMERICA,
INDIAN TERRITORY,
Central   DISTRICT

I   Nettie H Needham   on oath state that I am   24   years of age and a citizen by   Blood   of the   Choctaw   Nation, and as such have been placed upon the final roll of the   Choctaw   Nation, by the Honorable Secretary of the Interior my final enrollment number being   6340   ; that I am the lawful wife of   Enoch Needham   , who is a citizen of the   Choctaw   Nation, and as such has been placed upon the final roll of said Nation by the Honorable Secretary of the Interior, his final enrollment number being .... and that a   female   child was born to me on the   7   day of   April   190 3 ; that said child has been named   Helen Needham   , and is now living.

Nettie H Needham

WITNESSETH:
Must be two Witnesses who are Citizens.   Jno McIntosh
J N Leard

Subscribed and sworn to before me this   2nd   day of   March   190 5

J.P. Ward
Notary Public.

My commission expires   April 28/08

Applications for Enrollment of Choctaw Newborn
Act of 1905 Volume XII

Affidavit of Attending Physician or Midwife

UNITED STATES OF AMERICA,
INDIAN TERRITORY,
Central   DISTRICT

I,   Martha J McMurtry   a   Midwife
on oath state that I attended on Mrs. Nettie H Needham   wife of   Enoch Needham
on the 7   day of   April , 190 3, that there was born to her on said date a   Female   child, that said child is now living, and is said to have been named   Helen Needham

                                              Martha J McMurtry   M. D.

Subscribed and sworn to before me this the   2nd day of   March   1905

                                             J.P. Ward
                                                           Notary Public.

WITNESSETH:
Must be two witnesses who are citizens and know the child.
{ Jno McIntosh
  J.N. Leard

We hereby certify that we are well acquainted with   Martha J McMurtry   a   midwife   and know   her   to be reputable and of good standing in the community.

                                 Must be two citizen witnesses. { Jno McIntosh
                                                                               J.N. Leard

BIRTH AFFIDAVIT.

DEPARTMENT OF THE INTERIOR.
COMMISSION TO THE FIVE CIVILIZED TRIBES.

IN RE APPLICATION FOR ENROLLMENT, as a citizen of the   Choctaw   Nation, of   Helen Needham   , born on the 7   day of   April , 1903

Name of Father: Enoch Needham   a citizen of the   Choctaw   Nation.
Name of Mother: Nettie H Needham   a citizen of the   Choctaw   Nation.

                                       Postoffice   Hugo I.T.

Applications for Enrollment of Choctaw Newborn
Act of 1905 Volume XII

AFFIDAVIT OF MOTHER.

UNITED STATES OF AMERICA, Indian Territory,
....DISTRICT.

I, Nettie H Needham , on oath state that I am 24 years of age and a citizen by Blood , of the Choctaw Nation; that I am the lawful wife of Enoch Needham , who is a citizen, by Blood of the Choctaw Nation; that a Female child was born to me on 7" day of April , 1903; that said child has been named Helen Needham , and was living March 4, 1905.

Nettie H Needham

Witnesses To Mark:

Subscribed and sworn to before me this 5th day of April , 1905

J.P. Ward
Notary Public.

AFFIDAVIT OF ATTENDING PHYSICIAN OR MID-WIFE.

UNITED STATES OF AMERICA, Indian Territory,
Central DISTRICT.

I, G. B. Green , a Physician , on oath state that I attended on Mrs. Nettie H Needham , wife of Enoch Needham on the 7 day of April, 1903; that there was born to her on said date a Female child; that said child was living March 4, 1905, and is said to have been named Helen Needham

G.B. Green MD

Witnesses To Mark:

Subscribed and sworn to before me this 5th day of April , 1905

J.P. Ward
Notary Public.

Applications for Enrollment of Choctaw Newborn
Act of 1905 Volume XII

NEW-BORN AFFIDAVIT.

Number............

Choctaw Enrolling Commission.

IN THE MATTER OF THE APPLICATION FOR ENROLLMENT, as a citizen of the Choctaw Nation, of Herbert Enoch Needham

born on the 26 day of January 1905

Name of father   Enoch Needham   a citizen of   Choctaw
Nation final enrollment No............
Name of mother   Nettie H Needham   a citizen of   Choctaw
Nation final enrollment No   6340

Postoffice   Hugo I.T.

AFFIDAVIT OF MOTHER.

UNITED STATES OF AMERICA,
    INDIAN TERRITORY,
    Central   DISTRICT

I   Nettie H Needham   on oath state that I am 24 years of age and a citizen by Blood of the Choctaw Nation, and as such have been placed upon the final roll of the Choctaw Nation, by the Honorable Secretary of the Interior my final enrollment number being 6340 ; that I am the lawful wife of Enoch Needham , who is a citizen of the Choctaw Nation, and as such has been placed upon the final roll of said Nation by the Honorable Secretary of the Interior, his final enrollment number being .... and that a male child was born to me on the 26 day of January 1905 ; that said child has been named Herbert Enoch Needham , and is now living.

Nettie H Needham

WITNESSETH:
Must be two Witnesses who are Citizens.   Jno McIntosh
   J N Leard

Subscribed and sworn to before me this   2nd   day of   March   1905

J.P. Ward
Notary Public.

My commission expires   April 28/08

Applications for Enrollment of Choctaw Newborn
Act of 1905   Volume XII

Affidavit of Attending Physician or Midwife

UNITED STATES OF AMERICA,
INDIAN TERRITORY,
Central   DISTRICT

I, H. H. White   a   Physician on oath state that I attended on Mrs. Nettie H Needham   wife of   Enoch Needham   on the   26   day of   January , 190 5, that there was born to her on said date a   Male child, that said child is now living, and is said to have been named   Herbert Enoch Needham

H.H. White   M. D.

Subscribed and sworn to before me this the   2nd day of   March   1905

J.P. Ward
Notary Public.

WITNESSETH:
Must be two witnesses who are citizens and know the child.
{ Jno McIntosh
  J.N. Leard

We hereby certify that we are well acquainted with   H. H. White a   practicing physician   and know   him   to be reputable and of good standing in the community.

Must be two citizen witnesses.
{ Jno McIntosh
  J.N. Leard

BIRTH AFFIDAVIT.

DEPARTMENT OF THE INTERIOR.
COMMISSION TO THE FIVE CIVILIZED TRIBES.

IN RE APPLICATION FOR ENROLLMENT, as a citizen of the   Choctaw   Nation, of Herbert Enoch Needham   , born on the 26   day of   Jan , 1905

Name of Father: Enoch Needham   a citizen of the   Choctaw   Nation.
Name of Mother: Nettie H Needham   a citizen of the   Choctaw   Nation.

Postoffice   Hugo I.T.

Applications for Enrollment of Choctaw Newborn
Act of 1905   Volume XII

AFFIDAVIT OF MOTHER.

UNITED STATES OF AMERICA, Indian Territory, }
....DISTRICT. }

I, Nettie H Needham, on oath state that I am 24 years of age and a citizen by Blood, of the Choctaw Nation; that I am the lawful wife of Enoch Needham, who is a citizen, by Blood of the Choctaw Nation; that a Male child was born to me on 26 day of Jan, 1905; that said child has been named Herbert Enoch Needham, and was living March 4, 1905.

Nettie H Needham

Witnesses To Mark:
{

Subscribed and sworn to before me this 5th day of April, 1905

J.P. Ward
Notary Public.

AFFIDAVIT OF ATTENDING PHYSICIAN OR MID-WIFE.

UNITED STATES OF AMERICA, Indian Territory, }
Central   DISTRICT. }

I, H. H. White, a Physician, on oath state that I attended on Mrs. Nettie H Needham, wife of Enoch Needham on the 26 day of Jan, 1905; that there was born to her on said date a male child; that said child was living March 4, 1905, and is said to have been named Herbert Enoch Needham

H.H. White

Witnesses To Mark:
{

Subscribed and sworn to before me this 6th day of April, 1905

J.P. Ward
Notary Public.

Applications for Enrollment of Choctaw Newborn
Act of 1905   Volume XII

Choc New Born 841
   Rossie Glover Folsom   b. 5-19-04

7-288

Muskogee, Indian Territory, April 14, 1905.

Frank Folsom,
   Garland, Indian Territory.

Dear Sir:

   Receipt is hereby acknowledged of the affidavits of Charlotte Folsom and George W. St Clair to the birth of Rassie[sic] Glover Folsom, son of Frank and Charlotte Folsom, May 19, 1904, and the same have been filed with our records as an application for the enrollment of said child.

   Respectfully,

   Commissioner in Charge.

$W^m O.B.$

COMMISSIONERS:
TAMS BIXBY,
THOMAS B. NEEDLES,
C.R. BRECKINBRIDGE.

WM. O. BEALL
   Secretary

**DEPARTMENT OF THE INTERIOR,
COMMISSIONER TO THE FIVE CIVILIZED TRIBES.**

REFER IN REPLY TO THE FOLLOWING:

7-NB-841.

ADDRESS ONLY THE
COMMISSION TO THE FIVE CIVILIZED TRIBES.

Muskogee, Indian Territory, May 29, 1905.

Frank Folsom,
   Garland, Indian Territory.

Dear Sir:

   There is enclosed you herewith for execution application for the enrollment of your infant child.

   In the affidavits of January 12, 1905, heretofore filed in this office, the name of the applicant is given as Rossie Glover Folsom and the date of his birth as May 29, 1904, while in the affidavits of the 8th ultimo the name appears as Rassie Glover Folsom and the date of his birth as May 19, 1904. In the enclosed application the name of the applicant and the date of his birth are left blank. Please insert the correct name and date and, when the affidavits are properly executed, return them to this office.

Applications for Enrollment of Choctaw Newborn
Act of 1905 Volume XII

In having these affidavits executed care should be exercised to see that all names are written in full, as they appear in the body of the affidavit, and in the event that either of the persons signing the affidavit are unable to write, signatures by mark must be attested by two witnesses. Each affidavit must be executed before a Notary Public and the notarial seal and signature of the officer must be attached to each separate affidavit.

Respectfully,
Tams Bixby
Chairman.

VR 29-12.

7 N.B. 841.

Muskogee, Indian Territory, June 5, 1905.

Frank Folsom,
    Garland, Indian Territory.

Dear Sir:

Receipt is hereby acknowledged of the affidavits of Charlotte Folsom and G. W. St. Clair to the birth of Rossie Glover Folsom, son of Frank and Charlotte Folsom, May 19, 1904, and the same have been filed with our records in the matter of the enrollment of said child.

Respectfully,

Commissioner in Charge.

NEW-BORN AFFIDAVIT.

Number............

...Choctaw Enrolling Commission...

IN THE MATTER OF THE APPLICATION FOR ENROLLMENT, as a citizen of the Choctaw Nation, of Rossie Glover Folsom

born on the 29th day of __May__ 190 4

Name of father Frank Folsom   a citizen of   Choctaw
Nation final enrollment No. 13671
Name of mother Charlotte Folsom   a citizen of   Choctaw
Nation final enrollment No. 608

                                                    Postoffice   Garland

Applications for Enrollment of Choctaw Newborn
Act of 1905   Volume XII

AFFIDAVIT OF MOTHER.

UNITED STATES OF AMERICA
INDIAN TERRITORY
Central   DISTRICT

I   Charlotte Folsom   , on oath state that I am 32 years of age and a citizen by blood of the Choctaw Nation, and as such have been placed upon the final roll of the Choctaw Nation, by the Honorable Secretary of the Interior my final enrollment number being 608 ; that I am the lawful wife of Frank Folsom , who is a citizen of the Choctaw Nation, and as such has been placed upon the final roll of said Nation by the Honorable Secretary of the Interior, his final enrollment number being 13671 and that a male child was born to me on the 29th day of May 190 4; that said child has been named Rossie Glover Folsom , and is now living.

Charlotte Folsom

Witnesseth.
Must be two Witnesses who are Citizens.   *(Name Illegible)*
(Name Illegible)

Subscribed and sworn to before me this 12 day of Jan 190 5

C C Jones
Notary Public.

My commission expires: March 3^d 1907

AFFIDAVIT OF ATTENDING PHYSICIAN OR MIDWIFE

UNITED STATES OF AMERICA
INDIAN TERRITORY
Central   DISTRICT

I,   Dr. St. Clair   a   Physician on oath state that I attended on Mrs. Charlotte Folsom wife of Frank Folsom on the 29th day of May , 190 4 , that there was born to her on said date a male child, that said child is now living, and is said to have been named Rossie Glover Folsom

Dr Geo W. St. Clair

Subscribed and sworn to before me this, the   12   day of Jan   190 5

WITNESSETH:
Must be two witnesses who are citizens   J.S. Styles
Henry Cooper

C C Jones   Notary Public.

Applications for Enrollment of Choctaw Newborn
Act of 1905   Volume XII

We hereby certify that we are well acquainted with Geo W St. Clair a Physican[sic] and know him to be reputable and of good standing in the community.

Frank Garland _____

Ward Garland Jr _____

BIRTH AFFIDAVIT.

DEPARTMENT OF THE INTERIOR.
COMMISSION TO THE FIVE CIVILIZED TRIBES.

IN RE APPLICATION FOR ENROLLMENT, as a citizen of the Choctaw Nation, of Rassie[sic] Glover Folsom, born on the 19th day of May, 1904

Name of Father: Frank Folsom a citizen of the Choctaw Nation.
Name of Mother: Charlotte Folsom a citizen of the Choctaw Nation.

Postoffice Garland I.T.

AFFIDAVIT OF MOTHER.

UNITED STATES OF AMERICA, Indian Territory, }
Central DISTRICT. }

I, Charlotte Folsom, on oath state that I am 32 years of age and a citizen by Blood, of the Choctaw Nation; that I am the lawful wife of Frank Folsom, who is a citizen, by Blood of the Choctaw Nation; that a male child was born to me on 19th day of May, 1904; that said child has been named Rassie Glover Folsom, and was living March 4, 1905.

Charlotte Folsom

Witnesses To Mark:
{

Subscribed and sworn to before me this 8 day of April, 1905

C.C. Jones
Notary Public.

Applications for Enrollment of Choctaw Newborn
Act of 1905   Volume XII

AFFIDAVIT OF ATTENDING PHYSICIAN OR MID-WIFE.

UNITED STATES OF AMERICA, Indian Territory, }
Central   DISTRICT.

I, ..., a   Physician   , on oath state that I attended on Mrs.   Charlotte Folsom   , wife of   Frank Folsom   on the 19th day of   May , 1905; that there was born to her on said date a .... child; that said child was living March 4, 1905, and is said to have been named Rassie Glover Folsom

Dr Geo W. St Clair

Witnesses To Mark:
{

Subscribed and sworn to before me this 8   day of   April   , 1905

C.C. Jones
Notary Public.

BIRTH AFFIDAVIT.

DEPARTMENT OF THE INTERIOR.
COMMISSION TO THE FIVE CIVILIZED TRIBES.

IN RE APPLICATION FOR ENROLLMENT, as a citizen of the   Choctaw   Nation, of Rossie Glover Folsom   , born on the 19   day of   May , 1904

Name of Father: Frank Folsom   a citizen of the   Choctaw   Nation.
Name of Mother: Charlotte Folsom   a citizen of the   Choctaw   Nation.

Postoffice   Garland Ind. Ter.

AFFIDAVIT OF MOTHER.

UNITED STATES OF AMERICA, Indian Territory, }
Central   DISTRICT.

I,   Charlotte Folsom   , on oath state that I am   32   years of age and a citizen by   blood   , of the   Choctaw   Nation; that I am the lawful wife of Frank Folsom   , who is a citizen, by blood   of the   Choctaw   Nation; that a   male   child was born to me on   19th day of   May   , 1904; that said child has been named   Rossie Glover Folsom   , and was living March 4, 1905.

Charlotte Folsom

Witnesses To Mark:
{

Applications for Enrollment of Choctaw Newborn
Act of 1905   Volume XII

Subscribed and sworn to before me this 1ˢᵗ day of   June   , 1905

C.C. Jones
Notary Public.

AFFIDAVIT OF ATTENDING PHYSICIAN OR MID-WIFE.

UNITED STATES OF AMERICA, Indian Territory, }
Central   DISTRICT. }

I,   G. W. St Clair   , a   Physician   , on oath state that I attended on Mrs.   Charlotte Folsom   , wife of   Frank Folsom   on the 19ᵗʰ day of   May , 1905; that there was born to her on said date a .... child; that said child was living March 4, 1905, and is said to have been named Rossie Glover Folsom

G. W. St Clair Md

Witnesses To Mark:
{

Subscribed and sworn to before me this 1ˢᵗ day of   June   , 1905

C.C. Jones
Notary Public.

Choc New Born 842
    Nellie McCurtain Ridgeway
                      b. 10-26-02

7-4145

Muskogee, Indian Territory, April 14, 1905.

Sarah E. Ridgeway,
    Provence, Indian Territory.

Dear Madam:

    Receipt is hereby acknowledged of your letter of April 8, 1905, enclosing affidavits of Sarah E. Ridgeway and W. H. Campbell to the birth of Nellie McCurtain Ridgeway, daughter of George W. and Sarah E. Ridgeway, October 26, 1902, and the same have been filed with our records as an application for the enrollment of said child.

Applications for Enrollment of Choctaw Newborn
Act of 1905   Volume XII

Respectfully,

Commissioner in Charge.

BIRTH AFFIDAVIT.

DEPARTMENT OF THE INTERIOR.
COMMISSION TO THE FIVE CIVILIZED TRIBES.

IN RE APPLICATION FOR ENROLLMENT, as a citizen of the Choctaw Nation, of Nellie McCurtain Ridgeway, born on the 26 day of Oct, 1902

Name of Father: George W. Ridgeway   *Intermarried* a citizen of the Choctaw Nation.
Name of Mother: Sarah E Ridgeway   a citizen of the Choctaw Nation.

Postoffice   Provence I T

AFFIDAVIT OF MOTHER.

UNITED STATES OF AMERICA, Indian Territory,
Southern   DISTRICT.

I, Sarah E. Ridgeway, on oath state that I am 32 years of age and a citizen by Birth, of the Choctaw Nation; that I am the lawful wife of George W Ridgeway, who is a citizen, by Intermarriage of the Choctaw Nation; that a female child was born to me on 26 day of Oct, 1902; that said child has been named Nellie McCurtain Ridgeway, and was living March 4, 1905.

                        her
                Sarah E x Ridgeway
Witnesses To Mark: mark
  { W.H. Campbell
    James Walls

Subscribed and sworn to before me this 5 day of April, 1905

                W W Winans
                      Notary Public.

Applications for Enrollment of Choctaw Newborn
Act of 1905   Volume XII

AFFIDAVIT OF ATTENDING PHYSICIAN OR MID-WIFE.

UNITED STATES OF AMERICA, Indian Territory,
Southern   DISTRICT.

I, W.H. Campbell , a Practicing Physician , on oath state that I attended on Mrs. Sarah E Ridgeway , wife of George W Ridgeway on the 26 day of Oct , 1902; that there was born to her on said date a female child; that said child was living March 4, 1905, and is said to have been named Nellie McCurtain Ridgeway

W.H. Campbell

Witnesses To Mark:
{

Subscribed and sworn to before me this 5 day of April , 1905

W W Winans
Notary Public.

Choc New Born 843
    Clarice Maurine Brown b. 7-5-04

7-4145

Muskogee, Indian Territory, April 14, 1905.

William T. Brown,
    Kingston, Indian Territory.

Dear Sir:

Receipt is hereby acknowledged of your letter of April 10, 1905, enclosing affidavits of Susie Brown and E. A. Jones, to the birth of Clarice Morine[sic] Brown; also a certified copy of your marriage license and certificate to Susie Brooks and the same have been filed with our records in the matter of the enrollment of the above named child.

Respectfully,

Commissioner in Charge.

Applications for Enrollment of Choctaw Newborn
Act of 1905   Volume XII

7-4145

Muskogee, Indian Territory, April 15, 1905.

Susie Brown,
    Kingston, Indian Territory.

Dear Madam:

Receipt is hereby acknowledged of your letter of April 5, 1905, in which you state that you forwarded affidavits to Crawford & Bolin at Ada, Indian Territory, relative to the enrollment of your child, Clarice Morine Brown. You state that your maiden name was Brooks, and ask that if your child has not yet been enrolled that the necessary affidavits be sent you, and if she has been enrolled, you request a plat of the unallotted land in Township Seven (7) South Range, Six (6) East, in order that you may file on her allotment near your home.

In reply to your letter you are informed that your affidavit and the affidavit of E. A. Jones to the birth of your daughter, Clarice Morine Brown, has been filed with our records as an application for the enrollment of said child.

Relative to the selection of allotment for your child, you are advised that no reservation of land can be made or allotment selected for children for whom application has been made under the provisions of the act of Congress approved March 3, 1905, until their enrollment has been approved by the Secretary of the Interior.

As there are two persons on our records as applicants for enrollment as citizens of the Choctaw Nation by the name of Susie Brooks you are requested to state the names of your parents and if you have selected an allotment of the lands of the Choctaw or Chickasaw Nation give your roll number as the same appears upon your allotment certificate. it appears upon your allotment certificate.

        Respectfully,

                Chairman.

Applications for Enrollment of Choctaw Newborn
Act of 1905 Volume XII

7-4145

Muskogee, Indian Territory, May 5, 1905.

Susie Brown,
    Care of W. T. Brown,
        Kingston, Indian Territory.

Dear Madam:

    Receipt is hereby acknowledged of your letter of April 30, 1905, relative to the application for the enrollment of your child.

    In reply to your letter you are advised that the affidavits heretofore forwarded to the birth of Clarice Morine Brown child of W. T. and Susie Brown have been filed with our records as an application for the enrollment of said child.

                Respectfully,

                            [sic]

STATE OF TEXAS
MARRIAGE LICENSE
COUNTY OF GRAYSON

To any Judge of the District Court, Judge of the County Court, Ordained or Licensed Minister Jewish Rabbi or Justice of the Peace of Grayson County

GREETING:
YOU ARE HEREBY AUTHORIZED TO CELEBRATE THE
RITES OF MATRIMONY

Between   William T Brown
and   Miss Susie Brooks
and make due return to the Clerk of said Court within Sixty days thereafter certifying your action under this License,

Applications for Enrollment of Choctaw Newborn
Act of 1905 Volume XII

WITNESS my official signature and seal this 30th day of October 190 3

P F Ellis Clerk

By _____ Deputy

I A Minister certify that on the
4 day of Nov 190 3 I united in Marriage
Mr William T Brown and
Miss Susie Brooks the parties above named
Witness my hand this 5 day of Nov 190 3

J T Means
Woodville I.T.

Returned and filed for record the _____ day of _____ 190__
and recorded the _____ day of _____ 190__

_____ Deputy _____ County Clerk

The State of Texas:
County of Grayson: I, W. E. Baird Clerk of the County Court of Grayson County, Texas, do hereby certify that the above and foregoing is a true and correct copy of the original Marriage license issued to William T. Brown and Susie Brooks, together with the return thereof, as the same appears of record in my office in Book S.
Given under my hand and seal of office this 8" day of April 1905.

W. E. Baird, Clerk.
By *(Name Illegible)* Deputy.

BIRTH AFFIDAVIT. *#83*

IN RE-APPLICATION FOR ENROLLMENT, as a citizen of the Choctaw Nation, of Clarice Morine Brown , born on the 5th day of July , 190 4

Name of Father: Wm T. Brown a citizen of the Choctaw Nation.
Name of Mother: Susie Brown a citizen of the Choctaw Nation.

Postoffice Woodville, Ind. Ter.

Applications for Enrollment of Choctaw Newborn
Act of 1905   Volume XII

AFFIDAVIT OF MOTHER.

UNITED STATES OF AMERICA, INDIAN TERRITORY, }
Southern   District. }

I,   Susie Brown (nee Susie Brooks) , on oath state that I am   20   years of age and a citizen by   blood   , of the   Choctaw   Nation; that I am the lawful wife of   Wm T. Brown   , who is a citizen, by   marriage   of the   Choctaw   Nation; that a   female child was born to me on   the 5th   day of   July   , 1904 , that said child has been named Clarice Morine Brown   , and is now living.

Susie Brown (nee Brooks)

Witnesses To Mark:
{

Subscribed and sworn to before me this   22nd   day of   February   , 1905.

Robert St Bell
Notary Public.

AFFIDAVIT OF ATTENDING PHYSICIAN OR MID-WIFE.

UNITED STATES OF AMERICA, INDIAN TERRITORY, }
....   District. }

I,   E A Jones   , a   Physician   , on oath state that I attended on Mrs.   Susie Brown   , wife of   W.T. Brown   on the   5th day of   July   , 190 4; that there was born to her on said date a   Female   child; that said child is now living and is said to have been named   Clarice Morine Brown

E A Jones M.D.

Witnesses To Mark:
{

Subscribed and sworn to before me this   22nd   day of   February   , 1905.

Robert St Bell
Notary Public.

Applications for Enrollment of Choctaw Newborn
Act of 1905 Volume XII

BIRTH AFFIDAVIT.

DEPARTMENT OF THE INTERIOR.
COMMISSION TO THE FIVE CIVILIZED TRIBES.

IN RE APPLICATION FOR ENROLLMENT, as a citizen of the Choctaw Nation, of Clarice Maurine Brown, born on the 5th day of July, 1904

Name of Father: W. T. Brown a citizen of the .... Nation.
Name of Mother: Susie Brown (nee Brooks) a citizen of the Choctaw Nation.

Postoffice Kingston, I.T.

AFFIDAVIT OF MOTHER.

UNITED STATES OF AMERICA, Indian Territory,
Southern DISTRICT.

I, Susie Brooks, on oath state that I am 20 years of age and a citizen by blood, of the Choctaw Nation; that I am the lawful wife of W.T. Brown, who is a citizen, by intermarriage of the Choctaw Nation; that a female child was born to me on 5th day of July, 1904; that said child has been named Clarice Maurine Brown, and was living March 4, 1905.

Susie Brown

Witnesses To Mark:
{

Subscribed and sworn to before me this 6th day of April, 1905

D R Johnston
Notary Public.

AFFIDAVIT OF ATTENDING PHYSICIAN OR MID-WIFE.

UNITED STATES OF AMERICA, Indian Territory,
.... DISTRICT.

I, EA Jones, a Physician, on oath state that I attended on Mrs. Susie Brown nee Brooks, wife of W T Brown on the 5th day of July, 1904; that there was born to her on said date a female child; that said child was living March 4, 1905, and is said to have been named Clarice Maurine Brown

E A Jones M.D.

Witnesses To Mark:
{

Applications for Enrollment of Choctaw Newborn
Act of 1905   Volume XII

Subscribed and sworn to before me this 8th day of   April   , 1905

Ollie L Bean
Notary Public.

Choc New Born 844
    Annie Noah   b. 12-4-03

Choctaw 903[sic].

Muskogee, Indian Territory, April 14, 1905.

Hosea L. Fowler,
    Valliant, Indian Territory.

Dear Sir:

Receipt is hereby acknowledged of your letter without date transmitting the affidavits of Emma Noah and Jane Shotuby to the birth of Annie Noah, daughter of Foster and Emma Noah, December 4, 1903.

The other affidavits enclosed in your letter will be made the subject of a separate communication.

    Respectfully,

    Commissioner in Charge.

7-NB-844.

Muskogee, Indian Territory, June 6, 1905.

Foster Noah,
    Valliant, Indian Territory.

Dear Sir:

There is enclosed you herewith for execution application for the enrollment of your infant child, Annie Noah.

It is noted in the affidavits of February 23, 1905, heretofore filed in this office, that the date of the applicant's birth is given as December 4, 1902, while the affidavits of

Applications for Enrollment of Choctaw Newborn
Act of 1905   Volume XII

April 10, 1905, gives the date as December 4, 1903. Please insert the correct date and when the affidavits are properly executed return them to this office.

    In having these affidavits executed care should be exercised to see that all names are written in full, as they appear in the body of the affidavit, and in the event that either of the persons signing the affidavit are unable to write, signatures by mark must be attested by two witnesses. Each affidavit must be executed before a Notary Public and the notarial seal and signature of the officer must be attached to each separate affidavit.

                     Respectfully,

VR 6-6.   Commissioner in Charge.

---

                                                      7 NB 844

                    Muskogee, Indian Territory, June 24, 1905.

Foster Noah,
    Valliant, Indian Territory.

Dear Sir:

    Receipt is hereby acknowledged of the affidavits of Emma Noah and Selana Peter to the birth of Annie Noah, daughter of Foster Noah and Emma Noah (Bond) December 4, 1903, and the same have been filed with our records in the matter of the enrollment of said child.

                      Respectfully,

                              [sic]

NEW-BORN AFFIDAVIT.

            Number..................

...Choctaw Enrolling Commission...

    IN THE MATTER OF THE APPLICATION FOR ENROLLMENT, as a citizen of the Choctaw   Nation, of   Annie Noah

born on the   4th   day of   December   190 2

Name of father   Foster Noah   a citizen of   Choctaw
Nation final enrollment No. 2439
Name of mother   Emma Bond   a citizen of   Choctaw
Nation final enrollment No. 2424

Applications for Enrollment of Choctaw Newborn
Act of 1905   Volume XII

Postoffice   Valliant I.T.

AFFIDAVIT OF MOTHER.

UNITED STATES OF AMERICA
INDIAN TERRITORY
Central   DISTRICT

I   Emma Bond   , on oath state that I am 23 years of age and a citizen by blood of the Choctaw Nation, and as such have been placed upon the final roll of the Choctaw Nation, by the Honorable Secretary of the Interior my final enrollment number being 2424 ; that I am the lawful wife of Foster Noah , who is a citizen of the Choctaw Nation, and as such has been placed upon the final roll of said Nation by the Honorable Secretary of the Interior, his final enrollment number being 2439 and that a female child was born to me on the 4th day of December 190 2; that said child has been named Emma Noah , and is now living.

her
Emma x Bond
mark

Witnesseth.
Must be two Witnesses who are Citizens.   H B Jacobs
Jesse Christy

Subscribed and sworn to before me this 23rd day of Feb 190 5

W A Shoney
Notary Public.

My commission expires: Jan 10 1909

AFFIDAVIT OF ATTENDING PHYSICIAN OR MIDWIFE

UNITED STATES OF AMERICA
INDIAN TERRITORY
Central   DISTRICT

I, Foster Noah   a   attendant on oath state that I attended on Mrs. Emma Bond my wife of.................. on the 4th day of December , 190 2, that there was born to her on said date a female child, that said child is now living, and is said to have been named Annie Noah

Foster Noah attendant   ~~M.D.~~

WITNESSETH:
Must be two witnesses who are citizens and know the child.   H B Jacobs
Jesse Christy

Applications for Enrollment of Choctaw Newborn
Act of 1905 Volume XII

Feb Subscribed and sworn to before me this, the 23rd day of
1905

W A Shoney Notary Public.

We hereby certify that we are well acquainted with Foster Noah a Attendant and know him to be reputable and of good standing in the community.

{ H B Jacobs
{ Jesse Christy

BIRTH AFFIDAVIT.

DEPARTMENT OF THE INTERIOR.
COMMISSION TO THE FIVE CIVILIZED TRIBES.

IN RE APPLICATION FOR ENROLLMENT, as a citizen of the Choctaw Nation, of Annie Noah , born on the 4 day of Dec , 1903

Name of Father: Foster Noah a citizen of the Choctaw Nation.
Name of Mother: Emma Bond or Noah a citizen of the Choctaw Nation.

Postoffice Valliant IT

AFFIDAVIT OF MOTHER.

UNITED STATES OF AMERICA, Indian Territory,
Central **DISTRICT.**

I, Emma Bond or Noah , on oath state that I am 23 years of age and a citizen by Blood , of the Choctaw Nation; that I am the lawful wife of Foster Noah , who is a citizen, by Blood of the Choctaw Nation; that a Girl child was born to me on 4 day of Dec , 1902[sic]; that said child has been named Annie Noah , and was living March 4, 1905.

her
Emma x Noah
mark or Bond

Witnesses To Mark:
{ Lillian Wallace
{ John Fowler

Subscribed and sworn to before me this 10 day of April , 1905

H L Fowler
Valliant IT Notary Public.

Applications for Enrollment of Choctaw Newborn
Act of 1905   Volume XII

AFFIDAVIT OF ATTENDING PHYSICIAN OR MID-WIFE.

UNITED STATES OF AMERICA, Indian Territory, }
Central   DISTRICT.

I, Jane Shotuby , a ...., on oath state that I attended on Mrs. Emma Noah , wife of Foster Noah on the 4 day of Dec , 1903; that there was born to her on said date a Girl child; that said child was living March 4, 1905, and is said to have been named Annie Noah

Jane Shotuby
her x mark

Witnesses To Mark:
{ Lillian Wallace
{ John Fowler

Subscribed and sworn to before me this 10 day of April , 1905

H L Fowler
Notary Public.

BIRTH AFFIDAVIT.

DEPARTMENT OF THE INTERIOR.
COMMISSION TO THE FIVE CIVILIZED TRIBES.

IN RE APPLICATION FOR ENROLLMENT, as a citizen of the Choctaw Nation, of Annie Noah , born on the .... day of ...., 1........

Name of Father: Foster Noah   a citizen of the Choctaw Nation.
Name of Mother: Emma Noah (Bond)   a citizen of the Choctaw Nation.

Postoffice   Valliant Ind Ter

AFFIDAVIT OF MOTHER.

UNITED STATES OF AMERICA, Indian Territory, }
.... DISTRICT.

I, Emma Noah (Bond) , on oath state that I am 23 years of age and a citizen by blood , of the Choctaw Nation; that I am the lawful wife of Foster Noah , who is a citizen, by blood of the Choctaw Nation; that a female child was born to me on 4 day of Dec , 1903; that said child has been named Annie Noah , and was living March 4, 1905.

her
Emma x Noah (Bond)
mark

Applications for Enrollment of Choctaw Newborn
Act of 1905   Volume XII

Witnesses To Mark:
   { Houston Jacobs
    (Name Illegible)

    Subscribed and sworn to before me this 20 day of   Dec   , 1905

                             H L Fowler
                                  Notary Public.

AFFIDAVIT OF ATTENDING PHYSICIAN OR MID-WIFE.

UNITED STATES OF AMERICA, Indian Territory,
    Central   DISTRICT.

    I, Selana Peter , a Midwife , on oath state that I attended on Mrs. Emma Noah , wife of Foster Noah on the 4 day of Dec , 1903; that there was born to her on said date a female child; that said child was living March 4, 1905, and is said to have been named Annie Noah

                                  her
                            Selana x Peter
Witnesses To Mark: mark
   { John Fowler
    Simon Peter

    Subscribed and sworn to before me this 17 day of   June   , 1905

                             H L Fowler
                             Notary Public.

Choc New Born 845
    Clarence C McDaniel b. 6-23-04

Applications for Enrollment of Choctaw Newborn
Act of 1905   Volume XII

NEW-BORN AFFIDAVIT.

Number..............

...Choctaw Enrolling Commission...

IN THE MATTER OF THE APPLICATION FOR ENROLLMENT, as a citizen of the Choctaw   Nation, of   Clarence McDaniel

born on the   23   day of ____June____ 190 4

Name of father   Samuel McDaniel   a citizen of   Choctaw
Nation final enrollment No.   7466
Name of mother   Lou McDaniel   a citizen of   Choctaw
Nation final enrollment No.   7467

                                                     Postoffice   Tamaha IT

AFFIDAVIT OF MOTHER.

UNITED STATES OF AMERICA
INDIAN TERRITORY
   Central   DISTRICT

        I   Lou McDaniel   , on oath state that I am   34   years of age and a citizen by   blood   of the   Choctaw   Nation, and as such have been placed upon the final roll of the   Choctaw   Nation, by the Honorable Secretary of the Interior my final enrollment number being   7467 ; that I am the lawful wife of   Samuel McDaniel   , who is a citizen of the   Choctaw   Nation, and as such has been placed upon the final roll of said Nation by the Honorable Secretary of the Interior, his final enrollment number being   7466   and that a   Male   child was born to me on the   23rd day of   June   190 4; that said child has been named   Clarence McDaniel   , and is now living.

                                            Lou McDaniel

Witnesseth.
   Must be two   ⎱   George L Wadley
   Witnesses who
   are Citizens.   ⎰   J R Porch

      Subscribed and sworn to before me this   7   day of   January   190 5

                                   W^m B Davidson
                                            Notary Public.

My commission expires: 11th May 1907

Applications for Enrollment of Choctaw Newborn
Act of 1905   Volume XII

AFFIDAVIT OF ATTENDING PHYSICIAN OR MIDWIFE

UNITED STATES OF AMERICA
INDIAN TERRITORY
Central   DISTRICT

I,   A. T. Hill   a   Physician on oath state that I attended on Mrs.   Lou McDaniel   wife of   Samuel McDaniel on the   23rd   day of   June   , 190 4 , that there was born to her on said date a   Male child, that said child is now living, and is said to have been named   Clarence McDaniel

A.T. Hill   𝓂.𝒟.

Subscribed and sworn to before me this, the .... day of 7 January   190 5

WITNESSETH: W^m B Davidson   Notary Public.
Must be two witnesses who are citizens { George L Wadley
J R Porch

We hereby certify that we are well acquainted with   A.T. Hill a   Physician   and know   him   to be reputable and of good standing in the community.

John E McBrayer   George L Wadley

Rufus Bellew   J R Porch

BIRTH AFFIDAVIT.

DEPARTMENT OF THE INTERIOR.
COMMISSION TO THE FIVE CIVILIZED TRIBES.

IN RE APPLICATION FOR ENROLLMENT, as a citizen of the   Choctaw   Nation, of Clarence C McDaniel   , born on the   25   day of   June   , 1904

Name of Father: Samuel McDaniel   a citizen of the   Choctaw   Nation.
Name of Mother: Lou McDaniel   a citizen of the   Choctaw   Nation.

Postoffice   Tamaha I.T.

Applications for Enrollment of Choctaw Newborn
Act of 1905   Volume XII

AFFIDAVIT OF MOTHER.

UNITED STATES OF AMERICA, Indian Territory, }
    Central   DISTRICT. }

    I, Lou McDaniel, on oath state that I am 24 years of age and a citizen by Blood, of the Choctaw Nation; that I am the lawful wife of Samuel McDaniel, who is a citizen, by Blood of the Choctaw Nation; that a Male child was born to me on 23rd day of June, 1904; that said child has been named Clarence McDaniel, and was living March 4, 1905.

                                        Lou McDaniel

Witnesses To Mark:
{

    Subscribed and sworn to before me this 7 day of April, 1905

                                        W^m B Davidson
                                        Notary Public.

AFFIDAVIT OF ATTENDING PHYSICIAN OR MID-WIFE.

UNITED STATES OF AMERICA, Indian Territory, }
    Central   DISTRICT. }

    I, A T Hill, a Physician, on oath state that I attended on Mrs. Lou McDaniel, wife of Sam McDaniel on the 23 day of June, 1904; that there was born to her on said date a Male child; that said child was living March 4, 1905, and is said to have been named Clarence McDaniel

                                        A T Hill M.D.

Witnesses To Mark:
{

    Subscribed and sworn to before me this 7 day of April, 1905

                                        W^m B Davidson
                                        Notary Public.

Applications for Enrollment of Choctaw Newborn
Act of 1905 Volume XII

7-2572

Muskogee, Indian Territory, April 13, 1905.

Samuel McDaniel,
    Tamaha, Indian Territory.

Dear Sir:

    Receipt is hereby acknowledged of the affidavits of Lou McDaniel and A. T. Hill to the birth of Clarence C. McDaniel son of Samuel and Lou McDaniel, June 25, 1904, and the same have been filed with our records as an application for the enrollment of said child.

    Respectfully,

Commissioner in Charge.

Choc New Born 846
    Cleo Irene Ward   b. 10-3-04

7-2213

Muskogee, Indian Territory, April 13, 1905.

David Ward,
    Heavener, Indian Territory.

Dear Sir:

    Receipt is hereby acknowledged of the affidavit of M. A. Steward to the birth of Cleorine[sic] Ward, daughter of David and Gussie Ward, October 3, 1904, and the same has been filed with our records as an application for the enrollment of said child.

    Respectfully,

Commissioner in Charge.

Applications for Enrollment of Choctaw Newborn
Act of 1905   Volume XII

7-NB-846.

Muskogee, Indian Territory, June 6, 1905.

David Ward,
    Reichert, Indian Territory.

Dear Sir:

Referring to the application for the enrollment of your infant child, Cleo Irene Ward, born October 3, 1904, it is noted that the applicant claims through you.

In this event it will be necessary that you file with the Commission either the original or a certified copy of the license and certificate of your marriage to the applicant's mother, Gussie Ward.

Respectfully,

Commissioner in Charge.

---

7 NB 846

Muskogee, Indian Territory, June 14, 1905.

David Ward,
    Reichart[sic], Indian Territory.

Dear Sir:

Receipt is hereby acknowledged of the marriage license and certificate between David Ward and Gussie Crawford and the same have been filed in the matter of the enrollment of said child.

Respectfully,

Chairman.

Applications for Enrollment of Choctaw Newborn
Act of 1905   Volume XII

7-NB-846

Muskogee, Indian Territory, July 28, 1905.

David Ward,
    Reichert, Indian Territory.

Dear Sir:

    Referring to the application for the enrollment of your infant child, born October 3, 1904, it is noted in the affidavits of February 16 and April 5, 1905, that the name of the child is given as Cleo Irene Ward, while in the affidavit of the physician executed April 10, 1905, the name is given as Cleorine Ward.

    There is inclosed you herewith affidavit to be executed by the mother of the child, Gussie Ward, in which the name is left blank. Please insert the correct name of the child and when rproperly[sic] executed return, to this office immediately as no further action can be taken relative to the enrollment of your said child, until the evidence requested is supplied.

                        Respectfully,

LM 7/28   Commissioner.

---

7 N B 846

Muskogee, Indian Territory, August 14. 1905.

David Ward,
    Reichert, Indian Territory.

Dear Sir:

    Receipt is hereby acknowledged of the affidavits of Gussie Ward and M. A. Stewart, M. D. to the birth of Cleo Irene Ward, infant daughter of David and Gussie Ward, October 3, 1904, and the same have been filed with the record in the matter of the enrollment of said child.

                        Respectfully,

                                          Acting Commissioner.

Applications for Enrollment of Choctaw Newborn
Act of 1905 Volume XII

No. 1972

Certificate of Record of Marriages.

UNITED STATES OF AMERICA,
INDIAN TERRITORY, } SCT:
Central DISTRICT.

I, E.J. Fannin , Clerk of the United States Court in the Indian Territory and District aforesaid, do hereby CERTIFY, that the License for and Certificate of the Marriage of

Mr. David Ward and

Miss Gussie Crawford was

filed in my office in said Territory and District the 22" day of December A.D., 190___ and duly recorded in Book 1 of Marriage Record, Page 368

WITNESS my hand and seal of said Court, at *(Illegible)* , this 22" day of December A.D. 190 3

E.J. Fannin
Clerk.

By T.T. Varner *Deputy.*

P.O. Heavener

DEPARTMENT OF THE INTERIOR,
Commission to the Five Civilized Tribes.

FILED

JUN 13 1905

Tams Bixby CHAIRMAN.

Applications for Enrollment of Choctaw Newborn
Act of 1905   Volume XII

No. 1972

MARRIAGE LICENSE

United States of America, The Indian Territory,
Central DISTRICT, SS.

To any Person Authorized by Law to Solemnize Marriage, Greeting:

You are hereby commanded to Solemnize the Rite and publish the Banns of Matrimony between Mr.   David Ward
of   Heavener   *in the Indian Territory, aged*   23   *years, and M iss* Gussie Crawford   *of*   Heavener
in the Indian Territory., aged   21   *years, according to law, and do you officially sign and return this License to the parties therein named.*

WITNESS *my hand and official seal, this*   14th *day of*   December   *A. D. 190* 3

E.J. Fannin
Clerk of the United States Court.

By T T Varner   *Deputy*

Certificate of Marriage.

United States of America,
The Indian Territory,   } ss.
Central   *District.*

I,   Thos M Kimbro

a   Minister   *, do hereby certify, that on the*   20   *day of*   December   *A. D. 190* 3 *, I did, duly and according to law, as commanded in the foregoing License, solemnize the Rite and publish the Banns of Matrimony between the parties therein named.*

Witness my hand, this   20   *day of*   Dc   *A. D. 190* 3

My credentials are recorded in the office of the Clerk of the United States Court in the Indian Territory, Central District, Book   C   *, Page*   58

Thos M Kimbro

a   Minister

Note—This License and Certificate of Marriage must be returned to the Office of the Clerk of the United States Court of the Indian Territory, from whence it was issued, within sixty days from the date thereof, or the party to whom the License was issued will be liable in the amount of the One Hundred Dollars ($100.00).

Applications for Enrollment of Choctaw Newborn
Act of 1905 Volume XII

NEW BORN AFFIDAVIT

No ....

CHOCTAW ENROLLING COMMISSION

IN THE MATTER OF THE APPLICATION FOR ENROLLMENT as a citizen of the Choctaw Nation, of Cleo Irene Ward born on the 3 day of October 190 4

Name of father David Ward a citizen of Choctaw Nation, final enrollment No. 6417

Name of mother Gussie Ward a citizen of non Nation, final enrollment No.

Reichert I.T. Postoffice.

AFFIDAVIT OF MOTHER

UNITED STATES OF AMERICA
INDIAN TERRITORY
DISTRICT Central

I Gussie Ward , on oath state that I am 23 years of age and a citizen by non of the ——— Nation, and as such have been placed upon the final roll of the ——— Nation, by the Honorable Secretary of the Interior my final enrollment number being ———; that I am the lawful wife of David Ward , who is a citizen of the Choctaw by blood Nation, and as such have been placed upon the final roll of said Nation by the Honorable Secretary of the Interior, his final enrollment number being 6417 and that a Female child was born to me on the 3 day of October 190 4; that said child has been named Cleo Irene Ward , and is now living.

Gussie Ward

WITNESSETH:
Must be two witnesses { John Folsom
who are citizens   { Josephine Hill

Subscribed and sworn to before me this, the 16 day of February , 190 5

James Bower
Notary Public.

My Commission Expires:
Sept 23 - 1907

Applications for Enrollment of Choctaw Newborn
Act of 1905   Volume XII

Affidavit of Attending Physician or Midwife

UNITED STATES OF AMERICA,
INDIAN TERRITORY,
Central   DISTRICT

I,   M A Stewart   a   Practicing Physician on oath state that I attended on Mrs.   Gussie Ward   wife of   David Ward on the   3   day of   October   , 190 4, that there was born to her on said date a   female child, that said child is now living, and is said to have been named   Cleo Irene Ward

M.A. Stewart   M. D.

Subscribed and sworn to before me this the   16   day of   February   1905

James Bower
Notary Public.

WITNESSETH:
Must be two witnesses who are citizens and know the child. { John Folsom
Josephine Hill

We hereby certify that we are well acquainted with   M.A. Stewart a **Practicing Physician**   and know   him   to be reputable and of good standing in the community.

Must be two citizen witnesses. { John Folsom
Josephine Hill

AFFIDAVIT OF ATTENDING PHYSICIAN OR MID-WIFE.

UNITED STATES OF AMERICA, Indian Territory,
Central   DISTRICT.

I,   M A Stewart   , a   Practicing Physician   , on oath state that I attended on Mrs.   Gussie Ward   , wife of   David Ward   on the   3   day of   Oct   , 1904; that there was born to her on said date a   Girl   child; that said child was living March 4, 1905, and is said to have been named Cleorine Ward

MA Stewart

Witnesses To Mark:
{

Applications for Enrollment of Choctaw Newborn
Act of 1905   Volume XII

Subscribed and sworn to before me this 10th day of   Apr   , 1905

                         N S Costelow
                         Notary Public.
My Com Expr Mch 20-07

BIRTH AFFIDAVIT.

DEPARTMENT OF THE INTERIOR.
COMMISSION TO THE FIVE CIVILIZED TRIBES.

IN RE APPLICATION FOR ENROLLMENT, as a citizen of the   Choctaw   Nation, of Cleo Irene Ward   , born on the 3d day of October   , 1904

Name of Father: David Ward   roll 6417   a citizen of the   Choctaw   Nation.
Name of Mother: Gussie Ward   a citizen of the   U.S.A.   Nation.

                Postoffice   Reichert, Ind. Ter.

AFFIDAVIT OF MOTHER.

UNITED STATES OF AMERICA, Indian Territory,
     Central   DISTRICT.

     I,   Gussie Ward   , on oath state that I am   23   years of age and a citizen by ...., of the   U. S. A.   Nation; that I am the lawful wife of   David Ward   roll #6417   , who is a citizen, by blood   of the   Choctaw   Nation; that a Female   child was born to me on   3d day of October   , 1904; that said child has been named   Cleo Irene Ward   , and was living March 4, 1905.

                         Gussie Ward

Witnesses To Mark:

Subscribed and sworn to before me this   6th day of   April   , 1905

                         Lacey P Bobo
                         Notary Public.

Applications for Enrollment of Choctaw Newborn
Act of 1905   Volume XII

BIRTH AFFIDAVIT.   7- NB 846

DEPARTMENT OF THE INTERIOR.
COMMISSION TO THE FIVE CIVILIZED TRIBES.

IN RE APPLICATION FOR ENROLLMENT, as a citizen of the Choctaw Nation, of Cleo Irene Ward, born on the 3^d day of October, 1904

Name of Father: David Ward   Roll 6417   a citizen of the Choctaw Nation.
Name of Mother: Gussie Ward   a citizen of the   U.S.   ~~Nation~~.

Postoffice   Reichert, Ind. Ter.

AFFIDAVIT OF MOTHER.

UNITED STATES OF AMERICA, Indian Territory,
Central   DISTRICT.

I, Gussie Ward, on oath state that I am 23 years of age and a citizen by ~~blood~~ US, of the Choctaw Nation; that I am the lawful wife of David Ward, who is a citizen, by blood of the Choctaw Nation; that a female child was born to me on 3^d day of October, 1904; that said child has been named Cleo Irene Ward, and was living March 4, 1905.

Gussie Ward

Witnesses To Mark:
  Ida Naylor
  John Folsom

Subscribed and sworn to before me this 8th day of Aug, 1905

NS Costelow
Notary Public.
my com expr Mch 20-1907   Heavener I.T.

AFFIDAVIT OF ATTENDING PHYSICIAN OR MID-WIFE.

UNITED STATES OF AMERICA, Indian Territory,
Central   DISTRICT.

I, M A Stewart, a Physician, on oath state that I attended on Mrs. Gussie Ward, wife of David Ward on the 3rd day of Oct, 1904; that there was born to her on said date a Girl child; that said child was living March 4, 1905, and is said to have been named Cleo Irene Ward

M.A. Stewart M.D.

Applications for Enrollment of Choctaw Newborn
Act of 1905   Volume XII

Witnesses To Mark:
- Ida Naylor
- John Folsom

Subscribed and sworn to before me this 8th day of   Aug   , 1905

       NS Costelow
         Notary Public.

Choc New Born 847
  George J. Grant   b. 7-29-03

            7-4160.

    Muskogee, Indian Territory, April 13, 1905.

Tom Grant,
  Allen, Indian Territory.

Dear Sir:

  Receipt is hereby acknowledged of the affidavits of Mary E. (Grant) Crawford and W. C. Threlkeld to the birth of George J. Grant, son of Tom and Mary E. Grant, July 29, 1903, and the same have been filed with our records as an application for the enrollment of said child.

        Respectfully,

        Commissioner in Charge.

---

           7 NB 847

    Muskogee, Indian Territory, June 20, 1905.

R. E. Brians,
  Allen, Indian Territory.

Dear Sir:

  Receipt is hereby acknowledged of your letter of June 15, 1905, enclosing affidavits of Mary E. Crawford (Grant) and W. C. Threlkeld to the birth of George J.

Applications for Enrollment of Choctaw Newborn
Act of 1905   Volume XII

Grant, son of Thomas W. and Mary E. Grant, July 29, 1903, and the same have been filed with our records in the matter of the enrollment of said child.

                      Respectfully,

                                                Chairman.

                                                7-NB-847.

                    Muskogee, Indian Territory, May 31, 1905.

Mary E. Grant,
      Aleen[sic], Indian Territory.

Dear Madam:

      There is enclosed you herewith for execution application for the enrollment of your infant child, George J. Grant, born July 29, 1903.

      In the affidavits heretofore filed in this office you state that the father of the applicant is Tom Grant and give your husband's name as H. H. Crawford. The physician gives the name of the father as Tom Grant. In the enclosed application the name of the applicant's father and your husband is left blank. If Tom Grant is the father of the child and you have been divorced from him or that he is now dear you will please make the affidavit read that you were the wife of Tom Grant.

      In having these affidavits executed care should be exercised to see that all names are written in full, as they appear in the body of the affidavit, and in the event that either of the persons signing the affidavit are unable to write, signatures by mark must be attested by two witnesses. Each affidavit must be executed before a Notary Public and the notarial seal and signature of the officer must be attached to each separate affidavit.

                      Respectfully,

                                                Chairman.

VR 31-3.

Applications for Enrollment of Choctaw Newborn
Act of 1905   Volume XII

BIRTH AFFIDAVIT.

DEPARTMENT OF THE INTERIOR.
COMMISSION TO THE FIVE CIVILIZED TRIBES.

IN RE APPLICATION FOR ENROLLMENT, as a citizen of the   Choctaw   Nation, of George J Grant   , born on the 29 day of July , 1903

Name of Father: Tom Grant   a citizen of the U. S.   ~~Nation~~.
Name of Mother: Mary E Grant   a citizen of the Choctaw   Nation.

Postoffice ....

AFFIDAVIT OF MOTHER.

UNITED STATES OF AMERICA, Indian Territory, }
Central   DISTRICT.

I, Mary E Grant , on oath state that I am 32 years of age and a citizen by blood , of the Choctaw   Nation; that I am the lawful wife of B M Crawford , who is a citizen, by .... of the United States ~~Nation~~; that a male child was born to me on 29 day of July , 1903; that said child has been named George J Grant   , and was living March 4, 1905.

                                    Mary E (Grant) Crawford
Witnesses To Mark:
 {

Subscribed and sworn to before me this 8 day of   April   , 1905

My commission expires   J.L. Cart
June 29 1908   Notary Public.

AFFIDAVIT OF ATTENDING PHYSICIAN OR MID-WIFE.

UNITED STATES OF AMERICA, Indian Territory, }
Central   DISTRICT.

I, W. C. Threlkeld   , a physician   , on oath state that I attended on Mrs. Mary E Grant , wife of Tom Grant   on the 29 day of July , 1903; that there was born to her on said date a male   child; that said child was living March 4, 1905, and is said to have been named George J Grant

                                    W.C. Threlkeld M.D.

Applications for Enrollment of Choctaw Newborn
Act of 1905   Volume XII

Witnesses To Mark:
{

    Subscribed and sworn to before me this 3d day of   April   , 1905

My commission expires   J.L. Cart
June 29 1908   Notary Public.

BIRTH AFFIDAVIT.

DEPARTMENT OF THE INTERIOR.
COMMISSION TO THE FIVE CIVILIZED TRIBES.

IN RE APPLICATION FOR ENROLLMENT, as a citizen of the   Choctaw   Nation, of George J Grant   , born on the 29 day of July , 1903

Name of Father: Thomas W Grant   a citizen of the U. S.   ~~Nation~~.
Name of Mother: Mary E Grant   a citizen of the   Choctaw   Nation.

                 Postoffice   Aleen[sic], Ind Ter

AFFIDAVIT OF MOTHER.

UNITED STATES OF AMERICA, Indian Territory, }
    Central   DISTRICT. }

    I, Mary E Grant   , on oath state that I am 32   years of age and a citizen by blood , of the   Choctaw   Nation; that I am the lawful wife of   Thomas W Grant , who is a citizen, by Blood   of the   United States Nation; that a   male   child was born to me on   29   day of   July   , 1903; that said child has been named George J Grant   , and was living March 4, 1905.

                                          (Grant)
                               Mary E Crawford

Witnesses To Mark:
{

    Subscribed and sworn to before me this 9 day of   June   , 1905

                               R.E. Brians
                                   Notary Public.

Applications for Enrollment of Choctaw Newborn
Act of 1905   Volume XII

AFFIDAVIT OF ATTENDING PHYSICIAN OR MID-WIFE.

UNITED STATES OF AMERICA, Indian Territory, }
   Central   DISTRICT.

    I,   W. C. Threlkeld   , a Physician   , on oath state that I attended on Mrs.   Mary E Grant (now Mary E Crawford)   , wife of   Tom Grant   on the 29 day of   July   , 1903; that there was born to her on said date a   male   child; that said child was living March 4, 1905, and is said to have been named George J Grant

                                          W.C. Threlkeld

Witnesses To Mark:
{

    Subscribed and sworn to before me this 14 day of   June   , 1905

                                    R.E. Brians
                                        Notary Public.

Choc New Born 848
    Willie Uel Crowder b. 3-3-04

                                                      7 NB 848

                  Muskogee, Indian Territory, June 9, 1905.

Richard C. Crowder,
    Soper, Indian Territory.

Dear Sir:

    Receipt is hereby acknowledged of the affidavits of Mary Ellen Crowder and W. M. Wallace to the birth of Willie Uel Crowder son of Richard C. and Mary Ellen Crowder, March 3, 1904, and the same have been filed in the matter of the enrollment of said child.

                            Respectfully,

                                    Chairman.

Applications for Enrollment of Choctaw Newborn
Act of 1905 Volume XII

7-NB-848.

Muskogee, Indian Territory, May 31, 1905.

Richard Crowder,
    Soper, Indian Territory.

Dear Sir:

    There is enclosed you herewith for execution application for the enrollment of your infant child, Willie Uel Crowder.

    In the affidavits of January 19, 1905, heretofore filed in this office, the date of the applicant's birth is given as March 3, 1904, while in the affidavits of April 10, 1905, the physician gives the date of birth as April 3, 1904. In the enclosed application the date of birth is left blank. Please insert the correct date and, when the affidavits are properly executed, return them to this office.

    In having these affidavits executed care should be exercised to see that all names are written in full, as they appear in the body of the affidavit, and in the event that either of the p[sic] persons signing the affidavit are unable to write, signatures by mark must be attested by two witnesses. Each affidavit must be executed before a Notary Public and the notarial seal and signature of the officer must be attached to each separate affidavit.

                  Respectfully,

                          [sic]

NEW-BORN AFFIDAVIT.

        Number..................

Choctaw Enrolling Commission.

    IN THE MATTER OF THE APPLICATION FOR ENROLLMENT, as a citizen of the Choctaw   Nation, of   Willie Uel Crowder

born on the 3rd day of   March   190 4

Name of father   Richard Crowder   a citizen of   Choctaw
Nation final enrollment No   4034
Name of mother   Mary Ellen Crowder   a citizen of   Choctaw
Nation final enrollment No   810

                    Postoffice   Soper

Applications for Enrollment of Choctaw Newborn
Act of 1905   Volume XII

AFFIDAVIT OF MOTHER.

UNITED STATES OF AMERICA,
INDIAN TERRITORY,
Central   DISTRICT

I   Mary Ellen Crowder   on oath state that I am   25   years of age and a citizen by   Interm   of the   Choctaw   Nation, and as such have been placed upon the final roll of the   Choctaw   Nation, by the Honorable Secretary of the Interior my final enrollment number being   810   ; that I am the lawful wife of   Richard Crowder   , who is a citizen of the   Choctaw   Nation, and as such has been placed upon the final roll of said Nation by the Honorable Secretary of the Interior, his final enrollment number being   4034   and that a   male   child was born to me on the   3rd day of   March   190 4 ; that said child has been named   Willie Uel Crowder   , and is now living.

Mary Ellen Crowder

WITNESSETH:
Must be two Witnesses who are Citizens.   Joseph Cole
Robert Sanders

Subscribed and sworn to before me this   19   day of   Jan   190 5

W E Larcy
Notary Public.

My commission expires   July 9th 1908

Affidavit of Attending Physician or Midwife

UNITED STATES OF AMERICA,
INDIAN TERRITORY,
Central   DISTRICT

I,   W.M. Walace[sic]   a   Attending Physician   on oath state that I attended on Mrs.   Mary Ellen Crowder   wife of   Richard Crowder   on the   3rd day of   March   , 190 4, that there was born to her on said date a   Male   child, that said child is now living, and is said to have been named   Willie Uel Crowder

W.M. Wallace   M. D.

Subscribed and sworn to before me this the   19   day of   Jan   1905

WE Larecy
Notary Public.

WITNESSETH:
Must be two witnesses who are citizens and know the child.   Joseph Cole
Robert Sanders

Applications for Enrollment of Choctaw Newborn
Act of 1905   Volume XII

We hereby certify that we are well acquainted with   W. M. Walace[sic] a   Physician   and know   him   to be reputable and of good standing in the community.

Must be two citizen witnesses. { Joseph Cole
Robert Sanders

BIRTH AFFIDAVIT.

DEPARTMENT OF THE INTERIOR.
COMMISSION TO THE FIVE CIVILIZED TRIBES.

IN RE APPLICATION FOR ENROLLMENT, as a citizen of the   Choctaw   Nation, of Willie Uel Crowder   , born on the 3rd day of   March   , 1904

Name of Father: Richard Crowder   a citizen of the   Choctaw   Nation.
Name of Mother: Mary Ellen Crowder   a citizen of the   Choctaw   Nation.

Postoffice   Soper I.T.

AFFIDAVIT OF MOTHER.

UNITED STATES OF AMERICA, Indian Territory,
Central   DISTRICT.

I,   Mary Ellen Crowder   , on oath state that I am   25   years of age and a citizen by   Ent Marriage   , of the   Choctaw   Nation; that I am the lawful wife of   Richard Crowder   , who is a citizen, by   Blood   of the   Choctaw   Nation; that a   male   child was born to me on   3rd day of   March   , 1904; that said child has been named   Willie Uel Crowder   , and was living March 4, 1905.

Mary Ellen Crowder

Witnesses To Mark:
{

Subscribed and sworn to before me this   10th day of   April   , 1905

My commission expires
July 9th, 1908.   W.E. Larecy
                          Notary Public.

Applications for Enrollment of Choctaw Newborn
Act of 1905   Volume XII

AFFIDAVIT OF ATTENDING PHYSICIAN OR MID-WIFE.

UNITED STATES OF AMERICA, Indian Territory, }
Central   DISTRICT.

I, W. M. Walace, a Physician, on oath state that I attended on Mrs. Mary Ellen Crowder, wife of Richard Crowder on the 3rd day of April[sic], 1904; that there was born to her on said date a male child; that said child was living March 4, 1905, and is said to have been named Willie Uel Crowder

W.M. Wallace

Witnesses To Mark:
{

Subscribed and sworn to before me this 10th day of April, 1905

My commission expires
July 9th, 1908.
W.E. Larecy
Notary Public.

BIRTH AFFIDAVIT.

DEPARTMENT OF THE INTERIOR.
COMMISSION TO THE FIVE CIVILIZED TRIBES.

IN RE APPLICATION FOR ENROLLMENT, as a citizen of the Choctaw Nation, of Willie Uel Crowder, born on the 3 day of Mar, 1904

Name of Father: Richard Crowder   a citizen of the Choctaw Nation.
Name of Mother: Mary Ellen Crowder   a citizen of the Choctaw Nation.

Postoffice   Soper Ind. Ter.

AFFIDAVIT OF MOTHER.

UNITED STATES OF AMERICA, Indian Territory, }
Central   DISTRICT.

I, Mary Ellen Crowder, on oath state that I am 25 years of age and a citizen by intermarriage, of the Choctaw Nation; that I am the lawful wife of Richard Crowder, who is a citizen, by blood of the Choctaw Nation; that a ~~female~~ *male* child was born to me on 3rd day of March, 1904; that said child has been named Willie Uel Crowder, and was living March 4, 1905.

Mary Ellen Crowder

Witnesses To Mark:
{

Applications for Enrollment of Choctaw Newborn
Act of 1905   Volume XII

Subscribed and sworn to before me this 6th day of   June   , 1904[sic]

My commission expires
July 9th, 1908.   W.E. Larecy
                       Notary Public.

AFFIDAVIT OF ATTENDING PHYSICIAN OR MID-WIFE.

UNITED STATES OF AMERICA, Indian Territory, }
  Central   DISTRICT.   }

   I, W. M. Walace[sic]   , a   Physician   , on oath state that I attended on Mrs. Mary Ellen Crowder , wife of Richard Crowder   on the 3 day of March   , 1904; that there was born to her on said date a ~~female~~ *male* child; that said child was living March 4, 1905, and is said to have been named Willie Uel Crowder

                       W.M. Wallace M.D.

Witnesses To Mark:
{

   Subscribed and sworn to before me this 6th day of   June   , 1905

My commission expires
July 9th, 1908.   W.E. Larecy
                       Notary Public.

Choc New Born 849
     Gladys Aribell Gardner   b. 2-6-05

COPY

                       Muskogee, Indian Territory, March 31, 1905.

Robert L. Gardner,
     Jackson, Indian Territory.

Dear Sir:

   Receipt is hereby acknowledged of the affidavits of Fasie[sic] E. Gardner and J. W. Phillips to the birth of Glades[sic] A. Gardner, daughter of Robert L. and Fasie E. Gardner.

   It is stated in the affidavit of the mother that she is a citizen by blood of the Choctaw Nation and if this is correct you are requested to give her maiden name, the

Applications for Enrollment of Choctaw Newborn
Act of 1905   Volume XII

names of her parents, and state the name under which she was listed for enrollment and any other information which would lead to her identification upon our records as a citizen by blood of the Choctaw Nation.

Respectfully,
SIGNED
Tams Bixby
Chairman.

7-3807

Muskogee, Indian Territory, April 13, 1905.

Robert L. Gardner,
    Jackson, Indian Territory.

Dear Sir:

    Receipt is hereby acknowledged of the affidavits of Tasie E. Gardner and J. W. Phillips to the birth of Gladys Aribell Gardner, daughter of Robert L. and Tasie E. Gardner, February 6, 1905, and the same have been filed with our records as an application for the enrollment of said child.

Respectfully,

Commissioner in Charge.

7-NB-849.

Muskogee, Indian Territory, May 31, 1905.

Robert L. Gardner,
    Jackson, Indian Territory.

Dear Sir:

    Referring to the application for the enrollment of your infant child, Glades[sic] Gardner, born February 6, 1905, it is noted from the affidavits heretofore filed in this office that the applicant claims through you.

    In this event it will be necessary that you file with the Commission either the original or a certified copy of the license and certificate of your marriage to the applicant's mother, Tasie E Gardner.

Respectfully,
[sic]

Applications for Enrollment of Choctaw Newborn
Act of 1905 Volume XII

BIRTH AFFIDAVIT.

DEPARTMENT OF THE INTERIOR.
COMMISSION TO THE FIVE CIVILIZED TRIBES.

IN RE APPLICATION FOR ENROLLMENT, as a citizen of the Choctaw Nation, of Gladys Aribell Gardner, born on the 6th day of Feby, 1905

Name of Father: Robert L Gardner   a citizen of the Choctaw Nation.
Name of Mother: Tasie E. Gardner   a citizen of the Choctaw Nation.

Postoffice   Jackson IT

AFFIDAVIT OF MOTHER.

UNITED STATES OF AMERICA, Indian Territory, } Cent   DISTRICT.

I, Tasie E Gardner, on oath state that I am 22 years of age and a citizen by Intermarriage, of the Choctaw Nation; that I am the lawful wife of Robert L Gardner, who is a citizen, by blood of the Choctaw Nation; that a Female child was born to me on 6th day of Feby, 1905; that said child has been named Gladys Aribell Gardner, and was living March 4, 1905.

                         Tasie E Gardner

Witnesses To Mark:
{

Subscribed and sworn to before me this 10th day of April, 1905

                         B.W. Williams
                               Notary Public.

AFFIDAVIT OF ATTENDING PHYSICIAN OR MID-WIFE.

UNITED STATES OF AMERICA, Indian Territory, } Cent   DISTRICT.

I, J.W. Phillips, a Physician, on oath state that I attended on Mrs. Tasie E Gardner, wife of Robert L Gardner on the 6 day of Feb, 1905; that there was born to her on said date a Female child; that said child was living March 4, 1905, and is said to have been named Gladys Airbell[sic] Gardner

                         J.W. Phillips M.D.

Witnesses To Mark:
{

Applications for Enrollment of Choctaw Newborn
Act of 1905   Volume XII

Subscribed and sworn to before me this 10th day of April , 1905

B.W. Williams
Notary Public.

NEW-BORN AFFIDAVIT.

Number..........

Choctaw Enrolling Commission.

IN THE MATTER OF THE APPLICATION FOR ENROLLMENT, as a citizen of the Choctaw   Nation, of   Glades[sic] Gardner

born on the   6   day of   February   190 5

Name of father   Robert L Gardner   a citizen of   Choctaw
Nation final enrollment No   10746
Name of mother   Tasie E Gardner   a citizen of   Choctaw
Nation final enrollment No   ——

Postoffice   Jackson I.T.

AFFIDAVIT OF MOTHER.

UNITED STATES OF AMERICA, ⎫
   INDIAN TERRITORY,   ⎬
   Central   DISTRICT   ⎭

I   Tasie E Gardner   on oath state that I am 22 years of age and a citizen by Marriage   of the Choctaw   Nation, and as such have been placed upon the final roll of the —— Nation, by the Honorable Secretary of the Interior my final enrollment number being —— ; that I am the lawful wife of Robert L Gardner   , who is a citizen of the   Choctaw   Nation, and as such has been placed upon the final roll of said Nation by the Honorable Secretary of the Interior, his final enrollment number being 10746 and that a   Female   child was born to me on the 6 day of February   190 5 ; that said child has been named   Glades Gardner , and is now living.

Witnesses to mark Robert L Gardner   Tasie E x Gardner
WITNESSETH: mark
Must be two   ⎫   Jackson N Jones
Witnesses who ⎬
are Citizens. ⎭   Daniel H Gardner

Applications for Enrollment of Choctaw Newborn
Act of 1905 Volume XII

Subscribed and sworn to before me this 13 day of March 190 5

G W Adair

Notary Public.

My commission expires 10/16/06

Affidavit of Attending Physician or Midwife

UNITED STATES OF AMERICA,
   INDIAN TERRITORY,
Central   DISTRICT

I, J.W. Phillips a Physician on oath state that I attended on Mrs. Tasie E Gardner wife of Robert L Gardner on the 6 day of February , 190 5, that there was born to her on said date a Female child, that said child is now living, and is said to have been named Glades Gardner

J. W. Phillips   M. D.

Subscribed and sworn to before me this the 13 day of March 1905

G W Adair

Com expires 10/16/06   Notary Public.

WITNESSETH:
Must be two witnesses who are citizens and know the child. { Jackson N Jones
Daniel H Gardner

We hereby certify that we are well acquainted with J W Phillips a Physician and know him to be reputable and of good standing in the community.

Must be two citizen witnesses. { Jackson N Jones
Daniel H Gardner

BIRTH AFFIDAVIT.

DEPARTMENT OF THE INTERIOR.
COMMISSION TO THE FIVE CIVILIZED TRIBES.

IN RE APPLICATION FOR ENROLLMENT, as a citizen of the Choctaw Nation, of Glades A Gardner , born on the 6th day of Feby , 1905

Name of Father: Robert L Gardner   a citizen of the Choctaw Nation.
Name of Mother: Tasie E Gardner   a citizen of the Choctaw Nation.

Applications for Enrollment of Choctaw Newborn
Act of 1905 Volume XII

Postoffice   Jackson, I.T.

AFFIDAVIT OF MOTHER.

UNITED STATES OF AMERICA, Indian Territory, }
Central   DISTRICT. }

I, Tasie E Gardner, on oath state that I am 22 years of age and a citizen by blood, of the Choctaw Nation; that I am the lawful wife of Robert L Gardner, who is a citizen, by blood of the Choctaw Nation; that a Female child was born to me on 6th day of Feby, 1905; that said child has been named Gladie[sic] A Gardner, and was living March 4, 1905.

Tasie E Gardner

Witnesses To Mark:
{ Morris Smith
{ Daniel P. Williams

Subscribed and sworn to before me this 24th day of March, 1905

B.W. Williams
Notary Public.

AFFIDAVIT OF ATTENDING PHYSICIAN OR MID-WIFE.

UNITED STATES OF AMERICA, Indian Territory, }
Central   DISTRICT. }

I, J.W. Phillips, a Physician, on oath state that I attended on Mrs. Tasie E Gardner, wife of Robert L Gardner on the 6th day of Feby, 1905; that there was born to her on said date a Female child; that said child was living March 4, 1905, and is said to have been named Glades A Gardner

J.W. Phillips M.D.

Witnesses To Mark:
{ Morris Smith
{ Daniel P. Williams

Subscribed and sworn to before me this 24th day of March, 1905

B.W. Williams
Notary Public.

Applications for Enrollment of Choctaw Newborn
Act of 1905 Volume XII

No. 123

Certificate of Record of Marriages.

UNITED STATES OF AMERICA,
INDIAN TERRITORY, } SCT:
Central DISTRICT.

I, E.J. Fannin , Clerk of the United States Court in the Indian Territory and District aforesaid, do hereby CERTIFY, that the License for and Certificate of the Marriage of

Mr. Robert L Gardner and

Miss Tasie Holman was

filed in my office in said Territory and District the 22 day of December A.D., 190 2 and duly recorded in Book 1 of Marriage Record, Page 62

WITNESS my hand and seal of said Court, at Durant , this 22 day of December , A.D. 190 2

E.J. Fannin
Clerk.

By W.B. Stone *Deputy.*

Applications for Enrollment of Choctaw Newborn
Act of 1905   Volume XII

No. 123

FORM No. 598.

MARRIAGE LICENSE.

UNITES STATES OF AMERICA,
THE INDIAN TERRITORY,   } ss:
Central   DISTRICT.

To any Person Authorized by Law to Solemnize Marriage—Greeting:

You are hereby commanded to solemnize the Rite and publish the **Banns of Matrimony** *between* Mr. Robert Gardner *of* Bonty[sic] *in the Indian Territory, aged* 23 *years, and* Miss Lasie Halman *of* Bonty *in the Indian Territory, aged* 19 *years, according to law, and do you officially sign and return this License to the parties therein named.*

WITNESS my hand and official seal, this 20 day of November A. D. 190 2

E J Fannin
Clerk of the United States Court.

W B Stone
Deputy

CERTIFICATE OF MARRIAGE.

UNITES STATES OF AMERICA,
THE INDIAN TERRITORY,   } ss:
_____DISTRICT.

I, W.G.B. Lloyd
a Minister of the Gospel

do hereby CERTIFY, that on the 7 day of Dec A, D. 190 2 ; I did duly and according to law, as commanded in the foregoing License, solemnize the Rite and publish the BANNS OF MATRIMONY between the parties therein named.

Witness my hand this 13 day of Dec , A. D. 190 2

My credentials are recorded in the office of the Clerk of the United States Court in the Indian Territory, Central District, Book A   Page 201

WGB Lloyd
a   Minister of Gospel

Applications for Enrollment of Choctaw Newborn
Act of 1905   Volume XII

Choc New Born 850
 Chester G. Bohanan[sic]   b. 10-17-03

———

7-1620

Muskogee, Indian Territory, April 13, 1905.

Andrew Bohanan,
 Grand, Indian Territory.

Dear Sir:

 Receipt is hereby acknowledged of the affidavits of Rosie D. Bohanan and J. D. Brown to the birth of Chester G. Bohanan, son of Andrew and Rosie D. Bohanan, October 17, 1903, and the same have been filed with our records as an application for the enrollment of said child.

 Respectfully,

 Commissioner in Charge.

———

NEW-BORN AFFIDAVIT.

 Number............

...Choctaw Enrolling Commission...

———

 IN THE MATTER OF THE APPLICATION FOR ENROLLMENT, as a citizen of the Choctaw   Nation, of   Chester G. Bohanon

born on the   17   day of   Oct   190 3

Name of father   Andrew Bohanon   a citizen of   Choctaw
Nation final enrollment No.   4592
Name of mother   Rosie D. Bohanon   a citizen of   Choctaw
Nation final enrollment No.   85

 Postoffice   Grant I.T.

Applications for Enrollment of Choctaw Newborn
Act of 1905   Volume XII

AFFIDAVIT OF MOTHER.

UNITED STATES OF AMERICA
INDIAN TERRITORY
   Central   DISTRICT

I Rosie D. Bohanon , on oath state that I am 28 years of age and a citizen by Mariage[sic] of the Choctaw Nation, and as such have been placed upon the final roll of the Choctaw Nation, by the Honorable Secretary of the Interior my final enrollment number being 85 ; that I am the lawful wife of Andrew Bohanon , who is a citizen of the Choctaw Nation, and as such has been placed upon the final roll of said Nation by the Honorable Secretary of the Interior, his final enrollment number being 4592 and that a Male child was born to me on the 17th day of Oct 190 3; that said child has been named Chester G. Bohanon , and is now living.

                                            her
                                  Rosie D. x Bohanon
Witnesseth.   mark

Must be two Witnesses who are Citizens.
  B A Nelson
  Ben Wesly[sic]

Subscribed and sworn to before me this 14 day of Feb 190 5

                              D.O. Harold
                                      Notary Public.
My commission expires: Jan 26 1909   Grant IT

AFFIDAVIT OF ATTENDING PHYSICIAN OR MIDWIFE

UNITED STATES OF AMERICA
INDIAN TERRITORY
_____ DISTRICT

I, Dr J.D. Brown a physician on oath state that I attended on Mrs. Rosie D Bohanon wife of Andrew Bohanon on the 17th day of October , 190 3, that there was born to her on said date a male child, that said child is now living, and is said to have been named Chester G Bohanon

                              Dr. J. D. Brown   M.D.

WITNESSETH:
Must be two witnesses who are citizens and know the child.
  BA Nelson
  Anna L Durant

Subscribed and sworn to before me this, the 17th day of February 190 5

                             Rhodes S Baker   Notary Public.
                             Dallas County Texas

Applications for Enrollment of Choctaw Newborn
Act of 1905   Volume XII

We hereby certify that we are well acquainted with D^r. J. D. Brown a Practicing Physician and know him to be reputable and of good standing in the community.

> B A Nelson
> *(Name Illegible)*

BIRTH AFFIDAVIT.

DEPARTMENT OF THE INTERIOR.
COMMISSION TO THE FIVE CIVILIZED TRIBES.

IN RE APPLICATION FOR ENROLLMENT, as a citizen of the Choctaw Nation, of Chester G Bohanon , born on the 17 day of Oct , 1903

Name of Father: Andrew Bohanon   a citizen of the Choctaw Nation.
Name of Mother: Rosie D Bohanon   a citizen of the Choctaw Nation.

Postoffice   Grant I.T.

AFFIDAVIT OF MOTHER.

UNITED STATES OF AMERICA, Indian Territory,
Central   DISTRICT.

I, Rosie D. Bohanon , on oath state that I am 28 years of age and a citizen by Inter Mariadge[sic] , of the Choctaw Nation; that I am the lawful wife of Andrew Bohanon , who is a citizen, by Blood of the Choctaw Nation; that a Male child was born to me on 17 day of Oct , 1903; that said child has been named Chester G Bohanon , and was living March 4, 1905.

> her
> Rosie C x Bohanon
> mark

Witnesses To Mark:
  J.W. Wilson
  E.W. Sadler

Subscribed and sworn to before me this 30 day of Mch , 1905

> DP Harold
> Notary Public.
> Grant I.T.

Applications for Enrollment of Choctaw Newborn
Act of 1905   Volume XII

AFFIDAVIT OF ATTENDING PHYSICIAN OR MID-WIFE.

UNITED STATES OF AMERICA, Indian Territory, }
.... DISTRICT. }

I, J.D. Brown, a Physician, on oath state that I attended on Mrs. Rosie D Bohanon, wife of Andrew Bohanon on the 17 day of Oct, 1903; that there was born to her on said date a male child; that said child was living March 4, 1905, and is said to have been named Chester G Bohanon

J.D. Brown M.D.

Witnesses To Mark:
{ Leon Pearcy
{ W.J. Chester

Subscribed and sworn to before me this 10th day of April , 1905

JB Moreland
Notary Public.
Com exp Oct 21-1905

Choc New Born 851
     Willie Homer b. 9-10-03

BIRTH AFFIDAVIT.
DEPARTMENT OF THE INTERIOR.
COMMISSION TO THE FIVE CIVILIZED TRIBES.

IN RE APPLICATION FOR ENROLLMENT, as a citizen of the   Choctaw   Nation, of Willie Homer , born on the 10 day of Sept , 1903

Name of Father: Dana Homer   a citizen of the Choctaw Nation.
Name of Mother: Mollie Homer nee Bench   a citizen of the Choctaw Nation.

Postoffice   Bennington I.T.

Applications for Enrollment of Choctaw Newborn
Act of 1905 Volume XII

AFFIDAVIT OF MOTHER.

UNITED STATES OF AMERICA, Indian Territory, }
    Central   DISTRICT.

I, Dana Homer, on oath state that I am 23 years of age and a citizen by blood, of the Choctaw Nation; that I ~~am~~ *was* the lawful ~~wife~~ *husband* of Mollie Homer nee Bench, who ~~is~~ *was* a citizen, by blood of the Choctaw Nation; that a male child was born to me on 10 day of Sept, 1903; that said child has been named Willie Homer, and was living March 4, 1905. *and that Mollie Homer died Sept. 10, 1903*

                                   Dana Homer

Witnesses To Mark:
{ David C Byington
{ Sampson Byington

Subscribed and sworn to before me this 14 day of April, 1906

                                   J.C. Parker
                                   Notary Public.

AFFIDAVIT OF ATTENDING PHYSICIAN OR MID-WIFE.

UNITED STATES OF AMERICA, Indian Territory, }
                                   DISTRICT.

I, Kizzie Homer, a midwife, on oath state that I attended on Mrs. Mollie Homer nee Bench, wife of Dana Homer on the 10 day of Sept, 1903; that there was born to her on said date a male child; that said child was living March 4, 1905, and is said to have been named Willie Homer

Witnesses To Mark:
{
{

Subscribed and sworn to before me this ...... day of ...., 1905.

                                   Notary Public.

Applications for Enrollment of Choctaw Newborn
Act of 1905   Volume XII

BIRTH AFFIDAVIT.

DEPARTMENT OF THE INTERIOR.
COMMISSION TO THE FIVE CIVILIZED TRIBES.

IN RE APPLICATION FOR ENROLLMENT, as a citizen of the Choctaw Nation, of Willie Homer, born on the 10 day of September, 1903

Name of Father: Dana Homer   a citizen of the Choctaw Nation.
Name of Mother: Mollie Homer, nee Bench   a citizen of the Choctaw Nation.

Postoffice   Bennington, Ind. Ter.

AFFIDAVIT OF ######   Witness

UNITED STATES OF AMERICA, Indian Territory,
Central DISTRICT.

I, Sam Dyer, on oath state that I am 52 years of age and a citizen by Blood, of the Choctaw Nation; ~~that I am the lawful wife of~~, ~~who is a citizen, by~~ ~~of the~~ ~~Nation~~; that a Male child was born to ~~me~~ Dana Homer and Mollie Homer Sept 10, 1903; that said child has been named Willie Homer, and was living March 4, 1905.

Sam Dyer

Witnesses To Mark:

Subscribed and sworn to before me this 7th day of April, 1906

J.C. Parker
Notary Public.

BIRTH AFFIDAVIT.

DEPARTMENT OF THE INTERIOR.
COMMISSION TO THE FIVE CIVILIZED TRIBES.

IN RE APPLICATION FOR ENROLLMENT, as a citizen of the Choctaw Nation, of Willie Homer, born on the 10th day of Sept, 1903

Name of Father: Dana Homer   a citizen of the Choctaw Nation.
Name of Mother: Mollie Homer (nee Bench)   a citizen of the Choctaw Nation.

Postoffice   Bennington, I.T.

Applications for Enrollment of Choctaw Newborn
Act of 1905 Volume XII

AFFIDAVIT OF MOTHER.

UNITED STATES OF AMERICA, Indian Territory,
Cent   DISTRICT.

I, ... that I am .... years of age and a citizen by .... of the .... Nation; that I am the lawful wife of ...., who is a ci............ .... Nation; that a .... child was born to me on ...... day of ...., 1........, that said child has been named ....

Mollie Homer died on the 10th day of Sept A.D. 1903

and was living March 4, 1905.

                                  Dana Homer

Witnesses To Mark:
{ ....
  .... }

Subscribed and sworn to before me this 20th day of April, 1905.

                              B.W. Williams
                              Notary Public.

AFFIDAVIT OF ATTENDING PHYSICIAN OR MID-WIFE.

UNITED STATES OF AMERICA, Indian Territory,
Cent   DISTRICT.

I, Kizzie Homer, a Midwife, on oath state that I attended on Mrs. Mollie Bench (now Homer), wife of Dana Homer on the 10 day of Sept, 1903; that there was born to her on said date a Male child; that said child was living March 4, 1905, and is said to have been named Willie Homer

                                her
                         Kizzie x Homer

Witnesses To Mark: mark
{ Morris Smith

Subscribed and sworn to before me this 20th day of April, 1905.

                              B.W. Williams
                              Notary Public.

Applications for Enrollment of Choctaw Newborn
Act of 1905   Volume XII

7 NB 851
BIRTH AFFIDAVIT.

DEPARTMENT OF THE INTERIOR.
COMMISSION TO THE FIVE CIVILIZED TRIBES.

IN RE APPLICATION FOR ENROLLMENT, as a citizen of the   Choctaw   Nation, of Willie Homer   , born on the 10   day of Sept   , 1903

Name of Father: Dana Homer   a citizen of the   Choctaw   Nation.
Name of Mother: Mollie Homer   nee Bench   a citizen of the   Choctaw   Nation.

Postoffice   Bennington IT

AFFIDAVIT OF ~~MOTHER~~. Witness

UNITED STATES OF AMERICA, Indian Territory,
Central   DISTRICT.

I, Daniel Williams   , on oath state that I am   27   years of age and a citizen by   blood   , of the   Choctaw   Nation; that I ~~am the lawful wife of~~   was personally acquainted with Mollie Homer wife of Dana Homer , who ~~is~~ was a citizen, by blood   of the   Choctaw   Nation; that a   male   child was born to ~~me~~ her on   10   day of   September   , 1903; that said child has been named Willie Homer   , and was living March 4, 1905. and that said Mollie Homer died on Sept 10 1903

Daniel Williams

Witnesses To Mark:
{ ....
  .... }

Subscribed and sworn to before me this .... day of ...., 1905.

....
Notary Public.

AFFIDAVIT OF ATTENDING PHYSICIAN OR MID-WIFE.

UNITED STATES OF AMERICA, Indian Territory,
Central   DISTRICT.

I, Kizzie Homer   , a ...., on oath state that I attended on Mrs. Nancy[sic] Homer   , wife of   Dana Homer   on the 10th day of Sept ,

261

Applications for Enrollment of Choctaw Newborn
Act of 1905   Volume XII

1904[sic]; that there was born to her on said date a   Male   child; that said child was living March 4, 1905, and is said to have been named   Willie Homer

her
Kizzie x Homer
mark

Witnesses To Mark:
{ WO Byrd
{ (Name Illegible)

Subscribed and sworn to before me this *(illegible)* day of August , 1905

WO Byrd
Notary Public.

7-NB 851
BIRTH AFFIDAVIT.

DEPARTMENT OF THE INTERIOR.
COMMISSION TO THE FIVE CIVILIZED TRIBES.

IN RE APPLICATION FOR ENROLLMENT, as a citizen of the   Choctaw   Nation, of Willie Homer   , born on the 10   day of Sept , 1903

Name of Father: Dana Homer   a citizen of the   Choctaw   Nation.
Name of Mother: Mollie Homer,   nee Bench   a citizen of the   Choctaw   Nation.

Postoffice   Bennington IT

AFFIDAVIT OF <s>MOTHER.</s> Witness

UNITED STATES OF AMERICA, Indian Territory, }
Central   DISTRICT. }

I,   Daniel Williams , on oath state that I am 27 years of age and a citizen by   blood   , of the   Choctaw   Nation; that I ~~am the lawful wife of~~ *was personally acquainted* Mollie Homer *deceased wife of Dana Homer* , who ~~is~~ *was* a citizen, by   blood   of the   Choctaw   Nation; that a   male   child was born to ~~me~~ *her* on   10   day of   September   , 1903; that said child has been named Willie Homer   , and was living March 4, 1905. *that said Mollie Homer died on the 10th day of Sept 1903*

Daniel Williams

Witnesses To Mark:
{

Applications for Enrollment of Choctaw Newborn
Act of 1905 Volume XII

Subscribed and sworn to before me this 18 day of August , 1905

(Name Illegible)
Notary Public.

Kizzie Homer Died last February; the date 1904 in Affidavit of Kizzie Homer was a mistake made by the notary in filling out the Affidavit.

Dana A Homer

Subscribed and Sworn to before me this the 14th, day of April 1906.

J.C. Parker
Notary Public.

7-1649.

Muskogee, Indian Territory, April 26, 1905.

Dena[sic] Homer,
Bennington, Indian Territory.

Dear Sir:

Receipt is hereby acknowledged of the affidavit of Kizzie Homer to the birth of Willie Homer, son of Dena and Mollie Homer, September 10, 1903, and the same have been filed with our records as an application for the enrollment of said child.

Respectfully,

Chairman.

7-NB-851.

Muskogee, Indian Territory, May 31, 1905.

Dena Homer,
Bennington, Indian Territory.

Dear Sir:

Referring to the application for the enrollment of your infant child, Willie Homer, it is noted from the application heretofore filed in this office that the mother of the applicant is dead.

Applications for Enrollment of Choctaw Newborn
Act of 1905   Volume XII

If this is correct it will be necessary that you file with the Commission the affidavits of two persons, who are disinterested and not related to the applicant, who have actual knowledge of the facts that the child was born, the date of his birth; that he was living on March 4, 1905, and that Mollie Homer was his mother.

Respectfully,

[sic]

7-NB-851.

Muskogee, Indian Territory, August 18, 1905.

Kizzie Homer,
    Bennington, Indian Territory.

Dear Madam:

In the matter of the application for the enrollment of your grandson Willie Homer as a citizen by blood of the Choctaw Nation blood of the Choctaw Nation there is on file your affidavit only as to the birth of said child on September 10, 1903, and that affidavit is defective inasmuch as there is but one witness to your signature by mark must be attested by two witnesses.

You are advised that it will be necessary for you to furnish this Office with your affidavit and the affidavit of Dana Homer, the father of said child, relative to his birth and for that purpose there is inclosed herewith a blank for proof of birth.

The mother of said child being dead it will be necessary for you to furnish this office in lieu of her affidavit the affidavits of two disinterested persons as to the birth of said child. Said affidavits of the two disinterested persons must set forth said child's name, the date of his birth, the names of his parents and whether or not he was living on March 4, 1905.

Respectfully,

B C   Acting Commissioner.
Env.

Applications for Enrollment of Choctaw Newborn
Act of 1905   Volume XII

7- N B 851

Muskogee, Indian Territory, August 30, 1905.

Kizzie Homer,
Bennington, Indian Territory.

Dear Madam:

Receipt is hereby acknowledged of the affidavits of Daniel Williams of August 18, 1905, and of Kizzie Homer of August 26, 1905, in reference to the date of the birth of Willie Homer and the death of Mollie Homer.

These affidavits have been filed with the records of this office and will receive consideration in the disposition of the application of Willie Homer for enrollment as a new-born citizen by blood of the Choctaw Nation.

Respectfully,

Commissioner.

7-NB-851

Muskogee, Indian Territory, February 28, 1906.

Dana Homer,
Bennington, Indian Territory.

Dear Sir:

Receipt is hereby acknowledged of your letter of February 21, 1906, asking if your child Willie Homer is enrolled.

In reply to your letter you are advised that the application for the enrollment of your child Willie Homer has not yet been passed upon and before the same can receive consideration it will be necessary for you to forward the affidavits of two disinterested witnesses who know of the birth of this child, the names of his parents and that he was living March 4, 1905.

The affidavit of Daniel Williams heretofore forwarded did not bear the seal of the Notary Public before whom it was executed and if you will correct the same by having the Notary Public attach his seal thereto and forward the affidavit of another disinterested witness to the birth of this child, the matter will receive further consideration.

Respectfully,

KB 1-28.   Acting Commissioner.

Applications for Enrollment of Choctaw Newborn
Act of 1905 Volume XII

7-NB-851

Muskogee, Indian Territory, April 13, 1906.

Dana Homer,
    Bennington, Indian Territory.

Dear Sir:

    Receipt is hereby acknowledged of the affidavits of Sam Dyer and Daniel Williams to the birth of Willie Homer, child of Dana Homer and Mollie Homer deceased, September 10, 1903, and the same has been filed with the record in the matter of the enrollment of said child.

    There is inclosed herewith for execution by you and Kizzie Homer blanks partially filled out showing the birth of Willie Homer September 10, 1903. One affidavit of Kizzie Homer heretofore filed with this office gives the date of the birth of this child as September 10, 1904; all the other affidavits however, show the birth of this child September 10, 1903, and it this is correct you are requested to have the inclosed affidavits executed before a Notary Public and return the same to this office at the earliest practicable date.

                              Respectfully,

KB 2-12   Acting Commissioner.

7-NB-851

Muskogee, Indian Territory, July 27, 1906.

Dana A. Homer,
    Bennington, Indian Territory.

Dear Sir:

    Receipt is hereby acknowledged of your two letters of June 21 and July 23, 1904, asking if the enrollment of your child, Willie Homer, is approved.

    In reply you are advised that the name of your child, Willie Homer, has been placed upon a schedule of new born citizens of the Choctaw Nation, under the Act of Congress approved March 3, 1905, which is now being prepared for forwarding to the Secretary of the Interior, and you will be notified when his enrollment is approved.

                              Respectfully,

                                        Commissioner.

Applications for Enrollment of Choctaw Newborn
Act of 1905   Volume XII

<u>Choc New Born 852</u>
    Albert Jones   b.   12-25-04

7-NB-852.

Muskogee, Indian Territory, June 1, 1905.

Charley Jones,
    Dexter, Indian Territory.

Dear Sir:

    Referring to the application for the enrollment of your infant child, Albert Jones, born December 25, 1904, it is noted from the testimony taken on April 11, 1905, that you attended upon your wife at the time of birth of the applicant.

    In this event it will be necessary that you file in this office the affidavits of two persons, who are disinterested and not related to the applicant, who have actual knowledge of the facts that the child was born, the date of his birth; that he was living on March 4, 1905, and that Ellen Jones is his mother.

    The testimony of Rhoda Bohanan, in support of these facts, is on file in this office. It will, therefore, be necessary that you secure the affidavit of another person to the same facts.

Respectfully,

Chairman.

7-NB-852

Muskogee, Indian Territory, July 28, 1905.

Charley Jones,
    Dexter, Indian Territory.

Dear Sir:

    Your attention is called to a communication addressed to you by the Commission to the Five Civilized Tribes, under date of June 1, 1905, in which you were requested to furnish additional evidence relative to the enrollment of your child, Albert Jones, born December 25, 1904.

    In said letter you were requested to furnish the affidavit of one person who is disinterested and not related to the applicant, and who has actual knowledge of the facts,

Applications for Enrollment of Choctaw Newborn
Act of 1905   Volume XII

that the child was born, the date of his birth, that he was living March 4, 1905, and that Ellen Jones is his mother. No reply to this letter has been received.

This matter should receive your immediate attention as no further action can be taken relative to the enrollment of your said child until the evidence requested is supplied.

Respectfully,

Commissioner.

7-NB-852

Muskogee, Indian Territory, July 31, 1905.

F. M. Fuller,
    Attorney at Law.
    Nashoba, Indian Territory.

Dear Sir:

Receipt is hereby acknowledged of your letter of July 24, 1905, enclosing what porports[sic] to be a joint affidavit of Ben and Winnie Benjiman[sic] to the birth of Albert Jones, child of Charley and Ellen Jones, and the same are returned herewith for the reason that it is not signed by the affiants.

Kindly have Ben and Winnie Benjiman appear before you and sign and acknowledge the affidavit enclosed herewith and return the same to this office as early as practicable.

Respectfully,

Commissioner.

KB 1-13

Applications for Enrollment of Choctaw Newborn
Act of 1905   Volume XII

REFER IN REPLY TO THE FOLLOWING:

DEPARTMENT OF THE INTERIOR,
COMMISSIONER TO THE FIVE CIVILIZED TRIBES.

Tuskahoma, Indian Territory, February 20, 1906.

Rev. William H. McKinney,
    Tuskahoma, Indian Territory.

Dear Sir:

    Regarding the enrollment of Albert Jones, New Born Choctaw by blood, son of Charley and Ellen Jones, of Dexter, Indian Territory, I submit the following data:

    Ellen Jones, as lawful wife of Charley Jones, has made affidavit that the child was born on December 25, 1904.

    It appears that no mid-wife or physician attended the said Ellen Jones at the time of the birth of this child, and it is necessary to secure the affidavits of two disinterested parties as to the birth of the child. The affidavit and evidence of one disinterested party has already been procured by the Commission. I enclose you two birth proofs, one blank and one partly filled, which you get a disinterested party to make affidavit as to the birth, on the 25th of December 1904, of Albert Jones, the new born son of the aforesaid parties. The blank birth proof you use for any occasion that presents itself. I trust you will have an opportunity to procure this affidavit, as the enrollment of the child will be postponed until said affidavit is secured. There is enclosed herewith two official envelopes for you to transmit the affidavit when secured to the Commissioner at Muskogee.

    With best wished, I am

        Very truly yours,

            Lacey P. Bobo.

7-NB-852

        Muskogee, Indian Territory, March 2, 1906.

W. H. McKinney,
    Smithville, Indian Territory.

Dear Sir:

    Receipt is hereby acknowledged of your letter of February 26, 1906, inclosing the affidavit of Wade Bohanon to the birth of Albert Jones, child of Charles and Ellen Jones, December 25, 1904, and the same has been filed with the record in the matter of the enrollment of said child.

Applications for Enrollment of Choctaw Newborn
Act of 1905 Volume XII

Respectfully,

Acting Commissioner.

7-NB-852

Muskogee, Indian Territory, July 26, 1906.

Charles Jones,
    Nashoba, Indian Territory.

Dear Sir:

    Receipt is hereby acknowledged of your letter of May 21, 1906, in which you ask the status of the enrollment of your child Albert Jones.

    In reply you are advised that the name of your child, Albert Jones, has been placed upon a schedule of new born citizens of the Choctaw Nation, under the Act of Congress approved April 26, 1906, which is now being prepared for forwarding to the Secretary of the Interior and you will be notified when his enrollment is approved.

Respectfully,

Commissioner.

7-NB-852

Muskogee, Indian Territory, August 14, 1906.

Lacey P. Bobo,
    Talihina, Indian Territory.

Dear Sir:-

    Receipt is hereby acknowledged of your letter of July 23, 1906, asking to be advised if affidavits have been received to the birth of Albert Jones.

    In reply you are advised that affidavits have been received to the birth of said child, and his name has been placed upon a schedule of new born citizens of the Choctaw Nation, under the Act of Congress approved March 3, 1905, which has been forwarded to the Secretary of the Interior. It will not be necessary for you to take further steps to secure additional testimony in this case.

Respectfully,

Commissioner.

Applications for Enrollment of Choctaw Newborn
Act of 1905   Volume XII

DEPARTMENT OF THE INTERIOR,
COMMISSION TO THE FIVE CIVILIZED TRIBES.
TUSKAHOMA, IND. TER.,   APRIL 11, 1905.

In the matter of the application for the enrollment of Albert Jones as a citizen by blood of the Choctaw Nation.

Ellen Jones being sworn and examined through interpreter S. B. McKinney testifies as follows:

EXAMINATION BY THE COMMISSION:

Q What is your name? A Ellen Jones.
Q What is your age? A Twenty.
Q What is your post office address? A Dexter.
Q You have this day made application for the enrollment of your minor child Albert Jones as a citizen of the Choctaw Nation; when was this child born? A 25th day of December 1904.
Q What is the name of the father of this child? A Charley Jones.
Q Who attended you in the capacity of doctor or midwife when your child was born? A The father of the child.

Witness excused.

Charley Jones being sworn and esamined[sic] through S. B. McKinney interpreter testifies as follows:

EXAMINATION BY THE COMMISSION:

Q What is your name? A Charley Jones.
Q What is your age? A Over thirty years old.
Q What is your post office address? A Dexter.
Q Your wife, Ellen Jones, has this day made application for the enrollment of your minor child Albert Jones as a citizen of the Choctaw Nation; now when was Albert Jones born? A 25th of December 1904.
Q Was that child living on March 4, 1905? A Yes, sir.
Q Who attended you wife in the capacity of midwife or doctor when this child Albert Jones was born? A Himself.

Witness excused.

Applications for Enrollment of Choctaw Newborn
Act of 1905   Volume XII

Rhoda Bohanan being first duly sworn and examined through S. B. McKinney interpreter testifies as follows:

EXAMINATION BY THE COMMISSION:

Q What is your name? Rhoda Bohanan.
Q What is your age? A Twenty-five.
Q What is your post office address? A Nashoba.
Q Are you a citizen by blood of the Choctaw Nation? A Yes, sir.
Q Are you acquainted with Ellen Jones who has this day made application for the enrollment of her minor child Albert Jones as a citizen by blood of the Choctaw Nation? A Yes, sir.
Q Do you know when Albert Jones was born? A Yes, sir.
Q When? A December last year on Christmas day.
Q Was Albert Jones living on March 4, 1905? A Yes, sir.
Q How far does Ellen Jones live from you? A Five miles.
Q You see her frequently? A Yes, sir.

Witness excused.

Chas. T. Difendafer being first duly sworn states that the above and foregoing is a full, true and correct transcript of his stenographic notes taken in said cause on said date.

Chas. T. Difendafer

Subscribed and sworn to before me this 11th day of April 1905.

OL Johnson
Notary Public.

BIRTH AFFIDAVIT.

DEPARTMENT OF THE INTERIOR.
COMMISSION TO THE FIVE CIVILIZED TRIBES.

IN RE APPLICATION FOR ENROLLMENT, as a citizen of the   Choctaw   Nation, of Albert Jones   , born on the 25 day of December , 1904

Name of Father: Charles Jones   a citizen of the   Choctaw   Nation.
Name of Mother: Ellen Jones   a citizen of the   Choctaw   Nation.

Postoffice   Dexter, I.T.

Applications for Enrollment of Choctaw Newborn
Act of 1905 Volume XII

AFFIDAVIT OF ATTENDING PHYSICIAN OR MID-WIFE.

UNITED STATES OF AMERICA, Indian Territory, }
    Central   DISTRICT.

am acquainted with

I, Wade Bohanon , a disinterested person , on oath state that I ~~attended on~~ Mrs. Ellen Jones , wife of Charley Jones *I know* on the 25th day of December , 1904; that there was born to her on said date a male child; that said child was living March 4, 1905, and is said to have been named Albert Jones

                                  Wade Bohanon

Witnesses To Mark:
{

Subscribed and sworn to before me this 26 day of February , 1906

                          (Name Illegible)
                          Notary Public.

BIRTH AFFIDAVIT.

DEPARTMENT OF THE INTERIOR.
COMMISSION TO THE FIVE CIVILIZED TRIBES.

IN RE APPLICATION FOR ENROLLMENT, as a citizen of the Choctaw Nation, of Albert Jones , born on the 25th day of December , 1904

Name of Father: Charley Jones   a citizen of the Choctaw Nation.
Name of Mother: Ellen Jones   a citizen of the Choctaw Nation.

                    Postoffice   Dexter Ind. Ter.

AFFIDAVIT OF MOTHER.

UNITED STATES OF AMERICA, Indian Territory, }
    Central   DISTRICT.

I, Ellen Jones , on oath state that I am 20 years of age and a citizen by blood , of the Choctaw Nation; that I am the lawful wife of Charley Jones , who is a citizen, by blood of the Choctaw Nation; that a male child was born to me on 25th day of December , 1904; that said child has been named Albert Jones , and was living March 4, 1905.

                              Ellen Jones

Witnesses To Mark:
{

Applications for Enrollment of Choctaw Newborn
Act of 1905   Volume XII

Subscribed and sworn to before me this 11th day of   April   , 1905

         OL Johnson
         Notary Public.

Choc New Born 853
  Harry John b. 6-17-04

7- 5373 - 5081

BIRTH AFFIDAVIT.

DEPARTMENT OF THE INTERIOR.
COMMISSION TO THE FIVE CIVILIZED TRIBES.

  IN RE APPLICATION FOR ENROLLMENT, as a citizen of the   Choctaw   Nation, of Harry John   , born on the 17   day of June   , 1904

Name of Father: George John   a citizen of the   Choc   Nation.
Name of Mother: Sophia John (nee Carnes a citizen of the   Choc   Nation.

      Postoffice   Dexter Ind Ter

AFFIDAVIT OF MOTHER.

UNITED STATES OF AMERICA, Indian Territory, }
  Central   DISTRICT. }

  I,   Sophia John   , on oath state that I am   20   years of age and a citizen by blood   , of the   Choctaw   Nation; that I am the lawful wife of   George John , who is a citizen, by blood   of the   Choctaw   Nation; that a   male   child was born to me on   17   day of   June   , 1904; that said child has been named   Harry John   , and was living March 4, 1905.

        Sophia John

Witnesses To Mark:
{

  Subscribed and sworn to before me this   11 day of   April   , 1905

         OL Johnson
         Notary Public.

Applications for Enrollment of Choctaw Newborn
Act of 1905   Volume XII

AFFIDAVIT OF ATTENDING PHYSICIAN OR MID-WIFE.

UNITED STATES OF AMERICA, Indian Territory, }
   Central   DISTRICT. }

I, Lucinda Anderson, a midwife, on oath state that I attended on Mrs. Sophia John, wife of George John on the 17 day of June, 1904; that there was born to her on said date a male child; that said child was living March 4, 1905, and is said to have been named Harry John

                                              her
                                   Lucinda x Anderson

Witnesses To Mark: mark
   { Chas T. Difendafer
     OL Johnson

Subscribed and sworn to before me this 11 day of April, 1905

                                  OL Johnson
                                  Notary Public.

Choc New Born 854
      William Baker b. 1-31-03
      Raney Baker b. 2-27-05

7-3771-3770

BIRTH AFFIDAVIT.
                  DEPARTMENT OF THE INTERIOR.
             COMMISSION TO THE FIVE CIVILIZED TRIBES.

IN RE APPLICATION FOR ENROLLMENT, as a citizen of the Choctaw Nation, of Raney Baker, born on the 27 day of February, 1905

Name of Father: Hodgen Baker   a citizen of the Choctaw Nation.
Name of Mother: Lecy Anna Baker   a citizen of the Choctaw Nation.

                        Postoffice   Neshoba I.T.

Applications for Enrollment of Choctaw Newborn
Act of 1905   Volume XII

AFFIDAVIT OF MOTHER.

UNITED STATES OF AMERICA, Indian Territory, }
Central   DISTRICT.

I, Lecy Anna Baker, on oath state that I am 38 years of age and a citizen by blood, of the Choctaw Nation; that I am the lawful wife of Hodgen Baker, who is a citizen, by blood of the Choctaw Nation; that a male child was born to me on 27 day of February, 1905; that said child has been named Raney Baker, and was living March 4, 1905.

                              her
                       Lecy Anna x Baker

Witnesses To Mark: mark
  { Chas. T. Difendafer
    OL Johnson

Subscribed and sworn to before me this 10 day of April, 1905

                    OL Johnson
                    Notary Public.

AFFIDAVIT OF ATTENDING PHYSICIAN OR MID-WIFE.

UNITED STATES OF AMERICA, Indian Territory, }
Central   DISTRICT.

I, Jane Cooper, a midwife, on oath state that I attended on Mrs. Lecy Anna Baker, wife of Hodgen Baker on the 27 day of February, 1905; that there was born to her on said date a male child; that said child was living March 4, 1905, and is said to have been named Raney Baker

                              her
                       Jane x Cooper

Witnesses To Mark: mark
  { Chas. T. Difendafer
    OL Johnson

Subscribed and sworn to before me this 10 day of April, 1905

                    OL Johnson
                    Notary Public.

Applications for Enrollment of Choctaw Newborn
Act of 1905 Volume XII

7- 3771- 3770

BIRTH AFFIDAVIT.

DEPARTMENT OF THE INTERIOR.
COMMISSION TO THE FIVE CIVILIZED TRIBES.

IN RE APPLICATION FOR ENROLLMENT, as a citizen of the Choctaw Nation, of William Baker , born on the 31 day of January , 1903

Name of Father: Hodgen Baker   a citizen of the Choctaw Nation.
Name of Mother: Lecy Anna Baker   a citizen of the Choctaw Nation.

Postoffice   Neshoba I.T.

AFFIDAVIT OF MOTHER.

UNITED STATES OF AMERICA, Indian Territory, }
    Central   DISTRICT.

    I, Lecy Anna Baker , on oath state that I am 38 years of age and a citizen by blood , of the Choctaw Nation; that I am the lawful wife of Hodgen Baker , who is a citizen, by blood of the Choctaw Nation; that a male child was born to me on 31 day of January , 1903; that said child has been named William Baker , and was living March 4, 1905.

                                                 her
                                 Lecy Anna x Baker
Witnesses To Mark: mark
    { Chas. T. Difendafer
      OL Johnson

    Subscribed and sworn to before me this 10 day of April , 1905

                            OL Johnson
                                 Notary Public.

AFFIDAVIT OF ATTENDING PHYSICIAN OR MID-WIFE.

UNITED STATES OF AMERICA, Indian Territory, }
    Central   DISTRICT.

    I, Jane Cooper , a midwife , on oath state that I attended on Mrs. Lecy Anna Baker , wife of Hodgen Baker on the 31 day of January , 1903; that there was born to her on said date a male child; that said child was living March 4, 1905, and is said to have been named William Baker

Applications for Enrollment of Choctaw Newborn
Act of 1905   Volume XII

                                              her
                                       Jane x Cooper

Witnesses To Mark: mark
  { Chas. T. Difendafer
    OL Johnson

Subscribed and sworn to before me this   10   day of   April   , 1905

                                       OL Johnson
                                            Notary Public.

Choc New Born 855
    Gladys Baker   b. 2-4-04

                                                       7-NB-855.

                    Muskogee, Indian Territory, June 7, 1905.

Robison Baker,
    Neshoba, Indian Territory.

Dear Sir:

    Referring to the application for the enrollment of your infant child, Gladys Baker, born February 4, 1904, it is noted in the affidavits heretofore filed in this office that you are a Choctaw by Blood.

    If this is correct you will please state when, where and under what name you were listed for enrollment, the names of your parents and other members of your family who made application at the same time, and if you have selected your allotment give your roll number as it appears upon your allotment certificate.

    This matter should receive your immediate attention as no further action can be taken until this information is furnished the Commission.

                              Respectfully,

                                                    Commissioner in Charge.

Applications for Enrollment of Choctaw Newborn
Act of 1905   Volume XII

7-NB-855

Muskogee, Indian Territory, July 28, 1905

Annie Baker,
    Nashoba, Indian Territory.

Dear Madam:

    Referring to the application for the enrollment of your infant child, Gladys Baker, born February 4, 1904, it is noted in your affidavit, executed April 10, 1905, that you allege you are the wife of Robison Baker, who is a citizen by blood of the Choctaw Nation.

    If Robison Baker is a citizen by blood of the Choctaw Nation, you are requested to state when, where and under what name he was listed for enrollment, the names of his father and mother and other members of his family who made application at the same time, and if he has selected an allotment, give his roll number as it appears upon his allotment certificate.

    This matter should be given your immediate attention as no further action can be taken relative to the enrollment of your said child until the information requested is supplied.

                        Respectfully,

                                    Commissioner.

7-NB-855.

Muskogee, Indian Territory, September 5, 1905.

Annie Baker,
    Nashoba, Indian Territory.

Dear Madam:

    Receipt is hereby acknowledged of your letter of the 31st ultimo giving information relative to your enrollment as a citizen by blood of the Choctaw Nation blood of the Choctaw Nation in the matter of the application for the enrollment of your infant child, Gladys Baker, as a citizen by blood of said nation. You ask to be advised relative to the enrollment of your said child.

    In reply thereto, you are informed that the name of your child has been placed upon a schedule of citizens by blood of the Choctaw Nation and forwarded to the Department for the approval of the Secretary of the Interior and you will be advised in due time of his action.

Applications for Enrollment of Choctaw Newborn
Act of 1905 Volume XII

Respectfully,

Acting Commissioner.

(The affidavit below typed as given.)

United States of
America Central Dist
of Ind *(Illegible)*

      Personally appeared before me a Notary Public Silas Lewis and Roberson Shoat to me well known and being duly sworn deposes and says on oath that they are well acquainted with Annie Baker and Gladys Baker infant child of Annie Baker and know that Gladys Baker is the infant child of Annie Baker by seeing her nurse the child and com for it by supporting it and know Gladys Baker was living on the 4 of March 1905 and is still living and know Gladys Baker was born the 4 day of February 1904 and that they know these facts by living near Annie Baker residence and be *(illegible)* often at her house.

                                              Silas Lewis
                                                    his
                                           Roberson x Shoat
                                                   mark

Subscribed and sworn to before me this the 22 day of November 1905

                                                F M Fuller
                                                Notary Public

My commission expires April 18th 1908

BIRTH AFFIDAVIT.

DEPARTMENT OF THE INTERIOR.
COMMISSION TO THE FIVE CIVILIZED TRIBES.

      IN RE APPLICATION FOR ENROLLMENT, as a citizen of the   Choctaw   Nation, of Gladys Baker   , born on the 4 day of February , 1904

Name of Father: Roberson[sic] Baker   a citizen of the Choctaw   Nation.
Name of Mother: Annie Baker   a citizen of the Choctaw   Nation.

                                  Postoffice   Nashoba I T

Applications for Enrollment of Choctaw Newborn
Act of 1905   Volume XII

AFFIDAVIT OF MOTHER.

UNITED STATES OF AMERICA, Indian Territory,
Central   DISTRICT.

I, Annie Baker, on oath state that I am 20 years of age and a citizen by blood, of the Choctaw Nation; that I am the lawful wife of Roberson Baker, who is a citizen, by blood of the Choctaw Nation; that a Female child was born to me on 4 day of February, 1904; that said child has been named Gladys Baker, and was living March 4, 1905.

Annie Baker

Witnesses To Mark:
- Silas Lewis
- Nellie Halday

Subscribed and sworn to before me this 21 day of November, 1905

My Commission
Expires April 18th 1908

F M Fuller
Notary Public.

AFFIDAVIT OF ATTENDING PHYSICIAN OR MID-WIFE.

UNITED STATES OF AMERICA, Indian Territory,
Central   DISTRICT.

I, Emily Hardy, a mid wife, on oath state that I attended on Mrs. Annie Baker, wife of Roberson Baker on the 4 day of February, 1904; that there was born to her on said date a Female child; that said child was living March 4, 1905, and is said to have been named Gladys Baker

Emily x Hardy

Witnesses To Mark:
- Silas Lewis
- Nellie Halday

Subscribed and sworn to before me this .... day of ...., 1905.

Notary Public.

281

Applications for Enrollment of Choctaw Newborn
Act of 1905   Volume XII

BIRTH AFFIDAVIT.

DEPARTMENT OF THE INTERIOR.
COMMISSION TO THE FIVE CIVILIZED TRIBES.

IN RE APPLICATION FOR ENROLLMENT, as a citizen of the   Choctaw   Nation, of   Gladys Baker   , born on the   4   day of   February   , 1904

Name of Father: Robison Baker   a citizen of the   Choctaw   Nation.
Name of Mother: Annie Baker nee Hardy   a citizen of the   Choctaw   Nation.

Postoffice   Neshoba I. T.

AFFIDAVIT OF MOTHER.

UNITED STATES OF AMERICA, Indian Territory, }
   Central   DISTRICT.

I,   Annie Baker nee Hardy   , on oath state that I am   20   years of age and a citizen by   blood   , of the   Choctaw   Nation; that I am the lawful wife of   Robison Baker   , who is a citizen, by blood   of the   Choctaw   Nation; that a   female   child was born to me on   4th day of   February   , 1904; that said child has been named   Gladys Baker   , and was living March 4, 1905.

Annie Baker

Witnesses To Mark:
{

Subscribed and sworn to before me this   10   day of   April   , 1905

OL Johnson
Notary Public.

AFFIDAVIT OF ATTENDING PHYSICIAN OR MID-WIFE.

UNITED STATES OF AMERICA, Indian Territory, }
   Central   DISTRICT.

I,   Emily Hardy   , a   midwife   , on oath state that I attended on Mrs.   Annie Baker   , wife of   Robison Baker   on the 4th day of   February   , 1904; that there was born to her on said date a   female   child; that said child was living March 4, 1905, and is said to have been named   Gladys Baker

Applications for Enrollment of Choctaw Newborn
Act of 1905   Volume XII

Witnesses To Mark:
{ Chas. T. Difendafer
{ OL Johnson

                her
Emily x Hardy
                mark

Subscribed and sworn to before me this 10 day of April , 1905

            OL Johnson
                Notary Public.

Choc New Born 856
    Sidney Bohanan   b. 2-4-05

7- 5571

BIRTH AFFIDAVIT.

DEPARTMENT OF THE INTERIOR.
COMMISSION TO THE FIVE CIVILIZED TRIBES.

IN RE APPLICATION FOR ENROLLMENT, as a citizen of the Choctaw Nation, of Sidney Bohanon , born on the 4 day of February , 1905

Name of Father: Watson Bohanon   a citizen of the Choc Nation.
Name of Mother: Rhoda Bohanon nee Frazier   a citizen of the Choc Nation.

            Postoffice   Nashoba I.T.

AFFIDAVIT OF MOTHER.

UNITED STATES OF AMERICA, Indian Territory, }
    Central   DISTRICT. }

    I, Rhoda Bohanon , on oath state that I am 25 years of age and a citizen by blood , of the Choctaw Nation; that I am the lawful wife of Watson Bohanon , who is a citizen, by blood of the Choctaw Nation; that a male child was born to me on 4 day of February , 1905; that said child has been named Sidney Bohanon , and was living March 4, 1905.

                  her
            Rhoda x Bohanon
                mark

Applications for Enrollment of Choctaw Newborn
Act of 1905 Volume XII

Witnesses To Mark:
{ Chas. T. Difendafer
  OL Johnson

    Subscribed and sworn to before me this 11 day of April , 1905

                                OL Johnson
                                      Notary Public.

AFFIDAVIT OF ATTENDING PHYSICIAN OR MID-WIFE.

UNITED STATES OF AMERICA, Indian Territory, }
   Central   DISTRICT. }

    I, Ellen Jones , a midwife , on oath state that I attended on Mrs. Rhoda Bohanon , wife of Watson Bohanon on the 4 day of February , 1905; that there was born to her on said date a male child; that said child was living March 4, 1905, and is said to have been named Sidney Bohanon

                                Ellen Jones

Witnesses To Mark:
{

    Subscribed and sworn to before me this 11 day of April , 1905

                                OL Johnson
                                  Notary Public.

<u>Choc New Born 857</u>
    Martin Van Noah b. 10-3-03

7-5906
7-5907.

                DEPARTMENT OF THE INTERIOR,
        COMMISSION TO THE FIVE CIVILIZED TRIBES.
          TUSKAHOMA, IND. TER., APRIL 11, 1905.

    In the matter of the application for the enrollment of Martin Van Noah as a citizen by blood of the Choctaw Nation

Margaret J. Noah being first duly sworn testifies as follows:

Applications for Enrollment of Choctaw Newborn
Act of 1905   Volume XII

EXAMINATION BY THE COMMISSION:

Q What is your name? Margaret J. Noah.
Q What is your age? A Thirty-two.
Q What is your post office address? A Albion.
Q You have this day made application for the enrollment of your minor child Martin van Noah as a citizen of the Choctaw Nation; when was Martin Van Noah born? A October 3, 1903.
Q Who is the father of Martin Van Noah? A D. S. Noah.
Q Who attended you at the time this child was born in the capacity of doctor or midwife? A His father.
Q Is he a doctor? A No, sir.
Q You didn't have a doctor or midwife? A No, sir.
Q Was Martin Van Noah living on March 4, 1905?: A Yes, sir.

Witness excused.

D. S. Noah being first duly sworn testifies as follows:

EXAMINATION BY THE COMMISSION:

Q What is your name? A D. S. Noah.
Q How old are you? A Thirty-four.
Q What is your post office address? A Albion.
Q Your wife has this day made application for the enrollment of her child Martin Van Noah as a citizen of the Choctaw Nation; when was this child born? A 3rd day of October 1903.
Q Was this child living on March 4, 1905? A Yes, sir, living today.
Q Who attended your wife? A Nobody, I did myself.

Witness excused.

S. B. McKinney being first duly sworn and examined testifies as follows:

EXAMINATION BY THE COMMISSION:

Q What is your name? A S. B. McKinney.
Q What is your age? A Fifty-four.
Q What is your post office address? A Tuskahoma.
Q Are you a citizen by blood of the Choctaw Nation? A Yes, sir.
Q Are you acquainted with Margaret J. Noah and D. S. Noah who have this day made application for the enrollment of their child Martin Van Noah as a citizen of the Choctaw Nation? A Yes, sir.
Q Do you know about what time this child was born? A Yes, sir, October 3, 1903.
Q How far from Mr. Noah did you live at the time of the birth of this child? A About two hundred yards.

Applications for Enrollment of Choctaw Newborn
Act of 1905 Volume XII

Witness excused.

Chas. T. Difendafer being first duly sworn states that the above and foregoing is a full, true and correct transcript of his stenographic notes taken in said cause on said date.

Chas. T. Difendafer

Subscribed and sworn to before me this 12th day of April 1905.

OL Johnson
Notary Public.

Affidavit of Nancy McKinney

Indian Territory Central District.

Before me Robert D Francis, a Notary Public in and for the Central District and Territory personally appeared Nancy McKinney who being by me duly sworn upon oath state that I am 53 years of age and a citizen by blood of the Choctaw Nation, and my Post Office address is Tuskahoma, Indian Territory.

On or about the 3rd day of October 1903, I came to the residence of D. S. Noah and there I saw a male child who is said to be born just a few minutes before I came. And his mother Margaret J., Noah, wife of D. S. Noah, was in bed nursing the said child. I am well acquainted with both parents and applicant, and the said child is now living and is said to have been named Martin van Noah.

I am not interested neither related to the said applicant.

                                                                  her
Witness to Mark   Nancy x McKinney
By two { *(Name Illegible)*   mark
       { H.L. Hurdsick

Subscribed and sworn to before me this 16th day of June 1905.

RD Francis
My Commission expires   Notary Public
    Jan 8-1908

Applications for Enrollment of Choctaw Newborn
Act of 1905 Volume XII

7-5906-5907

BIRTH AFFIDAVIT.

DEPARTMENT OF THE INTERIOR.
COMMISSION TO THE FIVE CIVILIZED TRIBES.

IN RE APPLICATION FOR ENROLLMENT, as a citizen of the Choctaw Nation, of Martin Van Noah, born on the 3rd day of October, 1903

Name of Father: D. S. Noah   a citizen of the Choctaw Nation.
Name of Mother: Margaret J Noah   a citizen of the Choctaw Nation.

Postoffice   Albion, Ind. Ter.

AFFIDAVIT OF MOTHER.

UNITED STATES OF AMERICA, Indian Territory,
Central   DISTRICT.

I, Margaret J. Noah, on oath state that I am 32 years of age and a citizen by blood, of the Choctaw Nation; that I am the lawful wife of D. S. Noah, who is a citizen, by blood of the Choctaw Nation; that a male child was born to me on 3rd day of October, 1903; that said child has been named Martin Van Noah, and was living March 4, 1905.

Margaret J Noah

Witnesses To Mark:

Subscribed and sworn to before me this 11th day of April, 1905

OL Johnson
Notary Public.

Applications for Enrollment of Choctaw Newborn
Act of 1905   Volume XII

7 NB 857

Muskogee, Indian Territory, June 22, 1905.

D. S. Noah,
    Talihina, Indian Territory.

Dear Sir:

    Receipt is hereby acknowledged of the affidavit of Nancy McKinney to the birth of your child Martin Van Noah, son of D. S. and Margaret J. Noah, October 3, 1903, and the same has been filed with our records in the matter of the enrollment of said child.

        Respectfully,

                Chairman.

7-NB-857.

Muskogee, Indian Territory, June 1, 1905.

D. S. Noah,
    Albion, Indian Territory.

Dear Sir:

    Referring to the application for the enrollment of your infant child, Martin Van Noah, born October 3, 1903, it is noted from the testimony taken on April 11, 1904, that you attended upon your wife at the time of birth of the applicant.

    In this event it will be necessary that you file in this office the affidavits of two persons, who are disinterested and not related to the applicant, who have actual knowledge of the facts that the child was born, the date of his birth; that he was living on March 4, 1905, and that Margaret J. Noah is his mother.

    The testimony of S. B. McKinney, in support of these facts, is on file in this office. It will, therefore, be necessary that you secure the affidavit of another person to the same facts.

        Respectfully,

                Chairman.

Applications for Enrollment of Choctaw Newborn
Act of 1905   Volume XII

Choc New Born 858
    Ruth Anderson   b. 2-8-03

7-NB-858.

Muskogee, Indian Territory, June 1, 1905.

Watson Anderson,
    Tuskahoma, Indian Territory.

Dear Sir:

    Referring to the application for the enrollment of your infant child, Ruth Anderson, born February 8, 1903, it is noted from the testimony taken on April 12, 1905, that Mrs. Carnes, your sister, attended upon your wife at the time of birth of the applicant.

    If this is correct it will be necessary that you file in this office the affidavits of two persons, who are disinterested and not related to the applicant, who have actual knowledge of the facts that the child was born, the date of her birth; that she was living on March 4, 1905, and that Lucinda Anderson is her mother. The testimony of Josephine Bohanan, heretofore filed in this office, does not fulfill these requirements, as she failed to give the date of the applicant's birth.

    Respectfully,

    Chairman.

U.S. of America
Ind. Ter
Central District

We Rufus Allen and George W. Bell on oath states that they are personally acquainted with Ruth Anderson and that she was born Feby 8-1903 and that she was living on March 4th 1905, and Lucinda Anderson is her mother, In witness where of we sign our hand this the 24 day of June - 1905
    Signed   Rufus Allen
                    George W. Bell

Subscribed & sworn to before me this the 24 - 1905

    P.W. Hudson
My com expires 2/24/06   Notary Public
    Tuskahoma I.T.

Applications for Enrollment of Choctaw Newborn
Act of 1905   Volume XII

COMMISSIONERS:
TAMS BIXBY,
THOMAS B. NEEDLES,
C.R. BRECKINBRIDGE.

WM. O. BEALL
Secretary

DEPARTMENT OF THE INTERIOR,
COMMISSIONER TO THE FIVE CIVILIZED TRIBES.

Wm O.B.

REFER IN REPLY TO THE FOLLOWING:

7-NB-858.

ADDRESS ONLY THE
COMMISSION TO THE FIVE CIVILIZED TRIBES.

Muskogee, Indian Territory, June 1, 1905.

Watson Anderson,
    Tuskahoma, Indian Territory.

Dear Sir:

    Referring to the application for the enrollment of your infant child, Ruth Anderson, born February 8, 1903, it is noted from the testimony taken on April 12, 1905, that Mrs. Carnes, your sister, attended upon your wife at the time of birth of the applicant.

    If this is correct it will be necessary that you file in this office the affidavits of two persons, who are disinterested and not related to the applicant, who have actual knowledge of the facts that the child was born, the date of her birth; that she was living on March 4, 1905, and that Lucinda Anderson is her mother. The testimony of Josephine Bohanan, heretofore filed in this office, does not fulfill these requirements, as she failed to give the date of the applicants birth.

                      Respectfully,
                        TB Needles
                                Commissioner in Charge.

Choctaw N B 858

Muskogee, Indian Territory, June 28, 1905.

Watson Anderson,
    Tuskahoma, Indian Territory.

Dear Sir:

    Receipt is hereby acknowledged of the joint affidavit of Rufus Allen and George W. Bell to the birth of Ruth Anderson, daughter of Watson and Lucinda Anderson, February 8, 1903, and the same has been filed with the record in the matter of the enrollment of said child.

                      Respectfully,

                                Chairman.

Applications for Enrollment of Choctaw Newborn
Act of 1905 Volume XII

7-5301-5302. DEPARTMENT OF THE INTERIOR,
COMMISSION TO THE FIVE CIVILIZED TRIBES.
TUSKAHOMA, IND. TER., APRIL 11, 1905.

In the matter of the application for the enrollment of Ruth Anderson as a citizen by blood of the Choctaw Nation.

Josephine Bohanan being first duly sworn testifies as follows:

EXAMINATION BY THE COMMISSION:

Q What is your name? A Josephine Bohanan.
Q What is your age? A Twenty-six.
Q What is your post office address? A Tuskahoma.
Q Are you a citizen by blood of the Choctaw Nation? A Yes, sir.
Q Are you acquainted with Lucinda Anderson who has this day made application for her minor child Ruth Anderson? A Yes, sir.
Q Who is the husband of Lucinda Anderson? A Watson.
Q Do you know when Ruth Anderson was born? A Yes, sir.
Q When was Ruth Anderson born? A February.
Q How long ago was it - year or two years? A Two years ago.
Q Were you present when this child was born? A No.
Q Did you see this child shortly after it was born? A Yes, sir.
Q Was Ruth Anderson living on March 4, 1905? A Yes, sir.
Q How far do you live from Mrs. Anderson? A About three miles I guess.
Q How often do you see her? A Every week.

Witness excused.

Watson Anderson being first duly sworn testifies as follows:

EXAMINATION BY THE COMMISSION:

Q What is your name? A Watson Anderson.
Q How old are you? A About fifty-six I guess.
Q What is your post office address? A Tuskahoma.
Q Are you a citizen by blood of the Choctaw Nation? A Yes, sir.
Q Your wife Lucinda Anderson has this day made application for her child Ruth Anderson as a citizen of the Choctaw Nation; now when was this child born?
A February 8, 1903.
Q Who attended your wife when this child was born? A My sister, Mrs. Carnes.
Q Where is she now? A She is at home.
Q Is she able to appear here before us before Friday next? A I couldn't say, she has been sick nearly a year.
Q Mr. Anderson was this child Ruth Anderson living on March 4, 1905? A Yes, sir.

Applications for Enrollment of Choctaw Newborn
Act of 1905   Volume XII

Witness excused.

Chas. T. Difendafer being first duly sworn states that the above and foregoing is a full, true and correct transcript of his stenographic notes taken in said cause on said date.

Chas T Difendafer

Subscribed and sworn to before me this 12th day of April 1905.

OL Johnson
Notary Public.

BIRTH AFFIDAVIT.   7- 5301- 5302

DEPARTMENT OF THE INTERIOR.
COMMISSION TO THE FIVE CIVILIZED TRIBES.

IN RE APPLICATION FOR ENROLLMENT, as a citizen of the   Choctaw   Nation, of Ruth Anderson   , born on the 8   day of February   , 1903

Name of Father: Watson Anderson   a citizen of the   Choct   Nation.
Name of Mother: Lucinda Anderson   a citizen of the   Choctaw   Nation.

Postoffice   Tuskahoma

AFFIDAVIT OF MOTHER.

UNITED STATES OF AMERICA, Indian Territory, }
    Central   DISTRICT.

I, Lucinda Anderson   , on oath state that I am   43   years of age and a citizen by   blood   , of the   Choc   Nation; that I am the lawful wife of   Watson Anderson , who is a citizen, by blood   of the   Choc   Nation; that a   female child was born to me on   8   day of   February   , 1903; that said child has been named   Ruth Anderson   , and was living March 4, 1905.

her
Lucinda x Anderson
mark

Witnesses To Mark:
{ Chas T Difendafer
{ OL Johnson

Subscribed and sworn to before me this 11 day of   April   , 1905

OL Johnson
Notary Public.

Applications for Enrollment of Choctaw Newborn
Act of 1905 Volume XII

Choc New Born 859
    Bessie Anderson   b. 3-1-04

$W^m O.B.$

COMMISSIONERS:
TAMS BIXBY,
THOMAS B. NEEDLES,
C.R. BRECKINBRIDGE.

DEPARTMENT OF THE INTERIOR,
COMMISSIONER TO THE FIVE CIVILIZED TRIBES.

REFER IN REPLY TO THE FOLLOWING:

7-NB-859.

WM. O. BEALL
Secretary

ADDRESS ONLY THE
COMMISSION TO THE FIVE CIVILIZED TRIBES.

Muskogee, Indian Territory, June 1, 1905.

Norton Anderson,
    Tuskahoma, Indian Territory.

Dear Sir:

    Referring to the application for the enrollment of your infant child, Bessie Anderson, born March 1, 1904, it is noted from the affidavits heretofore filed in this office that you attended upon your wife at the time of birth of the applicant.

    In this event it will be necessary that you file in this office the affidavits of two persons, who are disinterested and not related to the applicant, who have actual knowledge of the facts that the child was born, the date of her birth; that she was living on March 4, 1905, and that Mary Anderson is her mother.

    The testimony of Lucinda Anderson to these facts has been filed. It will, therefore, be necessary that you secure an affidavit of another person to the same facts.

                            Respectfully,
                                TB Needles
                                      Commissioner in Charge.

Applications for Enrollment of Choctaw Newborn
Act of 1905   Volume XII

7 NB 859

Muskogee, Indian Territory, June 16, 1905.

Norton Anderson,
   Tuskahoma, Indian Territory.

Dear Sir:

   Receipt is hereby acknowledged of the joint affidavit of David Allen and Byington Ben to the birth of Bessie Anderson, daughter of Norton and Mary Anderson, March 1, 1904, and the same has been filed with the records in this case.

Respectfully,

Chairman.

NEW-BORN AFFIDAVIT.

Number..................

...Choctaw Enrolling Commission...

   IN THE MATTER OF THE APPLICATION FOR ENROLLMENT, as a citizen of the Choctaw   Nation, of   Bessie Anderson

born on the   1st day of ___March___ 190 4

Name of father   Norton Anderson   a citizen of   Choctaw
Nation final enrollment No.   13930
Name of mother   Mary Anderson   a citizen of   Choctaw
Nation final enrollment No.   5530

                                    Postoffice   Tuskahoma I.T.

AFFIDAVIT OF MOTHER.
UNITED STATES OF AMERICA
INDIAN TERRITORY
     Central   DISTRICT

         I   Mary Anderson   , on oath state that I am   28   years of age and a citizen by   Blood   of the   Choc   Nation, and as such have been placed upon the final roll of the   Choctaw   Nation, by the Honorable Secretary of the Interior my final enrollment number being   5530   ; that I am the lawful wife of   Norton Anderson   , who is a citizen of the   Choctaw   Nation, and as such has

294

Applications for Enrollment of Choctaw Newborn
Act of 1905 Volume XII

been placed upon the final roll of said Nation by the Honorable Secretary of the Interior, his final enrollment number being 13930 and that a Female child was born to me on the 1st day of March 190 5; that said child has been named Bessie Anderson, and is now living.

               her
            Mary x Anderson
Witnesseth.   mark
 Must be two   } W.H. Ishewood
 Witnesses who }
 are Citizens.   S.H. Bohanan

   Subscribed and sworn to before me this 3rd day of Mar 190 5

              Peter W Hudson
My Commission Expires Feb. 24, 1906.   Notary Public.
My commission expires:

AFFIDAVIT OF ATTENDING PHYSICIAN OR MIDWIFE

UNITED STATES OF AMERICA
INDIAN TERRITORY
 Central   DISTRICT

  I, Norton Anderson   a   Husband on oath state that I attended on Mrs. Mary Anderson wife of Norton Anderson on the 1st day of March , 190 5 , that there was born to her on said date a Female child, that said child is now living, and is said to have been named Bessie Anderson

             Norton Anderson *M.D.*
   Subscribed and sworn to before me this, the 3rd day of
   March   190 5

             Peter W Hudson Notary Public.
WITNESSETH:
 Must be two witnesses { W.H. Ishewood **My Commission Expires Feb. 24, 1906.**
 who are citizens   {
          S.H. Bohanan

  We hereby certify that we are well acquainted with Norton Anderson a Husband and know him to be reputable and of good standing in the community.

Applications for Enrollment of Choctaw Newborn
Act of 1905 Volume XII

U. S. of A
Ind. Ter
Central District

We David Allen and Byington Ben, Both citizen of the Choc Nation, on oath state that we are acquainted with Bessie Anderson and that she was born March 1, 1904, and that she was living March 4th 1905, and that Mary Anderson is her mother.

David Allen
Byington Ben

Subscribed & sworn to before me this 13th day of June 1905

My Commission Expires Feb. 24, 1906.   PW Hudson
Notary Public

7-13930-5530.
DEPARTMENT OF THE INTERIOR,
COMMISSION TO THE FIVE CIVILIZED TRIBES.
TUSKAHOMA, IND. TER., APRIL 11, 1905.

In the matter of the application for the enrollment of Bessie Anderson as a citizen by blood of the Choctaw Nation.

Mary Anderson being first duly sworn testifies as follows:

EXAMINATION BY THE COMMISSION:

Q What is your name? A Mary Anderson.
Q What is your age? A Twenty-eight.
Q What is your post office address? A Tuskahoma.
Q You have this day made application for your minor child Bessie Anderson as a citizen of the Choctaw Nation,; when was this child born? A March 1, 1904.
Q Who is the father of this child? A Norton Anderson.
Q Was this child living on March 4, 1905? A Yes, sir.
Q Who attended you when that baby was born? A My husband.
Q You didn't have any doctor or midwife? A No, sir.

Witness excused.

Norton Anderson being first duly sworn testifies as follows:

EXAMINATION BY THE COMMISSION:

Q What is your name? A Norton Anderson.
Q How old are you? A Thirty-three.

Applications for Enrollment of Choctaw Newborn
Act of 1905   Volume XII

Q What is your post office address? A Tuskahoma.
Q Your wife has this day made application for the enrollment of her child Bessie Anderson as a citizen of the Choctaw Nation; when was this child born? A March 1, 1904.
Q Was this child living on March 4, 1905? A Yes, sir.
Q Who attended your wife during her illness? A Myself.
Q You didn't have any doctor or midwife? A No, sir.

Witness excused.

Lucinda Anderson being first duly sworn testifies as follows:

EXAMINATION BY THE COMMISSION:

Q What is your name? A Lucinda Anderson.
Q How old are you? A Forty-three.
Q What is your post office address? A Tuskahoma.
Q Are you a citizen by blood of the Choctaw Nation? A Yes, sir.
Q Are you acquainted with Mary Anderson who has this day made application for the enrollment of her minor child Bessie Anderson as a citizen of the Choctaw Nation? A Yes, sir.
Q Who is the father of Bessie Anderson? A Norton Anderson
Q When was Bessie Anderson born? A March 1, 1904.
Q Were you present when this child was born? A Few minutes after it was born.
Q How far do you live from Mary Anderson? A Two miles.
Q Was Bessie Anderson living on March 4, 1905? A Yes, sir.

Witness excused.

Chas. T. Difendafer being first duly sworn states that the above and foregoing is a full, true and correct transcript of his stenographic notes taken in said cause on said date.

Chas. T. Difendafer

Subscribed and sworn to before me this 12th day of April 1905.

OL Johnson
Notary Public.

Applications for Enrollment of Choctaw Newborn
Act of 1905   Volume XII

7 - 13930 - 5530

BIRTH AFFIDAVIT.

DEPARTMENT OF THE INTERIOR.
COMMISSION TO THE FIVE CIVILIZED TRIBES.

IN RE APPLICATION FOR ENROLLMENT, as a citizen of the   Choctaw   Nation, of Bessie Anderson   , born on the 1   day of   March   , 1904

Name of Father: Norton Anderson   a citizen of the   Choc   Nation.
Name of Mother: Mary Anderson   a citizen of the   Choc   Nation.

Postoffice   Tuskahoma I.T.

AFFIDAVIT OF MOTHER.

UNITED STATES OF AMERICA, Indian Territory, }
     Central   DISTRICT.

I,   Mary Anderson   , on oath state that I am 28   years of age and a citizen by   blood   , of the   Choctaw   Nation; that I am the lawful wife of   Norton Anderson   , who is a citizen, by blood   of the   Choctaw   Nation; that a female   child was born to me on 1st day of   March   , 1904; that said child has been named   Bessie Anderson   , and was living March 4, 1905.

                                her
                        Mary x Anderson
Witnesses To Mark: mark
  { Chas T Difendafer
  { OL Johnson

Subscribed and sworn to before me this   11 day of   April   , 1905

                        OL Johnson
                            Notary Public.

Applications for Enrollment of Choctaw Newborn
Act of 1905 Volume XII

Choc New Born 860
Lillian Anderson b. 6-23-03

7-NB-860.

Muskogee, Indian Territory, May 31, 1905.

Reason Anderson,
Tuskahoma, Indian Territory.

Dear Sir:

There is enclosed you herewith for execution application for the enrollment of your infant child, Lillian Anderson, born June 23, 1903.

It is noted from the testimony taken in this case on the 12th ultimo that the mother of the applicant was sick at that time and unable to appear and give her testimony. Before this matter can be finally determined it will be necessary that you file the affidavit of the mother in this office.

In having these affidavits executed care should be exercised to see that all names are written in full, as they appear in the body of the affidavit, and in the event that either of the persons signing the affidavit are unable to write, signatures by mark must be attested by two witnesses. Each affidavit must be executed before a Notary Public and the notarial seal and signature of the officer must be attached to each separate affidavit.

Respectfully,

VR -31-11.   [sic]

7-5303-13389.

DEPARTMENT OF THE INTERIOR,
COMMISSION TO THE FIVE CIVILIZED TRIBES.
TUSKAHOMA, IND. TER.,   APRIL 11, 1905.

In the matter of the application for the enrollment of Lillian Anderson as a citizen by blood of the Choctaw Nation.

Reason Anderson being first duly sworn testifies as follows:

EXAMINATION BY THE COMMISSION:

Q What is your name? A Reason Anderson.
Q What is your age? A About twenty-seven.
Q What is your post office address? A Tuskahoma.

Applications for Enrollment of Choctaw Newborn
Act of 1905   Volume XII

Q For whom do you desire to make application today? A Lillian Anderson.
Q Who is the mother of Lillian Anderson? A Emeline Anderson.
Q What is the reason your wife is not here today to make application for her child? A Sick.
Q When was Lillian Anderson born? A Born June 23, 1903.
Q Is Lillian Anderson living today? A Yes, sir.

Witness excused.

Lucinda Anderson being first duly sworn testifies as follows:

EXAMINATION BY THE COMMISSION:

Q What is your name? A Lucinda Anderson.
Q How old are you? A Forty-three.
Q What is your post office address? A Tuskahoma.
Q Are you a citizen by blood of the Choctaw Nation? A Yes, sir.
Q Are you related in any way to Reason Anderson who has this day made application for the enrollment of his child Lillian Anderson? A Yes, sir.
Q In what way? A I am his mother.
Q Do you know when his child Lillian Anderson was born? A Yes, sir, June 23, 1903.
Q Were you present when that child was born? A Yes, sir.
Q What is the reason the mother is unable to appear here today? A Sick.
Q Is Lillian Anderson living today? A Yes, sir.

Witness excused.

Chas. T. Difendafer being first duly sworn states that the above and foregoing is a full, true and correct transcript of his stenographic notes taken in said cause on said date.

Chas. T. Difendafer

Subscribed and sworn to before me this 12th day of April 1905.

OL Johnson
Notary Public.

Applications for Enrollment of Choctaw Newborn
Act of 1905 Volume XII

7-5303   7-13389

BIRTH AFFIDAVIT.

DEPARTMENT OF THE INTERIOR.
COMMISSION TO THE FIVE CIVILIZED TRIBES.

IN RE APPLICATION FOR ENROLLMENT, as a citizen of the   Choctaw   Nation, of Lillian Anderson   , born on the 23   day of   June   , 1903

Name of Father: Reason Anderson   a citizen of the   Choc   Nation.
Name of Mother: Emeline Anderson   a citizen of the   Choc   Nation.

Postoffice   Tuskahoma

AFFIDAVIT OF ATTENDING PHYSICIAN OR MID-WIFE.

UNITED STATES OF AMERICA, Indian Territory,
.... DISTRICT.

I, Mary Anderson   , a   midwife   , on oath state that I attended on Mrs. Emeline Anderson   , wife of   Reason Anderson   on the 23   day of June   , 1903; that there was born to her on said date a   female   child; that said child was living March 4, 1905, and is said to have been named   Lillian Anderson

                                          her
                               Mary x Anderson
Witnesses To Mark: mark
   { Chas T Difendafer
   { OL Johnson

Subscribed and sworn to before me this 11 day of   April   , 1905

OL Johnson
Notary Public.

BIRTH AFFIDAVIT.

DEPARTMENT OF THE INTERIOR.
COMMISSION TO THE FIVE CIVILIZED TRIBES.

IN RE APPLICATION FOR ENROLLMENT, as a citizen of the   Choctaw   Nation, of Lillian Anderson   , born on the 23   day of   June   , 1903

Name of Father: Reason Anderson   a citizen of the   Choctaw   Nation.
Name of Mother: Emeline Anderson   a citizen of the   Choctaw   Nation.

Applications for Enrollment of Choctaw Newborn
Act of 1905 Volume XII

Postoffice   Tuskahoma Ind Ter

AFFIDAVIT OF MOTHER.

UNITED STATES OF AMERICA, Indian Territory, }
.... DISTRICT. }

I, Emeline Anderson, on oath state that I am 20 years of age and a citizen by blood, of the Choctaw Nation; that I am the lawful wife of Reason Anderson, who is a citizen, by blood of the Choctaw Nation; that a female child was born to me on 23 day of June, 1903; that said child has been named Lillian Anderson, and was living March 4, 1905.

Emeline Anderson

Witnesses To Mark:
{

Subscribed and sworn to before me this 6 day of July, 1905

My Com Expires 7/24/06   P.W. Hudson
Notary Public.

Choc New Born 861
    Lucius Hampton Enloe b. 3-10-03

COPY

Muskogee, Indian Territory, April 7, 1905.

J. Ernest Williams,
    Pauls Valley, Indian Territory.

Dear Sir:

There is returned you herewith affidavit of Wade Enloe in the matter of the application for enrollment of Lucius Hampton Enloe as a citizen by blood of the Choctaw Nation, in order that you may attach your signature thereto, as the affidavit appears to have been acknowledged before you.

Please return the affidavit as early as practicable.

Applications for Enrollment of Choctaw Newborn
Act of 1905 Volume XII

Respectfully,
SIGNED

T. B. Needles.
Commissioner in Charge.

AB 1-7

Choctaw N B 861

Muskogee, Indian Territory, May 20, 1905.

G. W. Enloe,
      Comanche, Indian Territory.

Dear Sir:

    Receipt is hereby acknowledged of your letter of May 17, requesting enrollment certificate of Lucious[sic] Hampton Enloe, who was enrolled at Chickasha, Indian Territory, April 4, 1905, by his mother Wade Mordis Enloe.

    In reply to your letter you are advised that the affidavits heretofore forwarded to the birth of Lucius Hampton Enloe, child of W. G. and Wade Enloe, have been filed with our records as an application for the enrollment of said child, but his name has not yet been placed upon a schedule of citizens by blood of the Choctaw Nation.

Respectfully,

Chairman.

7--861.

Muskogee, Indian Territory, June 19, 1905.

Commissioner in Charge,
    Chickasaw Land Office,
        Ardmore, Indian Territory.

Dear Sir:

    There is enclosed herewith the affidavit of Wade Enloe, the mother, to the birth of Lucius Hampton Enloe, which was executed before J. E. Williams, who was at that time an employe[sic] of your office. The affidavit states that the child was living on March 4, 1905, while it appears to have been executed on March 3, 1905. There is apparently an error in the date of execution.

Applications for Enrollment of Choctaw Newborn
Act of 1905   Volume XII

Please secure the proper correction and return the affidavit to this office by first mail.

Respectfully,

Chairman.

DeB--2/19

BIRTH AFFIDAVIT.

DEPARTMENT OF THE INTERIOR,
COMMISSION TO THE FIVE CIVILIZED TRIBES.

IN RE Application for Enrollment, as a citizen of the   Choctaw   Nation, of   Luchius[sic] H. Enloe , born on the   10   day of   March   , 1903

Name of Father: W^m G Enloe   a citizen of the United States Nation.
Name of Mother: Wade Enloe   a citizen of the   Choctaw   Nation.

Post-Office: Comanche I.T.

AFFIDAVIT OF MOTHER.

UNITED STATES OF AMERICA,
   INDIAN TERRITORY.
  Southern   District.

I,   Wade Enloe   , on oath state that I am............years of age and a citizen by............, of the ....Nation; that I am the lawful wife of ...., who is a citizen, by .... of the .... Nation; that a .... child was born to me on .... day of ...., 1........, that said child has been named ...., and is now living.

WITNESSES TO MARK:

{ ....
  .... }

Subscribed and sworn to before me this............*day of* ...., 190........

....
NOTARY PUBLIC.

304

Applications for Enrollment of Choctaw Newborn
Act of 1905   Volume XII

AFFIDAVIT OF ATTENDING PHYSICIAN OR MID-WIFE.

UNITED STATES OF AMERICA,
  INDIAN TERRITORY.
  Southern   District.

I, C. H. Howell, a Physician, on oath state that I attended on Mrs. Wade Enloe, wife of Wm G. Enloe on the 10 day of March, 1903; that there was born to her on said date a male child; that said child is now living and is said to have been named Luchius Hampton Enloe

Dr. C.H. Howell

WITNESSES TO MARK:

Subscribed and sworn to before me this 29 day of March, 1905.

J.B. Wilkinson
NOTARY PUBLIC.

BIRTH AFFIDAVIT.

DEPARTMENT OF THE INTERIOR.
COMMISSION TO THE FIVE CIVILIZED TRIBES.

IN RE APPLICATION FOR ENROLLMENT, as a citizen of the Choctaw Nation, of Lucius Hampton Enloe, born on the 10th day of March, 1903

Name of Father: William G. Enloe   a ~~non~~ citizen of the .... Nation.
Name of Mother: Wade Enloe   a citizen of the Choctaw Nation.

Postoffice   Commanche[sic] I.T.

AFFIDAVIT OF MOTHER.

UNITED STATES OF AMERICA, Indian Territory,
   Southern   DISTRICT.

I, Wade Enloe, on oath state that I am 29 years of age and a citizen by blood, of the Choctaw Nation; that I am the lawful wife of William G Enloe, who is a non citizen, ~~by~~ .... ~~of the~~ .... Nation; that a male child was born to me on 10th day of March, 1903; that said child has been named Lucius Hampton Enloe, and was living March 4, 1905.

Wade Enloe

Applications for Enrollment of Choctaw Newborn
Act of 1905   Volume XII

Witnesses To Mark:

{

Subscribed and sworn to before me this 3rd day of ~~March~~ *April*, 1905

         JE Williams
         Notary Public.

Choc New Born 862
  Dorothy Jessie Campbell   b. 1-20-05
  Mildred Audery[sic] Campbell   b. 10-8-02

              Choctaw 5729.

      Muskogee, Indian Territory, April 15, 1905.

Bond & Melton,
  Attorneys at Law,
    Chickasha, Indian Territory.

Gentlemen:

  Receipt is hereby acknowledged of your letter of April 3, enclosing the affidavits of Clare Campbell and Rebecca Dewitt to the birth of Mildred Audrey Campbell; also the affidavits of Clare Campbell and W. A. Eweng[sic] to the birth of Dorothy Jessie Campbell, children of Samuel S. and Clare Campbell, October 8, 1902 and January 20, 1905, respectively.

  The other affidavits referred to in your letter will be made the subject of a separate communication.

        Respectfully,

              Chairman.

Applications for Enrollment of Choctaw Newborn
Act of 1905   Volume XII

7-NB-862.

Muskogee, Indian Territory, May 31, 1905.

Samuel S. Campbell,
    Tuttle, Indian Territory.

Dear Sir:

    Referring to the applications for the enrollment of your infant children, Mildred Andrey[sic] Campbell and Dorothy Jessie Campbell, born October 8, 1902 and January 20, 1905, respectively, it is noted, from the applications heretofore filed in this office, that the applicants claim through you.

    In this event it will be necessary that you file in this office either the original or a certified copy of the license and certificate of your marriage to the applicant's mother, Clare Campbell.

Respectfully,

[sic]

---

7 NB 862

Muskogee, Indian Territory, June 12, 1905.

Samuel S. Campbell,
    Tuttle, Indian Territory.

Dear Sir:

    Receipt is hereby acknowledged of the certificate of J. W. Speake to the effect that he solemnized the marriage between S. S. Campbell and Clara Clayton, November 25, 1901, and the same has been filed with the record in the matter of the enrollment of Mildred Audrey and Dorothy Jessie Campbell as citizens by blood of the Choctaw Nation.

Respectfully,

Chairman.

Applications for Enrollment of Choctaw Newborn
Act of 1905 Volume XII

CERTIFICATE OF MARRIAGE.
--+++O+++--

UNITED STATES OF AMERICA,)
)
Indian Territory,)
)
Southern District.)

        I, J.W. Speake, a Deputy Clerk of the United States Court within and for the Southern District of the Indian Territory, do hereby certify that on the 25th day of November A.D. 1901, I did duly and according to law, as commanded in the marriage license issued out of the Clerks[sic] office of the United States Court for the Southern District of the Indian Territory on said date, solemnize the Rite and publish the Banns of Matrimony between Mr. S. S. Campbell and Clara Clayton.

        IN TESTIMONY WHEREOF, I have hereunto set my hand and affixed the seal of said Court at Chickasha, this the 7th day of June, A.D. 1905.

                                      J.W. Speake
                                  Deputy Clerk of U.S. Court,
                                  Southern District of Ind Ter.

BIRTH AFFIDAVIT.

DEPARTMENT OF THE INTERIOR.
COMMISSION TO THE FIVE CIVILIZED TRIBES.

        IN RE APPLICATION FOR ENROLLMENT, as a citizen of the   Choctaw   Nation, of Dorothy Jessie Campbell   , born on the 20th   day of January , 1905

Name of Father: Samuel S Campbell   a citizen of the   Choctaw   Nation.
Name of Mother: Clare Campbell   a citizen of the   ———   Nation.

                            Postoffice   Tuttle Ind Terr

AFFIDAVIT OF MOTHER.

UNITED STATES OF AMERICA, Indian Territory,)
     Southern   DISTRICT.)

        I, Clare Campbell   , on oath state that I am 21   years of age and a citizen by   ~~United States~~   , of the   ———   Nation; that I am the lawful wife of Samuel S. Campbell   , who is a citizen, by blood   of the   Choctaw Nation; that a   girl   child was born to me on 20th day of January   , 1905;

Applications for Enrollment of Choctaw Newborn
Act of 1905   Volume XII

that said child has been named   Dorothy Jessie Campbell   , and was living March 4, 1905.

Clare Campbell

Witnesses To Mark:
{

Subscribed and sworn to before me this 23rd day of March , 1905

(Name Illegible)
Notary Public.

Com Expires 10-17-1908

AFFIDAVIT OF ATTENDING PHYSICIAN OR MID-WIFE.

UNITED STATES OF AMERICA, Indian Territory, }
   Southern   DISTRICT.

I,   W.A. Ewing   , a   Physician   , on oath state that I attended on Mrs.   Clare Campbell , wife of   Samuel S Campbell   on the 20th day of January   , 1905; that there was born to her on said date a .... child; that said child was living March 4, 1905, and is said to have been named Dorothy Jessie Campbell

W.A. Ewing M.D.

Witnesses To Mark:
{

Subscribed and sworn to before me this 24th day of March , 1905

(Name Illegible)
Notary Public.

Com Expires 10-17-1908

BIRTH AFFIDAVIT.

DEPARTMENT OF THE INTERIOR.
COMMISSION TO THE FIVE CIVILIZED TRIBES.

IN RE APPLICATION FOR ENROLLMENT, as a citizen of the   Choctaw   Nation, of   Mildred Audrey Campbell , born on the 8th day of October , 1902

Name of Father: Samuel S Campbell   a citizen of the   Choctaw   Nation.
Name of Mother: Clare Campbell   a citizen of the   ———   Nation.

Postoffice   Tuttle I.T.

Applications for Enrollment of Choctaw Newborn
Act of 1905 Volume XII

AFFIDAVIT OF MOTHER.

UNITED STATES OF AMERICA, Indian Territory,
Southern DISTRICT.

I, Clare Campbell, on oath state that I am 21 years of age and a citizen by ~~United States~~, of the ———— Nation; that I am the lawful wife of Samuel S. Campbell, who is a citizen, by Blood of the Choctaw Nation; that a girl child was born to me on 8th day of October, 1902; that said child has been named Mildred Audrey Campbell, and was living March 4, 1905.

Clare Campbell

Witnesses To Mark:

Subscribed and sworn to before me this 23rd day of March, 1905.

(Name Illegible)
Notary Public.

Com Expires 10-17-1908

AFFIDAVIT OF ATTENDING PHYSICIAN OR MID-WIFE.

UNITED STATES OF AMERICA, Indian Territory,
Southern DISTRICT.

I, Rebecca Dewitt, a Mid wife, on oath state that I attended on Mrs. Clare Campbell, wife of Samuel S Campbell on the 8 day of Oct., 1902; that there was born to her on said date a Female child; that said child was living March 4, 1905, and is said to have been named Mildred Audrey Campbell

Rebecca Dewitt

Witnesses To Mark:

Subscribed and sworn to before me this 29 day of March, 1905.

A.T. Taylor
Notary Public.

MY COMMISSION EXPIRES 8/4 1908

Applications for Enrollment of Choctaw Newborn
Act of 1905   Volume XII

<u>Choc New Born 863</u>
      Florence Julius b. 8-9-03

COPY

Muskogee, Indian Territory, March 31, 1905.

Eli Julius,
    Bennington, Indian Territory.

Dear Sir:

    Receipt is hereby acknowledged of your letter of March 28th, transmitting affidavits of Eliza Julius and Serena Julius to the birth of Florence Julius, daughter of Eli and Eliza Julius, August 9, 1903. It is stated in the affidavit of the mother that she is a citizen by blood of the Choctaw Nation, and if this is correct you are requested to state her maiden name and when, where and under what name she was listed for enrollment, giving the names of other members of her family and such other information as will enable the Commission to identify her upon its records as a citizen by blood of the Choctaw Nation.

                            Respectfully,
                            SIGNED
                            Tams Bixby
                            Chairman.

Choctaw 3504.

Muskogee, Indian Territory, April 15, 1905.

Eli Julius,
    Bennington, Indian Territory.

Dear Sir:

    Receipt is hereby acknowledged of your letter of April 7, in which you state that the mother of your child, Florence Julius is a citizen by blood of the Choctaw Nation and is enrolled as Eliza Williams.

    In reply you are advised that this information has enabled the Commission to identify the mother of Florence Julius upon our records as an enrolled citizen by blood of the Choctaw Nation under the name of Eliza Williams, and the affidavits heretofore forwarded to the birth of Florence Julius have been filed with our records as an application for the enrollment of said child.

Applications for Enrollment of Choctaw Newborn
Act of 1905   Volume XII

Respectfully,

Chairman.

NEW-BORN AFFIDAVIT.

Number............

Choctaw Enrolling Commission.

IN THE MATTER OF THE APPLICATION FOR ENROLLMENT, as a citizen of the Choctaw Nation, of Florence Julius

born on the 9th day of August 190 3

Name of father   Eli Julius   a citizen of   Choctaw
Nation final enrollment No   10542
Name of mother   Eliza Julius   a citizen of   Choctaw
Nation final enrollment No   9972

Postoffice   Bennington IT

AFFIDAVIT OF MOTHER.

UNITED STATES OF AMERICA,
   INDIAN TERRITORY,
   Central   DISTRICT

I   Eliza Julius   on oath state that I am 24 years of age and a citizen by blood of the Choctaw Nation, and as such have been placed upon the final roll of the Choctaw Nation, by the Honorable Secretary of the Interior my final enrollment number being 9972 ; that I am the lawful wife of Eli Julius , who is a citizen of the Choctaw Nation, and as such has been placed upon the final roll of said Nation by the Honorable Secretary of the Interior, his final enrollment number being 10542 and that a female child was born to me on the 9th day of August 190 3 ; that said child has been named Florence Julius , and is now living.

Eliza Julius

WITNESSETH:
   Must be two
   Witnesses who   Dana Homer
   are Citizens.   JL Hampton

Subscribed and sworn to before me this   16th   day of   Jan   190 5

W. A. Shoney
Notary Public.

My commission expires Jan 10, 1909

Applications for Enrollment of Choctaw Newborn
Act of 1905   Volume XII

AFFIDAVIT OF ATTENDING PHYSICIAN OR MIDWIFE

UNITED STATES OF AMERICA
INDIAN TERRITORY
Central   DISTRICT

I,   Serena Julius   a   midwife on oath state that I attended on Mrs.   Eliza Julius   wife of   Eli Julius on the   9th   day of   August   , 190 3 , that there was born to her on said date a female   child, that said child is now living, and is said to have been named   Florence Julius

                            her
                     Serena x Julius   M.D.
                         mark

Subscribed and sworn to before me this, the   24   day of   Jan   190 5

                    JW Lloyd
                            Notary Public.

WITNESSETH:
Must be two witnesses   Dana Homer
who are citizens and
know the child.   JL Hampton

We hereby certify that we are well acquainted with   Serena Julius a   midwife   and know   her   to be reputable and of good standing in the community.

                    Dana Homer
                    JL Hampton

BIRTH AFFIDAVIT.

DEPARTMENT OF THE INTERIOR.
COMMISSION TO THE FIVE CIVILIZED TRIBES.

IN RE APPLICATION FOR ENROLLMENT, as a citizen of the   Choctaw   Nation, of   Florence Julius   , born on the   9th   day of   Aug   , 1903

Name of Father: Eli Julius   a citizen of the   Choctaw   Nation.
Name of Mother: Eliza Julius   a citizen of the   Choctaw   Nation.

                 Postoffice   Bennington IT

Applications for Enrollment of Choctaw Newborn
Act of 1905   Volume XII

AFFIDAVIT OF MOTHER.

UNITED STATES OF AMERICA, Indian Territory, }
Central   DISTRICT.

I, Eliza Julius, on oath state that I am 25 years of age and a citizen by blood, of the Choctaw Nation; that I am the lawful wife of Eli Julius, who is a citizen, by blood of the Choctaw Nation; that a female child was born to me on 9th day of Aug, 1903; that said child has been named Florence Julius, and was living March 4, 1905.

Eliza Julius

Witnesses To Mark:
{

Subscribed and sworn to before me this 27 day of March, 1905

Thomas H Bayless
Notary Public.

AFFIDAVIT OF ATTENDING PHYSICIAN OR MID-WIFE.

UNITED STATES OF AMERICA, Indian Territory, }
Central   DISTRICT.

I, Serena Julius, a midwife, on oath state that I attended on Mrs. Eliza Julius, wife of Eli Julius on the 9th day of Aug, 1903; that there was born to her on said date a female child; that said child was living March 4, 1905, and is said to have been named Florence Julius

her
Serena x Julius
mark

Witnesses To Mark:
{ Henry Byington
  ~~WO Byrd~~ WO Byrd

Subscribed and sworn to before me this 27 day of March, 1905

Thomas H Bayless
Notary Public.

Applications for Enrollment of Choctaw Newborn
Act of 1905 Volume XII

Choc New Born 864
    Daniel Bush b. 3-4-03

Choctaw 4580

Muskogee, Indian Territory, April 15, 1905.

Shelton Bush,
    Brooken, Indian Territory.

Dear Sir:

    Receipt is hereby acknowledged of the affidavits of Lindy Bush and J. N. Ritter to the birth of Daniel Bush, son of Shelton and Lindy Bush, March 4, 1903, and the same have been filed with our records as an application for the enrollment of said child.

        Respectfully,

        Chairman.

NEW-BORN AFFIDAVIT.

Number_____

...Choctaw Enrolling Commission...

IN THE MATTER OF THE APPLICATION FOR ENROLLMENT, as a citizen of the Chocktaw[sic] Nation, of Daniel Bush

born on the 4 day of ___March___ 190 3

Name of father Shelton Bush   a citizen of white
Nation final enrollment No..._____
Name of mother Lindy Bush   a citizen of Choctaw
Nation final enrollment No. 12680

        Postoffice   Brooken IT

Applications for Enrollment of Choctaw Newborn
Act of 1905 Volume XII

AFFIDAVIT OF MOTHER.

UNITED STATES OF AMERICA
INDIAN TERRITORY
Western   DISTRICT

I Malinda Bush , on oath state that I am 38 years of age and a citizen by Blood of the Chocktaw Nation, and as such have been placed upon the final roll of the Chocktaw Nation, by the Honorable Secretary of the Interior my final enrollment number being 12680 ; that I am the lawful wife of Shelton Bush , who is a citizen of the .... Nation, and as such has been placed upon the final roll of said Nation by the Honorable Secretary of the Interior, his final enrollment number being 12680 and that a Male child was born to me on the 4th day of March 190 3; that said child has been named Daniel Bush , and is now living.

                                              Malinda Bush x
Witnesseth.   mark

Must be two Witnesses who are Citizens.   T.J. Walls
                            Jess Walls

Subscribed and sworn to before me this 5 day of Jan 190 5

                                                John M Long
                                                      Notary Public.
My commission expires: Nov 27 1907

AFFIDAVIT OF ATTENDING PHYSICIAN OR MIDWIFE

UNITED STATES OF AMERICA
INDIAN TERRITORY
Western   DISTRICT

I, J.N. Ritter a Physician on oath state that I attended on Mrs. Lindy Bush wife of Shelton Bush on the 4 day of March , 190 3 , that there was born to her on said date a male child, that said child is now living, and is said to have been named Daniel Bush

                                                 J.N. Ritter   *M.D.*

Subscribed and sworn to before me this, the 5 day of January 190 5

WITNESSETH: John M Long   Notary Public.

Must be two witnesses who are citizens   Jess Walls
                                  (Name Illegible)

Applications for Enrollment of Choctaw Newborn
Act of 1905 Volume XII

We hereby certify that we are well acquainted with   Dr J. N. Ritter
a   Practicing Physician   and know   him   to be reputable and of good standing in the community.

T. J. Walls   _____

Jess Walls   _____

(The below note typed as given.)

Brooken I.T.
4/3 - 05

the commish Dear Sir you will fin the Lindy Bush Her name on the Role as Lindy Walker 12680

S P Davis

BIRTH AFFIDAVIT.

DEPARTMENT OF THE INTERIOR.
COMMISSION TO THE FIVE CIVILIZED TRIBES.

IN RE APPLICATION FOR ENROLLMENT, as a citizen of the   Choctaw   Nation, of Daniel Bush   , born on the 4   day of   March , 1903

Name of Father: Shelton Bush   a citizen of the   White   Nation.
Name of Mother: Lindy Bush   a citizen of the   Choctaw   Nation.

Postoffice   Brooken I.T.

AFFIDAVIT OF MOTHER.

UNITED STATES OF AMERICA, Indian Territory,
     Western   **DISTRICT.**

I, Linda[sic] Bush   , on oath state that I am about 38   years of age and a citizen by   Blood   , of the   Choctaw   Nation; that I am the lawful wife of Shelton Bush   , who is a citizen, by intermarrige[sic]   of the   Choctaw Nation; that a   male   child was born to me on   4 day of   March , 1903; that said child has been named   Daniel Bush   , and was living March 4, 1905.

                            her
                       Lindy x Bush
Witnesses To Mark: mark
  { E.T. Howell
  { J W Pesterfield

Applications for Enrollment of Choctaw Newborn
Act of 1905   Volume XII

Subscribed and sworn to before me this 3 day of   April   , 1905

S.P. Davis
Notary Public.

AFFIDAVIT OF ATTENDING PHYSICIAN OR MID-WIFE.

UNITED STATES OF AMERICA, Indian Territory,
Western   DISTRICT.

I,   J.N. Ritter   , a   Doctor   , on oath state that I attended on Mrs.   Mrs Lindy Bush   , wife of   Shelton Bush   on the 4 day of March , 1903; that there was born to her on said date a .... child; that said child was living March 4, 1905, and is said to have been named Daniel Bush

J.N. Ritter M.d.

Witnesses To Mark:

Subscribed and sworn to before me this 3 day of   April   , 1905

S.P. Davis
My commission expires Feb 9-07   Notary Public.

Choc New Born 865
  Pearl Hensley   b. 1-20-04

7-NB-865.

Muskogee, Indian Territory, May 31, 1905.

Columbus Hensley,
  Wynnewood, Indian Territory.

Dear Sir:

Referring to the application for the enrollment of your infant child, Pearl Hensley, born January 20, 1904, it is noted, from the affidavits heretofore filed in this office, that the applicant claims through you

Applications for Enrollment of Choctaw Newborn
Act of 1905   Volume XII

In this event it will be necessary that you file in this office either the original or a certified copy of the license and certificate of your marriage to the applicant's mother, Locy[sic] Hensley.

Respectfully,

[sic]

7 NB 865

Muskogee, Indian Territory, June 16, 1905.

Columbus Hensley,
    Dolberg, Indian Territory.

Dear Sir:

Receipt is hereby acknowledged of your letter of June 10, 1905, transmitting marriage license and certificate between Columbus D. Hensley and Lucy Morrison which you offer in support of the application for the enrollment of your child Pearl Hensley, and the same have been filed with the record in this case.

Respectfully,

Chairman.

BIRTH AFFIDAVIT.

DEPARTMENT OF THE INTERIOR.
COMMISSION TO THE FIVE CIVILIZED TRIBES.

IN RE APPLICATION FOR ENROLLMENT, as a citizen of the   Choctaw   Nation, of Pearl Hensley   , born on the 20th day of January   , 1904

Name of Father: Columbus Hensley   a citizen of the   Choctaw   Nation.
Name of Mother: Locy Hensley   a citizen of the United States Nation.

Postoffice   Wynnewood Ind. Tery

AFFIDAVIT OF MOTHER.

UNITED STATES OF AMERICA, Indian Territory,
Southern Judicial   DISTRICT.

I, Locy Hensley   , on oath state that I am 23   years of age and a citizen by ...., of the   United States   Nation; that I am the lawful wife of   Columbus

319

Applications for Enrollment of Choctaw Newborn
Act of 1905   Volume XII

Hensley   , who is a citizen, by blood   of the   Choctaw   Nation; that a female   child was born to me on   20th   day of   January   , 1904; that said child has been named   Pearl   , and was living March 4, 1905.

Lacy[sic] Hensley

Witnesses To Mark:
{

    Subscribed and sworn to before me this   7th   day of   April   , 1905

O.W. Patchell
Notary Public.

AFFIDAVIT OF ATTENDING PHYSICIAN OR MID-WIFE.

UNITED STATES OF AMERICA, Indian Territory, }
Southern Judicial   DISTRICT.   }

    I,   Mrs Laura Yates   , a   midwife   , on oath state that I attended on Mrs.   Lacey[sic] Hensley   , wife of   Columbus Hensley   on the   20th   day of   January   , 1904; that there was born to her on said date a   female   child; that said child was living March 4, 1905, and is said to have been named   Pearl

Laura Yates

Witnesses To Mark:
{

    Subscribed and sworn to before me this   7th   day of   April   , 1905

O.W. Patchell
Notary Public.

Applications for Enrollment of Choctaw Newborn
Act of 1905 Volume XII

DEPARTMENT OF THE INTERIOR,
Commission to the Five Civilized Tribes.
FILED
JUN 15 1905
Tams Bixby

FILED

FEB 4 1903 8AM

C. M. CAMPBELL, Clerk.
Southern Dist. Ind. Ter.

Certificate of Record of Marriage

United States of America, ⎫
   Indian Territory, ⎬ sct.
   Southern District. ⎭

I, C. M. CAMPBELL, Clerk of the United States Court, in the Territory and District aforesaid Do HEREBY CERTIFY, that the License for and Certificate of Marriage of

MR   C. H. Hensley   and

M   Lecy Morrison

were filed in my office in said Territory and District the   4"   day of   Feby   A.D., 190 3   and duly recorded in Book   T   of Marriage Record, Page   150

WITNESS my hand and Seal of said Court, at Ardmore, this   4"   day of   Feby   A.D. 190 3

C. M. Campbell
                               CLERK.

Return this License to the United States Clerk at Ardmore, that it may be recorded, when it will be mailed to the proper address.

Ardmoreite Steam Print.

Applications for Enrollment of Choctaw Newborn
Act of 1905 Volume XII

MARRIAGE LICENSE

N°. 2157

UNITED STATES OF AMERICA,
INDIAN TERRITORY, ss: To Any Person Authorized by Law to Solemnize Marriage, Greeting:
SOUTHERN DISTRICT.

𝔜ou are hereby commanded to solemnize the Rite and publish the Banns of Matrimony between Mr.   C. H. Hensley   of Wynnewood   in the Indian Territory, aged   23   years, and M   Lecy Morrison   of   Kiser   in the Indian Territory, aged   21   years, according to law; and do you officially sign and return this License to the parties therein named.

𝔚itness my hand and official Seal, this   28   day of   January   A. D. 190 3

C. M. CAMPBELL.
Clerk of the United States Court.

By: SH Woolton Dy

Certificate of Marriage.

UNITED STATES OF AMERICA,
INDIAN TERRITORY, ss:
SOUTHERN DISTRICT.   I,   J. B. Reaves

A Minister of the Gospel   do hereby certify that on the   29"   day of   January   , A. D. 190 3   , I did duly according to law, as commanded in the foregoing License, solemnize the Rite and publish the Banns of Matrimony between the parties therein named.

𝔚itness my hand this   2" day of   February   A. D. 190 3

My credentials are recorded in the office of the Clerk of the United States Court, Indian Territory, Southern District, at Ardmore, Book C , Page 23

(NOTE-The person officiating should fill in the spaces for book and page and sign here.)☞

J.B. Reaves
a   Minister of the Gospel

Applications for Enrollment of Choctaw Newborn
Act of 1905 Volume XII

Choc New Born 866
    Frances Henry b. 8-17-03

7-7555   7-7556
BIRTH AFFIDAVIT.

DEPARTMENT OF THE INTERIOR.
COMMISSION TO THE FIVE CIVILIZED TRIBES.

    IN RE APPLICATION FOR ENROLLMENT, as a citizen of the   Choctaw   Nation, of Frances Henry   , born on the 17th   day of   August , 1903

Name of Father: Matthew Henry   a citizen of the Choctaw   Nation.
Name of Mother: Lina Henry   a citizen of the Choctaw   Nation.

                Postoffice   Garland, Ind. Ter.

AFFIDAVIT OF MOTHER.

UNITED STATES OF AMERICA, Indian Territory, }
       Central   DISTRICT.

    I,   Lina Henry   , on oath state that I am 30   years of age and a citizen by blood   , of the   Choctaw   Nation; that I am the lawful wife of   Matthew Henry , who is a citizen, by blood   of the   Choctaw   Nation; that a   female   child was born to me on 17th   day of   August   , 1903; that said child has been named Frances Henry   , and was living March 4, 1905.

                                This is
                                Lina x Henry
Witnesses To Mark: my mark
  { J.L. Jones
    J.B. Jones

    Subscribed and sworn to before me this 7 day of   April   , 1905

                              J N Jones
                                  Notary Public.

Applications for Enrollment of Choctaw Newborn
Act of 1905 Volume XII

AFFIDAVIT OF ATTENDING PHYSICIAN OR MID-WIFE.

UNITED STATES OF AMERICA, Indian Territory,
Central   DISTRICT.

I, Louisa Hunt , a midwife , on oath state that I attended on Mrs. Lina Henry , wife of Matthew Henry on the 17th day of August , 1903; that there was born to her on said date a female child; that said child was living March 4, 1905, and is said to have been named Frances Henry

                         her
                         Louisa x Hunt

Witnesses To Mark: mark
   { AR Davis
   { JP Carl

Subscribed and sworn to before me this 5 day of April , 1905

my commission   Frank E Parke
expires 2/2/08   Notary Public.

AFFIDAVIT OF ATTENDING PHYSICIAN OR MIDWIFE

UNITED STATES OF AMERICA
INDIAN TERRITORY
Central   DISTRICT

I, Louisa Hunt a midwife on oath state that I attended on Mrs. Lina Henry wife of Matthew Henry on the 17th day of August , 190 3 , that there was born to her on said date a female child, that said child is now living, and is said to have been named Frances Henry

                         Louisa Hunt

Subscribed and sworn to before me this, the 6th day of Jan. 190 5

WITNESSETH: Jas A Rogers   Notary Public.

Must be two witnesses { James Hunt
who are citizens   { W.M. Hunt

We hereby certify that we are well acquainted with Matthew Henry a Choctaw By Blood and know him to be reputable and of good standing in the community.

          her
    Louisa x Hunt   James Hunt
       mark

                                  W.M. Hunt

Applications for Enrollment of Choctaw Newborn
Act of 1905   Volume XII

NEW-BORN AFFIDAVIT.

Number..............

...Choctaw Enrolling Commission...

IN THE MATTER OF THE APPLICATION FOR ENROLLMENT, as a citizen of the Choctaw Nation, of Frances Henry

born on the 12th day of __August__ 190 3

Name of father Matthew Henry	a citizen of	Choctaw
Nation final enrollment No. 7555		
Name of mother Lina Henry	a citizen of	Choctaw
Nation final enrollment No. 7556		
	Postoffice	Garland I.T.

AFFIDAVIT OF MOTHER.

UNITED STATES OF AMERICA
INDIAN TERRITORY
   Central   DISTRICT

I   Lina Henry   , on oath state that I am 36   years of age and a citizen by blood   of the   Choctaw   Nation, and as such have been placed upon the final roll of the   Choctaw   Nation, by the Honorable Secretary of the Interior my final enrollment number being   7556 ; that I am the lawful wife of   Matthew Henry   , who is a citizen of the   Choctaw   Nation, and as such has been placed upon the final roll of said Nation by the Honorable Secretary of the Interior, his final enrollment number being   7555   and that a   female   child was born to me on the   12th day of   August   190 3; that said child has been named   Frances Henry   , and is now living.

                                                                    her
                                            Lina x Henry

Witnesseth.   mark

Must be two ⎱ Osborne Cass
Witnesses who ⎰
are Citizens.   Wilson Christy

Subscribed and sworn to before me this   3   day of   Jan   190 5

                                      James Bower
                                              Notary Public.

My commission expires:
   Sept 23-1907

Index

ADAIR, G W 250
ALDRIDGE, S S 54,56
ALLEN
    David 294,296
    L D 24,25
    Rufus 174,177,289,290
    Thomas J 21
    Thomas J, MD 21
ANDERSON
    Bessie 293,294,295,296,297,298
    Emeline 300,301,302
    H D 181,182
    Levina 185
    Leviney 180
    Lillian 299,300,301,302
    Lucinda 275,289,290,291,292, 293,297,300
    Lucy 142,144,145
    Mary 293,294,295,296,297,298
    Norton 293,294,295,296,297,298
    Reason 299,300,301,302
    Robert 47
    Ruth 289,290,291,292
    Watson 290,291,292
    Wesley 174,177
ANDERSON WATSON 289
ANGELL, W H 44,118,119,122,191
ARMSTRONG
    J R 66,67
    M L 66
ARNOLD, C S 108

BAIRD, W E 216
BAKER
    Annie 279,280,281,282
    Gladys 278,279,280,281,282
    Hodgen 275,276,277
    Lecy Anna 275,276,277
    Raney 275,276
    Rhodes S 255
    Roberson 280,281
    Robison 278,279,282
    William 275,277
BAYLESS, Thomas H 314
BEALL, Wm O 109,114
BEAN, Ollie L 219
BECKWITH
    Francis 139,140
    Oliver 140
BELL
    Elsie A 158
    George W 289,290
BELLEW, Rufus 226
BELVIN, R S 65
BEN, Byington 294,296
BENCH, Mollie 257,258,259,260, 261,262
BENJIMAN
    Ben 268
    Winnie 268
BENTON, Phoeba 5,8
BERRY
    Allie Lorennie 160,161,162,163
    H H 161,162,163
    Rebecca 160,161,162,163
BILLY
    Austin 4,5,6,7,8
    Charles 180
    Charley 182
    Crawford 4,5,6,7,8
    Susan 4,5,6,7,8
BIXBY
    Mr 153,155
    Tams 16,17,34,57,61,107,108,129, 182,207,231,247,311,321
BOBO, Lacey P ... 72,80,109,115,141,142, 143,144,145,148,235,269,270
BOHANAN
    Andrew 158,254
    Chester G 254
    Josephine 289,290,291
    Matilda 157
    Rhoda 267,272
    Rosie D 254
    S H 295
    Sidney 283
BOHANON
    Andrew 158,159,254,255,256,257
    Chester G 254,255,256,257
    Disney 284
    Ellis 157,158
    Elsie A 158,159
    Emaline 156,157
    Matilda 157,158

Index

Rhoda 283,284
Robert 158,159
Rosie D 254,255,256,257
Sidney 283
Susan 157,158,159
Wade 269,273
Watson 283,284
BOND
   Emma 220,221,222,223
   Lizzie 169
   Mrs N E 111
BOND & MELTON 306
BOWER
   James 73,234,325
   John 233
BOWMAN
   W R 103
   W R, MD 103
BRADY, Denis C 49,54
BRANDON, Cora 61,62
BREAKER
   J J 82,84
   J J, MD 84
BREEDLOVE, R T 77,78,79
BRIANS, R E 237,240,241
BRITTON, Mary 71
BROOKS, Susie 213,214,215,216, 217,218
BROW
   J D 257
   J D, MD 257
BROWDER, J D 189,190
BROWN
   Celia 117,118
   Clarice Maurine 213,218
   Clarice Morine 213,214,215,216,217
   Dr J D 255,256
   Dr J D, MD 255
   Emra C 161
   J D 254
   Susie 213,214,215,216,217,218
   W E 137,138
   W T 215,217,218
   William T 213,215,216
   Wm T 216,217
BRUNSON, D D 21
BRYANT, Dan 9,180

BUCKHOLTS
   Jennette 163
   Rebecca 161,162,163
BURKS
   Burton Oran 20,21
   J M 20,21
   Joe M 22
   Lucinda 20,21,22
   Ora Velma 20,21,22
BURTAN, J S 69
BUSH
   Daniel 315,316,317,318
   Linda 317
   Lindy 315,316,317,318
   Malinda 316
   Shelton 315,316,317,318
BYINGTON
   David C 258
   Henry 314
   Sampson 258
BYRD, W O 262,314

CALHOUN
   C E 15,18
   C E, MD 15,18
CAMPBELL
   C M 61,62,321,322
   Clare 306,307,308,309,310
   Dorothy Jessie 306,307,308,309
   Mildred Andrey 307
   Mildred Audery 306
   Mildred Audrey 306,307,309,310
   Mr S S 308
   S S 307
   Samuel S 306,307,308,309,310
   W H 211,212,213
CANTERBURY, W M 92,93,94
CARL, J P 324
CARLETON, C H 62
CARNES
   Jimmie 168,169
   Molsie 168,169
   Mrs 289,290,291
   Sophia 274
CART, J L 239,240
CARTLEDGE
   Albert 192

Index

John Thomas.................... 192
Nancy 192
CARTLIDGE
   Albert....................... 193,194,195
   John Thomas............ 192,193,194,195
   Nancy 193,194,195
CASS, Osborne..................... 325
CHAPMAN
   J J.. 68
   J J, MD 68
   John J...............................69,70
   John J, MD 69
CHESTER, W J 257
CHOAT, Gilbert...................35,37
CHRISTY
   Jesse..............................221,222
   Wilson 325
CLARDY, Josh......................... 60
CLARK, Perry M 140
CLAY, Jincy.......................... 186
CLAYTON, Clara 307,308
COCHRAN, J V 195
COLBERT
   Alexander 176
   Annie 174,175,176,177,178
   Ellis 174,175,176,177,178
   T28,29,31,32
   Temelius 175,176,177,178
   W E 175
COLE, Joseph....................243,244
COLEY
   Celin 23
   Sophie...............................23,24
COOPER
   G W 67,69
   Henry 208
   Jane 276,277,278
COSTELOW, N S 73,235,236,237
COVINGTON, W P 148
COWEN
   Frances 134,135
   Francis 134,136,137
   J R..............................134,135,136,137
   Myrtle Susie 134,135,136,137
CRAIGO, W A, MD................. 22
CRAWFORD
   B M.................................... 239

Gussie 229,231,232
H H 238
Mary E......................237,240,241
Mary E (Grant) 239
CRAWFORD & BOLIN 214
CRONISTER, Ida 115
CRONITZER, Ida................... 115
CROWDER
   Mary Ellen ... 241,242,243,244,245,246
   Richard 242,243,244,245,246
   Richard C............................ 241
   Willie Uel 241,242,243,244,245,246
CULBERTSON
   Bengamin F 27
   Bengamon F 28,29,30
   Benjamin F 27
   C E...............3,4,28,29,30,31,32,33
   Charles E 27,28,29,31,32
   Chas E 29,30,32,33
   Ida J 27,31,32,33
   Sophia A............27,28,29,30,31,32,33
   Bengamon F 29

DANEY
   Adaline 181,182
   Adaline Johnson 180,181,182
   Adeline 183
   Allie 179,181,182,183
   Arthur Lee 184,185
   Daniel 184,185
   Rebecca 184,185
   Soloman 182
   Solomon 180,181,182
DANIELS, Turner 55
DANY
   Adaline 179
   Adaline Johnson 180
   Allie 179,180
   Solomon 179
DAVIDSON, Wm B................225,227
DAVIS
   Ella 22,23,24
   Eller 23
   A R 324
   Rosa 23,24
   S P 317,318
   Tom 23,24

Index

DEVER
  C M... 53
  E M...50,51
DEVERS
  E M... 49
  Mrs E M 53
DEWITT, Rebecca 306,310
DICKEN
  Mrs W E 109
  W E................... 108,109,110,112
  W E, MD 109
DIFENDAFER, Chas T........157,169,171,
172,173,177,178,184,185,186,272,275,
276,277,278,283,284,286,292,297,298,
300,301
DILBECK, Alvarado 60
DOCTOR
  James 185,186
  Levina....................................185,186
  Wilkin....................................185,186
DRAKE, Rosa 23,24
DUKES
  Loren D 9,10
  Mabel...9,10
  Pallie..9,10
DURANT
  Anna L.. 255
  Isaac..99,100
DWIGHT, E T 65
DYER
  E E... 135
  Sam..259,266

ELAPASHABBE
  Barnett......................................36,37
  T Barnett... 35
ELLIOTT, J H 52,55
ELLIS
  Anna S..81,82
  Floyde...81,82
  Mitchell 81,82
  P F 216
ENLOE
  G W 303
  Luchius H 304
  Luchius Hampton 305
  Lucious Hampton 303

  Lucius Hampton 302,303,305
  W G 303
  Wade........................302,303,304,305
  Wade Mordis 303
  William G.. 305
  Wm G 304,305
EWENG, W A 306
EWING
  W A 309
  W A, MD.. 309

FANNIE, E J 232
FANNIN, E J 129,130,231,252,253
FINLEY, Joe 44
FLEMING
  Geo N 194,195
  Geo N, MD 194,195
  George N 192
FLOYD, J W 313
FOLSOM
  Charlotte 206,207,208,209,210,211
  A E 120,121
  Frank........... 206,207,208,209,210,211
  John 233,234,236,237
  Rassie Glover 206,209,210
  Rossie Glover 206,207,208,210,211
FOSS, Mrs H N 109
FOSTER
  Bonnie B................................137,138
  Mary A 137,138
  W F 138
  William F................................137,138
FOWLER
  D A..89,90
  Emma 219
  H L 222,223,224
  Hosea L 219
  John 222,223,224
FRANCIS
  R D 286
  Robert D 286
FRANKLIN, Wirt..............................47,71
FRAZIER, Rhoda............................... 283
FREENEY, Benjamin Baxton 100
FREENY
  Benjamin B................................102,103
  Benjamin Baxter........ 100,101,103,104,

Index

105
   Josephine 100,102,103,104,105
   R C 100
   Robert C 100,101,103,104,105
   Robt C 102,103
FREY, E W 84
FULLER
   F M 26,131,132,133,268,280,281
   M A 26
   Olie G 128,129,130
FULTZ, Jos R 129

GARDENHIRE, A J 142,144
GARDNER
   Carrie 88,89,90
   Daniel H 249,250
   E J 90,91
   Edmund 89,90
   Edward 89
   Fasie E 246
   Glades 247,249,250
   Glades A 246,250,251
   Gladie A 251
   Gladys Airbell 248
   Gladys Aribell 246,247,248
   Robert 253
   Robert L 246,247,248,249,250,
251,252
   Tasie E 247,248,249,250,251
GARDNER-TYLER, Carrie 89
GARLAND
   Deliah 26
   Delilah 25,26
   Frank 209
   Rachel 26
   Ward, Jr 209
GILL
   Jno J 79
   John J 80
   John J, MD 80
GOFORTH, W H 102,103
GRANT
   George J 237,238,239,240,241
   Mary E 237,238,239,240,241
   Thomas W 238,240
   Tom 237,238,239,241
GREEN

G B 199,202
G B, MD 202
GUDE, David 198,199
GUESS
   John M 82,83,84
   Maud 82,83,84
   Minnie 82,83,84
GUS, Sina 2,3

HALDAY, Nellie 281
HALMAN, Lasie 253
HALSTEAD, Martha 123,124,126
HAMMONS
   Cleo Inez 187,188,189,190,191,192
   John 187,188,190,191,192
   John W 189,190
   Lizzie 188,189,190,191,192
HAMPTON
   J L 312,313
   Watson 145,150,152,155
HARDY
   Annie 282
   Emily 281,282,283
   Washington 132
HARKINS, William M 135
HARLIN, Logan 87
HARMON
   M J 100,104
   Montie Jane 100,105
HAROLD
   D O 255
   D P 256
HARRIS
   Byington 46
   J M 140
   Johnson 46
   Nicey 46,47
   W L 97,98
HART, John 86
HEISTEIN, Milton 191,192
HEKIA
   John E ... 106,107,108,109,110,111,112
   Sibbie 111
   Sibby 106,107,108,109,110,111,112
HENDON, R S 68,69
HENDRIX, Myra 120,121,122
HENRY

Frances 323,324,325
Lina............................323,324,325
Matthew....................323,324,325
HENSLEY
  C H 321,322
  Columbus......................318,319,320
  Columbus D.......................... 319
  Lacey 320
  Lacy..................................... 320
  Locy..................................... 319
  Pearl.............................318,319,320
  T M 134
HILL
  Josephine 233,234
  A T 226,227,228
  A T, MD 226,227
HINSLEY, T M 136,137
HOLMAN
  Alferd 36
  Alfred 34,35,36,37,38
  Eliza............................34,35,36,37,38
  Eliza A................................... 38
  Moses 34,35,36,37,38
  Tasie 252
HOMER
  Byington 45,46,47,48
  Dana 257,258,259,260,261,262, 264,265,266,312,313
  Dana A...............................263,266
  Dena 263
  J H 72
  J W 142,144
  Jacob 145,146
  Johnson 45,47,48
  Kizzie 258,260,261,262,263, 264,265,266
  Mollie 257,258,259,260,261, 262,263,265,266
  Nancy 261
  Nicey 45,47,48
  Sol J 102
  Willie 257,258,259,260,261, 262,263,264,265,266
HOMES
  Dana 259
  Mollie 259
  Sol J 103

Willie..................................... 259
HONER, Jacob 147
HOOVER
  Andrew J 167,168
  Andrew J, MD 165,167,168
  A J 165
HOPKINS, D W 193,194,195
HOWELL
  C H 305
  Dr C H 305
  E T 317
HUDLOW, W H................41,42,43,44
HUDSON
  Chas H 86
  P W 178,289,296,302
  Peter J 130
  Peter W 176,295
HUNT
  James 324
  Louisa 324
  W M................................... 324
HUNTER
  T W...................................... 65
  Thos W 65
HURDSICK, H L 286

IMPALUMBI, Lovina 46
IMPSON
  L 41,42,43
  M 41,42
  Minnie 42,43
ISH, W W 87,88
ISHEWOOD, W H 295

JACOBS
  H B 221,222
  Houston 224
JAMES
  Austin W 6
  Jincy 139,140
  Johnie N..........................139,140
  Johnnie N............................ 139
  Laura A...........................139,140
  A W 46
JEFFERSON
  Cephus............................79,80
  Sackey 79,80

Sam 141,147,150,152,155
Wallace 79,80,146,148
JOHN
  George 274,275
  Harry 274,275
  Sophia 274,275
JOHNSON
  Adaline 179
  Adeline 183
  Henry 5,7
  Ivey May 70,71,72,73
  Martha 71,72,73
  O L .... 156,157,158,159,169,171, 172,173,177,178,184,185,186,272,274 ,275,276,277,278,282,283,284,286, 287,292,297,298,300,301
  Sam 71,72,73
  Victor M 135
JOHNSTON
  D R 218
  E D 92,93
JOLLY, W D 82
JONES
  Acy Louis 91,93,94
  Adna 94,96,99,100
  Albert 267,268,269,270,271,272,273
  Amelia Mae 197,198
  Amelia May 196,197
  Arthur N B 97,98
  C C 208,209,210,211
  Charles 269,270,272
  Charley 267,268,269,271,273
  E A 213,214,217,218
  E A, MD 217,218
  Edna 95,98
  Edna May 48,49,51,52
  Edney May 49,51,53,54
  Ella 49,53
  Ella E 53
  Ellar 50,51
  Ellen 268,269,271,272,273,284
  Ellis 196,197,198
  Gracie Sybil 48,49,50,54,55,56
  J B 323
  J L 323
  J N 198,199,323
  Jackson N 249,250

James A 91,92,93,94
John F 49,50,51,52,53,54,55,56
John T 50
Lizzie 196,197,198
Lou 91,92,93,94
Louis 97,98
Malinda 198,199
Mary 49,50,51,52,53,54,55,56
Melinda 196,197
Russell Ray 91,92
T W 59
JULIUS
  Eli 311,312,313,314
  Eliza 311,312,313,314
  Florence 311,312,313,314
  Serena 311,313,314

KELLEY
  Gracie 123
  Jewel 123
  Jewell 123
  A S 162
KELLY
  Gracie 123,124
  Jewel 123,125,126
  Mollie 123,124,125,126
  W W 123
  William 125
  William W 124,125,126
KENNEDY, D S 57
KILGORE, Carl 18
KIMBRO, Thos M 232
KING
  Mrs N O 77
  N O 75,77,78
  Robert 180

LARCY, W E 243
LARECY, W E 243,244,245,246
LARRABEE, C F 153,155
LAWRENCE, Rosa 57,58
LEARD, J N 200,201,203,204
LEE, Robert E 96,97,99
LEFLORE
  Allen 65
  Bertha 94,95,96,97,98,99
  Lou 94,95,96,97,98,99

Index

M W 65
Mach H 95
Mack H 94,95,96,97,98,99
LESTER, C L 48
LEWALLEN
   W P 188,189,191,192
   W P, MD 189,191,192
LEWIS
   Allie 126
   Judith 84,86
   Lena Moria 127
   Leona Maria 126
   Leona Moria 126,127,128,131,132, 133
   Moria Leona 128
   Ollie 126,127,133
   Ollie G 131,132
   Silas 126,127,128,131,132,133, 280,281
   Silas B 129,130
LINEBAUGH, Jno H 119
LLOYD, W G B 253
LOMAN, Emeline 132,133
LOMAR, Emeline 126
LONG
   Dr T J 119
   John M 316
   T J 118,119
   T J, MD 118,119
LUNTZ, Henry 126

MACKEY
   E M 164,165
   Sarah Margaret 164,165
   Wayne Lee............................. 164,165
MANSFIELD, MCMURRAY &
   CORNISH 16
MAPLES
   Dr J B 162
   Frank 162
   J B 161
   J B, MD 162
   M F 162
MATTHEWS, Abbie 111
MAULDIN
   Betse 67
   Betsey 68

Betsie 68,69,70
Jack 67,68,69,70
Roy 68
Roy Jackson 67,68,69,70
MCBRAYER, John E 226
MCCLAIN, George 71
MCCLARD, C C 197
MCCOOLE, John I 53,54
MCCURTAIN
   Elum 113,116
   Ruth 113,116
MCDANIEL
   Clarence 225,226,227
   Clarence C 224,226,228
   Lou 225,226,227,228
   Sam 227
   Samuel 225,226,227,228
   Wm 76
MCGAHEY
   Alexander J 117,118
   Celia 117,118
   Johnie F 117
   Johnie Franklin 117
   Johnnie F 118
   L L 117,119
MCGOWAN, G E 59
MCINTOSH
   Alex 8
   Jno 200,201,203,204
MCKEEL, J F 77
MCKINNEY
   Mattie 197
   Nancy 286,288
   Rev William H 269
   S B 170,271,272,285,288
   W H 269
MCMORRIET
   L W, MD 29,32
   Lee W 33
   Lee W, MD 30
MCMORRIS, Dr L W 27,29,30,32,33
MCMURTRY, Martha J 201
MCVEAN, Margaret 109,111,112
MEANS, J T 216
MERRYMAN, Leonidas E 71
MILLER
   Geo W 163

Index

W B 9,10,12,13,14,19
W B, MD 10,13,14,19
MILTON, George 5,7
MITCHEL, Martha 73
MITCHELL
   Alice 1,2,3,4
   Dellie 4
   Jane 1,2,3,4
   Luster 1,2,3,4
   M A 4
   Martha 73
MORELAND, J B 257
MORESON, J A 67
MORRIS
   Mary 170,171,173
   Temelius 178
   Will 170,173
MORRISON
   Lecy 321,322
   Lucy 319
MURPHY, Jane 1,2,3

NAYLOR, Ida 236,237
NEEDHAM
   Enoch 196,199,200,201,202,203, 204,205
   Helen 199,200,201,202
   Herbert Enoch 199,203,204,205
   Nettie H 199,200,201,202,203, 204,205
NEEDLES, T B 290,293,303
NELSON, B A 255,256
NICAR
   Amanda E 39,40,42,43,44
   Amanda Ellen 40,41
   Christie 40,41
   Christy 39,42,43,44
   Cristie 41,42
   Ella 39,41,44
   Ellia 40
   Ellie 42,43,44
   Ola P 39,40,41,42,43,44
NIHKA, Solomon 38,39
NOAH
   Annie 219,220,221,222,223,224
   D S 285,286,287,288
   Emma 219,220,221,222,223,224

Foster 219,220,221,222,223,224
Margaret J 284,285,286,287,288
Martin Van 284,285,286,287,288

OTOOLE, Jno 189,190,192
OTT
   Rosa 57,58,59
   Roy 57,58,59
   Sam 57,58,59

PARKE, Frank E 324
PARKER, J C 258,259,263
PARRISH, W M 112
PATCHELL, O W 320
PEARCY, Leon 257
PEERY, Clifford V 86
PERKINS, Alice 74
PERRY
   Emeline 114,115
   Hampton 112,113,114
   William 112,113,114,115,116
PESTERFIELD, J W 317
PETER
   Selana 220,224
   Simon 224
PHILIP, Tom 2,3
PHILLIPS
   J W 246,247,248,250,251
   J W, MD 248,250,251
   John 2
PLUMBBI, Lovina 47
PORCH, J R 225,226
POUND, Geo W 28,29,31,32
PRIDDY, Melvin 189,190

RAPPOLEE, J L 104
REAVES, J B 322
REED, James N 193,194
REMISE, John 139
RICE, O W 81,82
RICHARD, W T 75
RICHARDSON
   Lucinda C 166,167,168
   Mattie C 166
   Mattie Codelia 166
   S O 166,168
   Samuel O 166,167

Index

Samuel Oliver 166,167,168
RICHEY, A E 105,106
RIDGEWAY
   George W 211,212,213
   Nellie McCurtain 211,212,213
   Sarah E 211,212,213
RITTER
   Dr J N 317
   J N 315,316,318
   J N, MD 316,318
ROBERTS, Sam T, Jr ... 6,7,9,10,13,14,15,
16,17,18,19,20,180
ROGERS
   B F 117,119
   Jas A 324
   W F 117
ROSE
   Alcy 1,2,3,4
   Vester 47
ROSS, A Frank 135
ROWLEY, H B 2
RUSHING
   Caraline 75,76,77,78
   Joe 75,76,77,78
   Mary Elizabeth 75,76,77,78
RYAN, Thos 152,155

SADLER, E W 256
SAGE
   Carrie 12,13,14,15,18,19
   Claud 11,12,13,14,18,19
   Claude 11,14
   Clyde 11,12,13,14,18
   Leroy 11,15,16,17,18
   Mrs 18
   Sidney 11,12,13,14,15,16,17,18,19
SAM
   Lula 141,142,143,144,145,147,
148,149,150,151,152,153,154,155
   Stanford 141,143,144,146,147,150,
152,155
   Susan 142,143,144,145,146,147,
150,152,155
SANDERS, Robert 243,244
SHOAT, Roberson 280
SHONEY, W A 89,90,221,222,312
SHOTUBY, Jane 219,223

SILER, Otto 195
SIMMONS, O A 66
SIMS, Columbus 36,37
SMALLWOOD, Lizzie 196,198
SMITH
   C B 63,65,66
   C B, MD 63,64,65,66
   Morris 251,260
SPEAKE, J W 307,308
SPRING, Buster 168,169
ST BELL, Robert 217
ST CLAIR
   Dr 208
   Dr Geo W 208,210
   G W 207,211
   G W, MD 211
   Geo W 209
   George W 206
STEPHENSON
   A, MD 75
   A 74,75
STEWARD, M A 228
STEWART
   M A 234,236
   M A, MD 230,234,236
STONE, W B 252,253
STRANGE, I L 59
STYLES, J S 208
SUDDATH, T M 92,93

TALBERT
   Jno E 36,37,38,39
   John E 37
TATE, E V 88,89,90,91
TAYLOR
   Cora 59,60
   Emeline 114,115
   Eulafay 59,60
   John 59,60,61,62
   A S 137,138
   A T 310
THOMAS
   Allie J 112
   D 6,180
   Jno J 7,8,9,180,181
THOMPSON
   Joseph P 38,39

Index

Minerva B 27
R A 125,126
Wallie 121
Wilburn 120,121
THRELKELD
   W C 237,239,241
   W C, MD 239
TOM, Sampson 132
TROUTT
   M A 134,137
   Mary A 134,135
   Mary E 134
   Mrs M A 137
TRUITT
   Alice 74
   William L 74
   William M 74
TURNER
   A P 77
   Robt F 192
TYLER
   Butte 133
   Carrie 88,89,90,91
   George 88,89
   George W 88,90,91
   William W 88,90,91
   William Ward 88,89

VARNER, T T 232

WADE, Wicey 57,59
WADLEY, George L 225,226
WALACE, W M 243,244,245,246
WALKER
   J C 76
   Lindy 317
WALL
   Elma May 156,157
   Phoebe A 156
   Tandy 156
WALLACE
   Lillian 222,223
   W M 241,245
   W M, MD 243,246
WALLS
   James 212
   Jess 316,317

Mulcy 170,171,172,173
Muley 170
Sam 170,171,172,173
Sibbl 171
Sibby 170,172,173
T J 316,317
WARD
   Cleo Irene 228,229,230,233,234, 235,236
   Cleorine 228,230,234
   David 73,228,229,230,231,232, 233,234,235,236
   Gussie ... 228,229,230,233,234,235,236
   J P 200,201,202,203,204,205
   Sallie 99,100
WESLY, Ben 255
WHEELER, J S 167,168
WHITE
   H H 199,204,205
   H H, MD 204
   J M 83
WILKIN
   Lean 25,26
   Levi 25,26
   Margret 25,26
WILKINSON
   C S 91,92,94
   J B 305
WILLIAMS
   B W 198,248,249,251,260
   Daniel 261,262,265,266
   Daniel P 251
   E F 162
   Eliza 311
   J E 58,303,306
   J Ernest 302
WILLIS, Ben 8
WILSON
   Elizabeth 120,121,122
   J W 256
   Lark A 121,122
   Lark H 120,121
   Mary 49,50,52,55,56
   Sallie 46,47
   Samuel R 73
   Simpson 46,47
   Zel Ora 120,121,122

Zell Ora 120,121
WINANS, W W..........................212,213
WOOLEY, Sam................................52,55
WRIGHT
    Bency...............................84,85,86,87
    J P..193,194
    Mary Ann 84,85,86,87
    Sampson 84,85,86,87

YANDELL
    Dora..................................63,64,65,66
    John 64,65
    John M..................................63,64,66
    Nettie 63,64,65,66
YATES, Laura..................................... 320
YOUNG, J M 116

www.ingramcontent.com/pod-product-compliance
Lightning Source LLC
Chambersburg PA
CBHW020243030426
42336CB00010B/585